Jewels of the Doctrine

SUNY Series in Buddhist Studies
Kenneth Inada, Editor

Jewels of the Doctrine

Stories of the Saddharma Ratnāvaliya

Dharmasēna Thera

translated by

Ranjini Obeyesekere

State University of New York Press

Published by
State University of New York Press, Albany

Printed in the United States of America

For information, address the State University of New York Press,
State University Plaza, Albany, NY 12246

Library of Congress Cataloging-in-Publication Data

Dharmasena, Thera, 13th cent.
[Saddharmaratnāvaliya. English]
Jewels of the doctrine : stories of the Saddharma Ratnavaliya / Dharmasena Thera : translated by Ranjini Obeyesekere.
p. cm. — (SUNY series in Buddhist studies)
Includes bibliographical references.
ISBN 0-7914-0489-7 (alk. paper). — ISBN 0-7914-0490-0 (pbk. : alk. paper)
1. Dhammapadaṭṭhakathā. 2. Tipitaka. Suttapiṭaka. Khuddakanikāya. 3. Dhammapada—Commentaries—Early works to 1800.
I. Title. II. Series.
BQ1375.D5413 1991 90-9579
294.3'823—dc20 CIP

10 9 8 7 6 5 4 3 2 1

In memory of my grandfather, Dingiri Banda Ällepola of the village of Ällepola in Mātale, who lived his ninety years by the simple humane values of Buddhism.

Contents

Acknowledgments

The preparation of this volume was made possible in part by a grant from the National Endowment for the Humanities, an independent federal agency.

I wish to thank Professor G. D. H. Wijewardene of the school of Oriental and African studies, London, who gave generously of his time and scholarship, helped me through the intricacies of Buddhist philosophical concepts and Pali terminology, and painstakingly went through my translations. Thanks are also due to my colleague Hildred Geertz and my friends of the Princeton Research Forum translation group, who read, edited, and often provided inspired suggestions for endless versions of these stories; to Pauline Caulk, who with infinite patience and clarity, cut through my constant tangles with the computer; and finally to my husband, Gananath Obeyesekere, whose chance request for a "quick translation of two pages" of this text first triggered my interest, and who then encouraged my venture into this more ambitious project.

I wish to thank the SUNY press for the speed and efficiency with which they undertook the work of publication.

Introduction

THE PLACE OF THE SADDHARMARATNĀVALIYA IN SINHALA CULTURE

A Personal Note

My own first encounter with the *Saddharmaratnāvaliya* (The Jewel Garland of the True Doctrine) was as a child. Growing up in Sri Lanka, in the city of Colombo, we considered the high point of our lives to be the school vacations, which we spent in our grandfather's house in the small village of Palapathwela in the central hill country. There, often of an evening, after the first lamp was lit, my grandfather would sit at the dining table, relaxed after his day's work, take out a fat leather bound book and read aloud. At that twilight hour, when it was too dark to do anything more exciting and dinner was still only a matter of curry smells wafting from the kitchen, we would slowly gather round grandfather and his lamp, a motley group of children of all ages drawn like moths to a flame, and we would listen to his sonorous voice reading from the *Saddharmaratnāvaliya* or the *Jātaka Tales*. We didn't always understand all that he read. Some of my younger cousins often fell asleep at the table. Others, bored, would disappear after a while into the more interesting world of the kitchen. But a few of us older ones stayed and listened. We were his faithful. Sometimes we would interrupt with a question. His answers were always short and simple, and seemed then to be eminently sensible. He rarely stopped to explain at any length. For the most part he just read on and we listened.

He read, I now realize, mainly for himself, and reading aloud was only his way of reading. But he didn't mind our collecting round him and even acknowledged our presence by every now and then interrupting the flow of the text with a "ā puthā," which I can only translate as, "Isn't that so my child?"

The reading would stop abruptly when grandmother brought the steaming rice and curries to the table. Grandfather would close the book without protest, at whatever point he happened to be, and give up his place and lamp so that we children could eat.

Many of the stories grew very familiar with time. We heard them told and retold in many different contexts; in the temples, when the elders observed the eight precepts on full moon nights, as illustrations in the sermons of monks, and in schools where they were often assigned in the literature classes. But the stories I remembered best, and the bits and pieces that remained stuck in my mind were those that had fired my imagination as a child—Cunda, running about mad, screaming like a pig and boiling in hell fires; Devidat being sucked into the earth; the distraught bride following after prince Nanda, who in turn reluctantly followed behind the Buddha; or the majestic elephant Pāralīya, broken-hearted, watching the Buddha depart.

This I think is how most Sinhala children (at least those growing up before the fifties) came to know these stories. In a paper on "The Conscience of King Duṭṭhagāmani Abhaya" (1987), Gananath Obeyesekere remarks: "The abstract ethics and the abstruse concepts of the doctrinal tradition were given an immediacy, a concreteness and an ethical salience in peasant society through storytelling." Looking back on my childhood, I realize we were never given religious instruction as such, either in school or at home. We participated in Buddhist rituals and ceremonies, mostly with the extended kin group, went to temple on full moon days (that, too, mainly during vacations), and listened to many, many Buddhist stories. That was how we learned to be Buddhists.

The stories of the *Saddharmaratnāvaliya* and the *Jātaka Tales* have, I think, always performed this function, ever since they were translated into Sinhala. They have been central to the dissemination of Buddhist values and doctrine, and for this very reason were preserved and cherished, copied and recopied by monks, and passed on from generation to generation. In recent years their role has diminished. Buddhism is taught as a subject in schools, in Sunday Schools or *Daham pāsäl*, that have sprung up all over the country, and children study doctrinal texts and understandably, are extremely bored with them. Ours was a much more exciting way to come to the Teachings.

ON TEXTS WITHIN TEXTS AND TRANSLATIONS OF TRANSLATIONS

The *Saddharmaratnāvaliya* is one of the best known and best loved books of the Sinhala literary canon. It is the work of a thirteenth century monk, Dharmasēna Thera, and is a translation of the fifth century Pāli work the *Dhammapadaṭṭhakata* or Dhammapada Commentary. For Sinhala readers over the centuries, however, it has taken on an identity and life of its own. Its connection with the earlier Pāli work hardly surfaces in the consciousness of the general Sinhala reader or listener. To them, it is essentially a Sinhala Buddhist work, rooted in the culture, the world view and the very texture of Sinhala society. This is not surprising because the world of reference of both the Pāli and Sinhala works is agrarian, feudal, medieval, and profoundly Buddhist. In spite of five hundred years of western colonial contact, the world and value systems of the Sinhala Buddhist peasant, even as late as the nineteen fifties, was not too far removed from that thirteenth century world and so the stories had an immediacy and relevance. For the Sinhala scholar and for those who have come to be identified as the "vernacular intelligentsia" (in contrast to the western educated intelligentsia of postcolonial times), the *Saddharmaratnāvaliya* was an important Sinhala literary work that resonated with the deep rooted values of their Buddhist past.

There was perhaps yet another reason for this resonance. Long before the fifth century A.D. the text had existed in Sri Lanka, and had been known to Buddhist scholars as an important commentarial work on the *Dhammapada* (one of the central texts of the Buddhist canon). Thus, it was originally a Sinhala work.

This Sinhala commentary or collection of stories, was translated into Pāli in the fifth century by a foreign Buddhist monk; he was popularly believed to be the scholar monk Buddhaghōsa.[1] The Pāli translation was entitled the *Dhammapadaṭṭhakatha* and soon became known throughout the Buddhist world. I shall refer to this text from now on for convenience as the *Dhammapada Commentary.*

Then in the thirteenth century A.D., perhaps because the pre-fifth century Sinhala work was lost by that time, the Sri Lankan monk Dharmasēna Thera, decided to retranslate the Pāli *Dhammapada Commentary* back into Sinhala, creating the text known as the "*Saddharmaratnāvaliya.*"

The translation of Buddhist texts and commentaries, from the classical languages of Pāli and Sanskrit into the vernacular languages, and vice versa, has been an ongoing activity throughout the Buddhist world. Translations were generally of two kinds; either close textual translations of primary canonical material, or freer adaptations or transformations of secondary materials such as commentaries or illustrative stories.

Both the *Dhammapada Commentary* and the *Saddharmaratnāvaliya* belong to the latter category. In prologues to their works, each of the two authors indicates how he approached his task. The translator of the fifth century *Dhammapada Commentary* states he was told by a Senior Monk that:

> A subtle commentary thereon [the *Dhammapada*] has been handed down from generation to generation in the island of Sri Lanka. But be-

> cause it is composed in the language of the island it is of no profit or advantage to foreigners. [If it were translated into Pāli] It might perhaps conduce to the welfare of mankind. This was the wish expressed to me by the Elder Kumāra Kassapa, self-conquered, living in tranquillity, steadfast in resolve. His earnest request was made to me because of his desire that the Good Law might endure.[2]

Then, with the slightly dismissive impatience of a classicist for the stylistic involutions of an indigenous vernacular, he adds:

> Therefore I shall discard this dialect and its diffuse idioms and translate the work into the pleasing language of the Sacred Texts. Whatever in the *[Dhammapada]* Stanzas has not been made clear in the Stanzas themselves, whether in letter or in word, all that will I make clear. The rest I will also tell in Pāli, in accordance with the spirit of the Stanzas. Thus will I bring to the minds of the wise joy and satisfaction in matters both temporal and spiritual.[3]

While the original Sinhala text on which the Pāli version was based was probably lost long before the thirteenth century, the fifth century Pāli translation remained in circulation in Sri Lanka and in the larger Buddhist world. It was translated into English by E. W. Burlingame in 1921 and published by the Pāli Text Society in 1969 and again in 1979.

Dharmasēna Thera's *Saddharmaratnāvaliya*, too, has remained in circulation in Sri Lanka since the thirteenth century. It was preserved originally in the form of palm leaf *(ōla)* manuscripts stored in Buddhist temples throughout the country. But since the late nineteenth century it has been edited and published in book form. The most recent is a two volume edition published in 1985 by the Oriental Languages Association and the Sinhala Department of the Colombo University.

The author of the *Saddharmaratnāvaliya* states in *his* introduction how *he* approached the task of translation. He says:

> We have abandoned the strict Pāli method and taken only the themes, in composing this work. It may have faults and stylistic shortcomings but [you the reader should] ignore them. Be like the swans who separate milk from water even though the milk and water have been mixed together, or like those who acquire learning and skills even from a teacher of low status, because it is only the acquisition of knowledge with which they are concerned, . . . So, consider only its usefulness and apply the healing salve of the *Saddharmaratnāvaliya* to remove the hazy film of Delusion that clouds the Eye of Wisdom, and go happily and with clear sight along the highway of Right Actions to the city of *nirvāṇa*.[4]

Thus, with mock modesty and a subtle irony, he seems determined to restore the "diffuse idioms" of his native tongue, which his august predecessor had so assiduously eliminated! The *Saddharmaratnāvaliya*, not surprisingly then, is much more than a translation and turns out to be three times as long as its original. Like the *Dhammapada Commentary* it is a reworking of its sources. Both writers work in terms of the feel and flow of their respective languages. The *Saddharmaratnāvaliya* contains additional stories, expanded descriptions, new metaphors, and elaborate images not in the Pāli *Dhammapada Commentary*, which are intended to capture the imagination of his thirteenth century *Sinhala* readers and listeners. It is written in an easy flowing, colorful prose, in the half-colloquial, half-literary, style still used by Buddhist monks in their sermons. The speaking voice and narrative persona of the author/translator cuts into the text constantly, revealing his humanity and humor, his narrative gifts, and above all the intellectual and psychological subtlety with which he explores and illuminates abstract elements of Buddhist doctrine, relating them to the everyday needs and actions of ordinary people.

THE BUDDHIST STORY TRADITION

The stories in this collection are very much in the Buddhist storytelling tradition. However, since they were meant to illustrate and illuminate abstract philosophical doctrines for lay audiences, they are also contextualized in the everyday world of the medieval Sinhala peasant and of the author/translator. Thus, while they conform to the larger pattern of Buddhist storytelling, in their descriptive details and imagery they provide valuable sociological insights into the life and times of their author.

Paula Richman in her recent book *Women, Branch Stories and Religious Rhetoric in a Tamil Buddhist Text* (1988), has an excellent description of the Buddhist story tradition. There is generally a main central story that is linked to several minor or "branch" stories. The latter do not, however, relate to the former in the manner of a plot and subplots knit into a tightly organized whole but rather in the tradition somewhat of the picaresque novel that relates the adventures of the central character in a variety of changing situations and contexts. In the Buddhist tradition (as for example with the *Jātaka Tales*) the situations become even more diverse and far-flung because they range over several "lives" (i.e. previous rebirths) lived in a variety of contexts, human, animal, divine, or demonic.

Again, unlike the *Arabian Nights* tradition, where one story leads to another and moves constantly outward, these Buddhist stories always turn back to their central characters, often with an explicit statement such as: "The physician at the time is now the Senior Monk Cakkhupāla." In the process, the "branch" stories reflect and refract on central themes of the Buddhist Teachings, expounding, and illuminating them for the lay reader and listener. The intention is always didactic, conveyed sometimes explicitly through sermons, sometimes implicitly through the story itself and the manner of its telling.

In the introduction to his translation of the *Dhammapada Commentary,* E. W. Burlingame remarks on the nature of Buddhist commentaries. He says that in the Hindu tradition stories are introduced as illustrations, and are always subordinated to the main purpose, which is the exegesis of the doctrinal text. In the Pāli Buddhist commentaries by contrast,

> The verbal glosses begin to shrink both in size and importance and the stories begin to grow. Finally as in the case of the *Dhammapada Commentary* the exegesis of the text becomes a matter of secondary importance . . . to all intents and purposes what was once a commentary has become nothing more or less than a huge collection of legends and folk tales.[5]

The *Saddharmaratnāvaliya* then, which claims to be a translation of the Pāli *Dhammapada Commentary,* is also a collection of such stories. This no doubt accounts for the wide popularity the work has enjoyed with generations of readers and listeners, both monks and lay individuals. A close comparison of the Sinhala and Pāli works, however, reveals a marked difference in how they handle the commentarial function, which, though minimized, is implicitly recognized by both translators.

In the *Dhammapada Commentary* this is done by initially presenting a stanza of text from the *Dhammapada* followed by an illustrative narrative as commentary. For example, the first story, that of "The Monk Cakkhupāla," begins with the opening stanza of the *Dhammapada* followed by the story of the monk. As pointed out by Burlingame, we thus have a pattern of text followed by a narrative illustration, but no formal exegesis.

In the *Saddharmaratnāvaliya,* however, religious and philosophical commentary is reintroduced, but it is closely incorporated into the body of the narratives. Sometimes the commentary is in the form of expanded descriptive imagery, as in the opening image of the Kāḷī story.

> As a bush fire burning out of control stops only when it reaches a vast body of water, so the rage of one who vows vengeance cannot be

quelled except by the waters of compassion that fill the ocean of Omniscience.[6]

At other times, the commentary is in the form of discourses spoken by characters within the story, or of authorial remarks at relevant points in the story, or sometimes even as sermons preached by the Buddha, when he appears as a character in a story. The long sermon on the three basic requirements for a Buddhist (Generosity, Moral Conduct, and Contemplation), which the Buddha preaches to Mahāpāla, the protagonist in the Cakkhupāla story, (p. 12) is one such example. So also is the sermon on Forgiveness that is preached to the demoness Kāḷī when she enters the monastery to devour her victim's child. (pp. 102–103)

The commentaries are thus skillfully contextualized and carefully incorporated into the narrative framework, thereby becoming an integral element of the story. The exegesis is made internal to the story, and because it is framed, as in the example quoted above, it allows for additional subtleties, nuances, explanations, and insights.

In the story of Tissa the Fat, the pigheaded stubbornness of the monk is deplored by his fellows, who seem at a loss to understand why the Buddha tolerates such disobedience from a junior monk. The Buddha responds with a marvelous metaphor that both explains the action and illuminates his understanding of the complexities of human psychology.

"Listen O monks. If one says, 'That man scolded me, tried to kill me, beat me, defend me in argument or stole what belonged to me,' and if, whatever the cause, one harbors thoughts of hatred and vengeance, one then deposits that treasure [vengeance], which is of significance only to oneself, inside the container of one's mind and binds it tightly with the rope of one's thoughts. The result is fearful for the person concerned. Therefore in such a situation, wise men like the Buddhas do not undo that rope with a single tug. Instead they untie it slowly, take the pot in their hands and place it where it cannot be knocked over. If they do not do so, since the bonds are strong, even if the ropes were to disintegrate and the pot to break, the person concerned will merely transfer his treasure [vengeance] into another pot and tie it still more tightly with rope. Thus it [vengeance] would never die."[7]

The contrast with the corresponding passage in the *Dhammapada Commentary* is illuminating:

Then he addressed the Elder Tissa as follows, "Tissa if a monk allows himself to think, 'So and So abused me, So and So struck me, So and So defeated me, So and So robbed me of my goods,' his hatred never

> ceases. But if he does not cherish such thoughts his hatred ceases." So saying he pronounced the following stanzas.[8]

The doctrinal imput can also come in the form of authorial comment when the author explicates a specific Buddhist philosophical concept for the benefit of a lay audience. In the Cakkhupāla story, the *Dhammapada Commentary* merely describes the merchant Mahāsumana in the following terms:

> He was rich, possessed of great wealth, possessed of ample means of enjoyment but at the same time was childless.[9]

The Saddharmaratnāvaliya expands these lines with the following image in order to explain the manner in which the Buddhist doctrine of *karma* operates:

> Though blessed with much wealth he had no offspring to enjoy its benefits. Trees that bear fruit do so only in due season. Perhaps the good deeds of his past existences had not sufficiently matured to provide him with the blessing of a son.[10]

Implicit in the explanation is the question, if a man is blessed with so much, his past *karma* must have been good. Why then is he childless? Here the explanation is given (as is so often the case in this text) as an authorial comment as well as through a simple image drawn from a worldly totally comprehensible to his rural agricultural audience.

The *Saddharmaratnāvaliya* is a written not an oral text so the language used is the written (as opposed to the colloquial) form.[11] The style is that of classical Sinhala literary works of the medieval period. The tone in which the stories are told however, often suggests the speaking voice of a storyteller. Thus, the imagery is of two kinds. Sometimes there is a brief but telling simile drawn from the familiar world of agricultural peasant living. "If a man wraps himself in a monk's robe while his mind is stained with Defilements, it is as if he were to decorate the outside of a pot containing feces." Sometimes, as in the description of the Buddha on p. 41, there is a highly formalized account in the classical style of ornamental prose where image is added to image creating an overall impression of rich elaboration:

> Thus on the dawn of the second day the Buddha rose from his meditative trance. . . . He put on his robe, which was like a garland of Kobōlīla flowers dipped in lacquer and glowed like a coral embedded in a piece of red lacquer. He draped his robe from his navel to the knee-cap

> so as to cover three parts of his body and emerged like a full moon partly hidden by rosy clouds. Over the robe he tied a belt, glistening with pearls, strung on a golden chain that looked like a lightening bolt. Over that he wore the outer robe, which was like a spread of red Hibiscus flowers, or Ficus fruits, or like a red carpet thrown over the forehead of an elephant, or a net of pearls encasing a golden lampstand, or a red carpet covering a golden *stūpa,* or a rosy cloud covering a full moon, or molten lacquer flowing down a golden mountain or like the Sithulpauva mountain in the Himalayas, encircled with a garland of Hibiscus flowers.[12]

Again the contrast with the relevant passage in the *Dhammapada Commentary* is revealing:

> Accordingly, on the following day, having attended to his toilet, he surrounded himself with a large company of monks and entered Sāvatthi for alms . . . [13]

It is the one phrase, "having attended to his toilet" that the narrator of the *Saddharmaratnāvaliya* builds into a one page description. It is as if the very profuseness and stylistic hyperbole suggest the impossibility of the narrator's task, fumbling to find words to describe the indescribable beauty of the Buddha's person. By contrast, when the intended effect is different, the descriptions, though still in the rhetorical literary style, are devoid of that element of ornateness. Thus, the dying child Maṭṭakuṇḍalī's vision of the Buddha is conveyed in formal, but simple, moving terms. The effect again is cumulative but the language and imagery work very differently.

> Maṭṭakuṇḍalī saw the Buddha, who soothes the eye of those who look upon him, calms the minds of those who think of him, lulls the ear of those who hear him, whose goodness, acquired through a hundred million eons, is as if moulded together and sculpted into a single form.[14]

While some of the stories are richly elaborated and provide fascinating interpretations of philosophical and doctrinal issues as well as insights into Sri Lanka peasant life in the thirteenth century, others in the collection are a close rendering of the Pāli originals, sometimes almost verbatim translations. (e.g. the tale of the pig-killer Cunda, p. 189) It is possible that Dharmasēna occasionally got tired of his task (as is understandable), or his creativity flagged. However, the work as a whole has the stamp of his identity, is suffused with rare insight, and a deeply Buddhist compassion for the human condition.

The *Saddharmaratnāvaliya* can be read at many levels. Its seemingly simple stories can provide a commentary on profound philosophical questions of doctrinal Buddhism. For example, the Kāḷī story is not just a tale of violence, vengeance, and their final resolution. It is a study, in Buddhist terms, of the complex and pervasive nature of violence, its inevitable counterpart — vengeance, and the increasing momentum of their interaction that enmeshes both the initial aggressor and the victim. As the action develops, the narrative flow speeds up until the reader soon loses track of who initiated the violent acts or who was the original victim. Distinctions between protagonist and antagonist or the "good" one and the "evil" one are consciously blurred. Their roles are successively reversed. Both become trapped in a cycle of violence and vengeance, propelled by "justifications" until the question as to who was initially guilty or innocent ceases to be relevant. In this instance, the narrative structure itself provides the intended doctrinal commentary. (See the story of Kāḷī, p. 97)

Again, in this particular story, rewards and punishments are not evenly handed out according to who was initially guilty or who initially innocent. The karmic doctrine as illustrated here is far more complex. The initial victim is in fact reborn as the demoness, while it is the cruel first wife who is reborn as the woman with the child. The moral of the story does not turn on the question of guilt or innocence. Once they both resort to acts of violence such distinctions cease to matter. Instead the action of the story shows that, tied as they are in their interpersonal acts of violence, they now have to work out their salvation jointly.

The story also illustrates how such a cycle of cumulative hatred and vengeance *can* be broken. A daring gesture of trust and generosity on the part of one toward the other, whether by the victim or by the evildoer, is needed if the violence is to stop and goodness and security be restored. Nor does the story end with the cessation of the violence. It goes on to illustrate the slow arduous process of restoration by which the demonic is transformed into the divine and becomes a potential for active good.

In most folk or fairy tales, such transformations are usually instantaneous. Given the Buddhist karmic framework, the consequences of an evil action must be worked out. Even the Buddha's active involvement, as in this case, does not result in a forgiveness of sin or instant redemption. Through his discourse, the Buddha leads the demoness to the path of Enlightenment. However, her evil karma accumulated through her past actions continues to work itself out, and she suffers a series of hardships over a period of time. Finally, she arrives at a state of tranquillity and from then on engages only in acts that are beneficial to those around her. Kāḷī the demoness becomes transformed into Kāḷī the benevolent, a guardian deity, a power for good.

For the anthropologist, this particular story provides an insight into the process by which demons and figures from folk cults are absorbed and made ethical in a Buddhist framework. In neither the *Dhammapada Commentary* nor the *Saddharmaratnāvaliya* is the demoness identified as Kāḷī in the body of the text. She is merely referred to as the demoness. However, by the time of the *Saddharmaratnāvaliya,* not only is the story entitled "The Tale of the demoness Kāḷī," but the identification is clearly stated in the final paragraph. Thus, the demoness story of early legend becomes an origin myth for Kāḷī who, by the time of the text, seems already to be incorporated into popular Buddhism.

It is interesting that demon exorcistic rituals even today, enact a process similar to that described in the Kāḷī story, whereby evil or demonic influences are banished, stage by stage, from within an individual or a household into the outer environment.

Dharmasēna's work is an important resource for scholars from many disciplines. All kinds of information can be gleaned about thirteenth century attitudes and relationships, whether between individuals and social groups, between kings and subjects, or men and women. A comparison of the text of the *Saddharmaratnāvaliya* with that of the *Dhammapada Commentary* also provides insights into some of the changes and shifts that might have occurred in political and social institutions between the fifth and thirteenth centuries.

For example, in the story of "The Monk Tissa the Fat" a quarrel between two ascetics results in one exercising his magical powers to prevent the sun from rising. The people, disturbed by this event, rush to the king. The fifth century *Dhammapada Commentary* version is as follows:

> When the sun failed to rise the citizens assembled before the gate of the king's palace and wailed, "Your Majesty, the sun has not risen and you are king. Make the sun rise for us." The King surveyed his own deeds, words, and thoughts and, seeing no impropriety, thought to himself, "What can be the cause?"[15]

The *Saddharmaratnāvaliya* version introduces a subtle shift that suggests a very different relationship between king and people:

> When the sun did not rise that day the citizens of that town went to the king and said, "Your Majesty, the sun that has risen every morning ever since the beginning of your reign has not yet risen today. Just as you collect taxes regularly from all your provinces and outer regions before the year is out, so before this day is over make the sun rise." On hearing them the king wondered at first if it could be because of some lapse, such as lack of impartiality on his part. He called to mind his own past actions and could find nothing that he had done wrong.[16]

In the fifth century text, a terrified populace stands at the palace gate and humbly begs an all-powerful monarch to exercise his divine or magical powers to make the sun rise. In the thirteenth century version by contrast, one clearly hears the tone of a demand. Kingship is seen as a contractual arrangement. Just as citizens must pay taxes by a due date, so now it is the king's duty to make the sun rise, without delay. While underlying both versions is the assumption that the king is responsible for the welfare of his subjects and that natural disasters are caused by some lapse in kingly duty or conduct, yet the markedly different tone of the later version (heightened by the choice of image) suggests that certain subtle changes may have occurred in the relationship between rulers and ruled. Alternatively one could interpret it as Dharmasēna Thera's statement of the Buddhist view of that relationship.

One of the earliest records of the practice of exercising choice by individual vote and the acceptance of the decision of the majority on an issue, occurs in the Buddhist texts of the *Vinaya Piṭaka*. It is one of the rules laid down for the organization of the monastic order. Scholars while accepting its basically democratic feature in early Buddhist organizations, tended to regard it primarily as a system of endorsement, through voting, of accepted or popular decisions.

In the *Saddharmaratnāvaliya* story of the *Ochre Robe* we see how powerful the concept had become in the Buddhist world and how it had percolated through into situations of ordinary daily living. In this story, so entrenched is the idea that a majority decision must be upheld that it is carried out even when the choice is clearly wrong. The *Saddharmaratnāvaliya* text reads as follows:

> The organizer of the food offering said, "The golden robe, which a certain nobleman gifted is still left. To whom should we give it?"
>
> Like a man who, when asked about rice-fields, points out the most fertile field he knows, so someone suggested it be given to the Senior Monk Säriyut, who was like a fertile field fed by the waters of Discipline, which he had cultivated for over one incalculable and one hundred thousand eons in order to become the Buddha's chief disciple. But others, worthless themselves, as if pointing out an abandoned field that has lain fallow for so long that it had become an uncultivable marsh, said, "This monk Säriyut is like the man who visits only when the pot of rice is cooked. He comes to stay for a week or a month and then leaves. The monk Devidat on the other hand is constantly with us. He is like a medicinal plant, of great use to us."
>
> Since usefulness is something that everyone always likes, those who considered it a significant virtue asked that the robe be given to him. In this debate, those in favor of giving the robe to Devidat were in a majority. Therefore, in spite of the fact that the monk Devidat did

> not belong to the order of the Ariyas, and so was lower in rank than the Senior Monk Säriyut, and was inferior in goodness, since he did not possess the virtues of Moral Conduct and Contemplation, and though he was lower in status, since he had not achieved the position of a disciple, and was full of wickedness, since he had nursed a grievance unassuaged over a period of five eons, swearing vengeance over a golden plate (as related in the *Serivāṇija Jātaka*), they still gave the robe to him. He cut it up like a monk's robe and wore it.[17]

Giving the robe to Devidat was clearly the wrong choice, yet it was the wish of the majority and so had to be done. Thus, the incident illustrates the percolation of the concept of majority choice which was a monastic practice, into everyday Buddhist life.

Several incidents in the *Saddharmaratnāvaliya* stories substantiate the theory that Buddhism resulted in a spread of learning into the wider society, unlike with the Brahmanic tradition where religious knowledge was the preserve of a small elite. I shall quote two incidents from the story of Nāgasēna.

The young monk Nāgasēna is on his way to the city of Pälaḷup when he encounters a rich merchant returning from a business trip. The merchant invites the monk to travel with him and in the course of conversation, asks, "Did you become a monk only because of the exigencies of time and place or do you know the Teachings?"

Nāgasēna replies that, since he did not go through the normal period of apprenticeship with a preceptor, he has not studied the *Vinaya Piṭaka* or the *Sutta Piṭaka,* which contains the Scriptural texts. He only knows the *Abhidhamma Piṭaka* (which of course is the most abstract and complex book of the canon). The merchant is delighted. "That is indeed excellent, because I, too, am familiar with the *Abhidhamma Piṭaka,*" he replies.

The text continues:

> Just as one who knows Tamil, when addressed in Tamil, is excited at the chance to speak the language, so the merchant said, "It is fortunate that we met. We may not be equal in learning but it is always possible to learn from one who knows more, so please preach to me from the *Abhidhamma.*"
>
> Since the merchant had said he was familiar with the text, the monk wished to disclose the full range of his powers. So, like teaching an artisan, who knows his craft, he preached from the *Abhidhamma Piṭaka* holding nothing back of its profoundities. The merchant heard the sermon and in addition to his worldly wealth he now acquired the wealth of Spiritual Attainments.[18]

Again, in another incident in the same story an old woman offers Nāgasēna alms. The monk accepts and in return, as is customary, he is about to preach a short sermon. Before he can begin the old woman interrupts saying,

> "I am old. Simple little sermons are not of much use to me. Preach to me a sermon of profound and complex Teachings." Nāgasēna then took what he considered a subject of complexity, the doctrine of "no-soul" from the *Abhidhamma Piṭaka.* The aged devotee heard the sermon and though she was old at the time, became a Stream-Enterer, a state in which one never grows old.[19]

These incidents, even though only casual references, illustrate what has been substantiated by other evidence, as for example the seventh century graffiti verses at Sigiriya, that in Sri Lanka, learning and education had spread beyond the confines of monks and scholars to a wider selection of society.

Quite apart from the wealth of information the stories provide about the life and customs of the time, Dharmasēna's narrative power and sense of dramatic timing, coupled with his instinct for the homely but pointed, sometimes even poignant image, make his work eminently readable. A brief passage from the Kāḷī story illustrates this:

> She finished her bath, climbed back on to the bank and was sitting suckling her child while her husband took his bath. Suddenly she saw the demoness approach. Having seen her twice before, she recognized her instantly. She shouted, "Quick! Come ashore, the child-eating ogress is coming," and without waiting for him, she ran to the temple and rushed in through the door. At this time the Buddha, accompanied by a retinue of forty monks, was seated preaching in the temple. The terrified woman cut through the crowds, rushed right up to the Buddha, and, as if placing a water jar on a pillow covered in a wondrously colored spread, laid the tiny infant down and placed the child's head on his feet, which were resplendent with the one hundred and eight auspicious marks.[20]

The mother's panic is contrasted with the serenity associated with the Buddha and brilliantly captured in the juxtaposition of the briefly described, hurried actions with the elaborate extended image, all tied together by the rolling rhythms of the long sentences. By contrast the *Dhammapada Commentary* version reads:

> Now at this time, the Teacher was preaching the Law in the midst of the congregation. The young wife laid her boy at the feet of the Tathagata and said, "I give this child to you. Spare the life of my son."[21]

The *Saddharmaratnāvaliya* has proved entertaining reading (and listening) for generations of Sri Lankans. Like all great works of literature it deals with the vicissitudes of the human condition, so although written in the thirteenth century and very much a work of its time it is timeless in its relevance and appeal.

At present the work is known only to the Sinhala reader. In making a case for the need for an English translation I can but quote the words of the Elder, Kumāra Kassapa to the original translator: "Because it is composed in the language of the island it is of no profit or advantage to foreigners."

As far back as the fifth century A.D., the stories were thought worthy to be translated into the language of international Buddhism. There is at present an English translation only of the Pāli *Dhammapada Commentary.* A translation of the thirteenth century Sinhala *Saddharmaratnāvaliya* will, I believe, provide an interesting comparative base.

I have tried to stay closer to my original than my fifth century or thirteenth century predecessors have done. I chose to do so in an attempt to convey something of the flavor and the rich elaboration of the original, the piquant mixture of a colloquial tone with the formalism of literary style that characterizes the Sinhala work. It is an almost impossible task however to hit that fine balance between readability in English and faithfulness to the flavor and character of the Sinhala. If I were translating these stories only for the general English reader, I would perhaps have done what my predecessors did, translate freely in a style and rhetoric accessible to such an audience. However, since I see my work also as a resource, providing students of Buddhism, Asian historians, and social scientists with access to the thirteenth century Sinhala *text,* I have chosen to stay as close to the original as it is possible to do without making it unreadable.

This manuscript contains only the fifteen stories that comprise the first section of the *Saddharmaratnāvaliya.* I decided to translate the fifteen stories in sequential order, not only because they stand together to form the first unit in the book, illustrating the stanzas from the first section of the *Dhammapada,* the *Yamaka Vagga* [Twin Verses], but because some of these early stories have linked passages that make the sequential order important.

I have decided however *not* to try to translate the rest of the *Saddharmaratnāvaliya* in its entirety. To translate the entire work (which I had rashly imagined I could do in two years), I now realize will probably take me the rest of my life. Instead, I hope to bring out a second volume of *selected* stories. The two volumes together should then give readers some sense of what the *Saddharmaratnāvaliya* is like.

THE TEXT

My translation is based on the most recent edition (1985) of the *Saddharmaratnāvaliya* that has been published by the Association for Oriental Languages and edited by the Colombo University's Sinhala Department. This text, the editors claim, was based on a careful examination of eleven extant *ōla* manuscripts, and seven earlier published versions of 1894, 1914, 1925, 1928, 1936, and 1954. I shall summarize their comments.

The palm leaf manuscripts studied belonged to the following libraries:

1. Talagama Rājamahā Vihāra library at Ambēpussa.
2. Padumārāma Vihāra library at Polhēna, Mātara.
3. Agrabōdhi Rājamahā Vihāra library at Väligama. (This was an incomplete manuscript.)
4. Tupārāma Vihāra library at Gintoṭa, Galle.
5. Toṭagamuva Rājamahā Vihāra library at Telvatta, Toṭagamuva.
6. Siyambalāgoda Potgul Vihāra library at Kaḍugannāva. (This, too, was an incomplete manuscript with a section missing at the end. The work concluded with the story of King Pasēnadi of Kosol.)
7. Sūriyagoda Sri Narendrārāma Rājamahā Vihāra library at Murutalāva, Kandy. (Another incomplete manuscript, but the missing section was attached to the beginning of the manuscript, so that the work begins with the story of The Copper-pot Thief.)
8. Gaṅgātilaka Vihara library at Puhuvala, Mīvanapalāna. (This, too, had a section missing at the beginning. It began with the story of Prince Anitthigandha.
9. Pälmadulla Rājamahā Vihāra library at Pälmadulla.
10. Pahalagama Vidyāravinda Pirivena library at Yaṭavatta, Gampaha.
11. Doṁbovela Rājamahā Vihāra library at Mātale. (This had a small section missing in the middle, that is, fifteen pages from the story of the Four Novices to the middle of the story of the Senior Monk Jaṭila.

The editors further state that the copies at the Padumārāma, Agrabōdhi, Tupārāma, Totagamuva, and Pälmadulla temple libraries were found to be almost identical, which seemed to suggest the possibility that they were copied from a single manuscript. The fact that four of them came from the South of Sri Lanka lent further support to this position. They found that the copies at the Pahalagama and Doṁbavela temple libraries though not as closely similar, had many resemblances. Those at Toṭagamuva, Siyambalāgoda and Gaṅgātilaka temple libraries seemed to belong to a very different tradition. The manuscript at the Agrabōdhi temple library was badly preserved and the letters difficult to read. However, it had marked differences from the other manuscripts and in some instances much more felicitious usages. It was clear this manuscript belonged to a completely different tradition.

Of the published editions, the one by Sir D. B. Jayatilleke seemed to them to be the most accurate because its editor had given priority to the manuscript version and not attempted to change the text according to what he thought was correct. Important words were footnoted. Three of the other editions, those of Baṭuvantudāve, Wēragama, and Indajōti Thera, seemed to have come from a single manuscript. However they stayed close to their text. The edition by Bentara Saddhātissa Thera was based on a manuscript from a different tradition. While all the editors had not attempted to change or "amend" the text, they had tried to keep close to the earlier versions. Vēragoda Amaramōli Thera, in his edition, seemed to consider some of the manuscripts he had consulted as erroneous and sought to amend the text to provide what he considered a better reading.[22]

My translation is based mainly on the 1985 edition, but I have also used the editions by Kiriälle Ñāṇavimala Thera (1971), D. B. Jayatilleke (1936), and L. Gunaratne's text for schools for their notes, comments, and variant readings.

THE AUTHOR: DHARMASĒNA THERA

The *Saddharmaratnāvaliya* ends with a specific reference to its author. The colophon to the work, a four-lined Pāli stanza, states, "The Senior Monk Dharmasēna desiring to firmly establish the True Doctrine composed this great work known as the Saddharmaratnāvali."[23] Such statements of authorship are not unusual. Several early Sinhala literary works carry similar references. It is a characteristic perhaps of cultures where authors and their works were respected, honored and even venerated. It is also a mark of the difference between an oral and a written tradition. The moment a particular individual decides to "write" a work —even a work that may have existed earlier in an oral form—the writer puts the stamp of authorship on it. The process is distinct from scribal activity and never confused with it. The one is an accurate transcribing of an extant work, the other is a "writing" of it, which then transforms it. Such a "recreated" work was often given a distinctive title. The *Saddharmaratnāvaliya* well illustrates the latter process.

Apart from the fact that we are given the author's name and informed that he was a monk, we are told nothing more, not even where he lived or the name of his monastery (the kind of additional information that many texts do carry). A later work, the *Nikāya Saṅgrahaya*, which lists the names of monks and laymen writing between the fifth and thirteenth centuries A.D. does however have one other reference. The list consists of twenty-two names of monks which concludes thus:

> Similarly monks such as Slōkasiddārtha, Sāhitya-Vilgammula, Anuruddha, Dīpaṅkara, Mayurapāda, Dharmasēna, as well as Sūrapāda . . . and other lay scholars, wrote sermons, collections of verses, commentaries, exegeses of various concepts and several philosophical works.[24]

Scholars believe that the Dharmasēna referred to is the author of the *Saddharmaratnāvaliya*. Not only does the name end the list, follow that of Mayurapāda, author of the *Pūjāvaliya*, but the two works are also stylistically very close and mark a break with an older tradition of writing. The *Pūjāvaliya* states, within the text itself, the date of its composition,[25] the events that led to the composition, and names Parakramabahu II as the king who was reigning at the time. Scholars are agreed on the basis of linguistic and other evidence, that the *Pūjāvaliya* and the *Saddharmaratnāvaliya* belong to roughly the same period (thirteenth century), a period of considerable literary activity under a king who was himself known to be a scholar, poet, and a patron of the arts.[26] Sinhala literature flourished during the period and several extant works document this.

Whatever other information we can find is what we can glean from the text itself. The stories reveal a man of considerable scholarship, profound psychological insight, and a familiarity with the lives and concerns of lay society of all classes, whether nobles, merchants, or peasants. We gather, too, that he was very likely a *granthadura* monk, involved in an active life of scholarship and preaching, rather than a reclusive *Vanavāsin* monk engaged in a life of meditation.

The numerous references to medical lore, the detailed knowledge of its theory and practice, which permeate the text of the *Saddharmaratnāvaliya*, suggest that he was familiar with medical texts and theories, (considered part of classical Sanskritic literature) and was perhaps a practitioner himself. It was not uncommon for monks to practice medicine. We know that the monk Mayurapāda, author of the *Pūjāvaliya* and Dharmasēna's contemporary, wrote two treatises on medicine and was very likely a medical practitioner. Many Sri Lankan Buddhist monks actively practice medicine even today.

The style of the writing, the pithy, earthy images, the lengthy digressions, interpolated sermons, and the flair with which he explains abstruse doctrinal concepts to a lay audience, all suggest a skilled teacher, who no doubt spent a lifetime perfecting his art.

It is significant that not only is a specific author mentioned for the *Saddharmaratnāvaliya* but that the work, though based on the *Dhammapada Commentary,* was also given a distinctive title. For the author, this work is not just a translation of the earlier *Dhammapada Commentary* (as he takes pains to state in his introduction). The stories are Jewels *(ratna),* rare, faceted, reflecting and refracting light. They are strung together in a garland or necklace *(āvaliya),* linked, so that both individually and together they can illuminate profound truths of the *Saddharma,* the True Doctrine or Teachings. Thus, the work is more than a religious commentary on a text, which is what the *Dhammapada Commentary* claims to be. In giving his work the title *Saddharmaratnāvaliya,* Dharmasēna is making a statement about the inherent unity and artistic coherence of his work. He achieves this unity by conscious effects such as passages and cross references that link and counterpoint the stories one with another.

It is achieved also through the distinctive voice of the author that permeates the text. It is a voice that shifts easily from homely colloquialisms to resonant rhetoric, and pithy aside to the lofty cadence, and is suffused with a humor and humanity that is characteristic of the best tradition of Buddhist sermons, a tradition that has come down even to the present times. As I read the *Saddharmaratnāvaliya,* the monk Dharmasēna's voice seems to blend in with other voices of other monks whose sermons I have listened to during my childhood, growing up in Sri Lanka. It is a voice that is both distinctive *and* familiar because it is very much part of a continuing and living tradition.

NOTES ON THE ORGANIZATION OF THIS WORK

The Prologue

I have not translated, in its entirety, the opening prologue or *Sūvisi Vivaraṇa kathā* and the *Buddha Carita kathā.* They are accounts of the twenty-four occasions when the Buddha Gōtama in his previous lives as a Bōdhisatva, performed acts of sacrifice and obtained a "prophetic revelation" *(vivaraṇa)* from other Buddhas, a form of legitimation enabling him to pursue his own quest for Buddhahood. This is followed by an account of the life of the Buddha. The incidents are familiar to most Buddhist readers and tend to have a repetitive and formal quality. I decided therefore to translate only a few sections of this formal preamble to give the reader a sense of the author's style and intentions.

Buddhist Terms and Concepts

All Buddhist philosophical terms and concepts, which I have rendered into English, are capitalized and glossed. Sometimes they are the phrases in current usage in Buddhist literature, and sometimes I have used my own translations of a word or concept, which I feel convey the meaning better in the given context. For example, for the concept *lovī lovuturā säpa* I have used the simple phrase 'blessings of the world as well as Spiritual Attainments.' *Lovuturā* is generally translated in the literature as "Supramundane" or "Transcendental." I decided to use the less technical phrase and give the exact meaning in the glossary.

In the case of some concepts such as *karma, nirvāṇa, saṃsāra* and so forth, which are already familiar to most readers, I have decided to keep the Pāli term and gloss the meaning. It makes for a less cumbersome translation.

Sinhala Forms of Proper Names

I have retained the Sinhala form of most of the proper names even though they differ somewhat from the Pāli, by which they are more popularly known. I did this intentionally to keep something of the flavor of the original Sinhala. For example, I have used Sävät for Sāvatthi and Anēpiḍu for Anātapindika.

Notes and Comments

Notes and Comments have been placed at the end of each story. This allows me to cater to two (possible) categories of readers. Those who do not need further explanations can read the stories without the distraction of footnotes while those who need them will find them at the end of the story. For convenience, in the sections of notes and comments the *Saddharmaratnāvaliya* is referred to as the SR and the *Dhammapadaṭṭhakatha* as the DA.

Pāli Stanzas Quoted in the Text

I have decided to retain the Pāli stanzas within the body of the English translation, for that is how they appear interpolated in the Sinhala text. I have given the English translation of the Pāli verse in a footnote. I decided on this format partly because it follows to some degree the pattern of the Sinhala original. The author inserts the Pāli stanzas within the Sinhala text (no doubt intending them to be sonorously chanted when read aloud) but being aware that Sinhala lay readers and listeners of his time probably knew very little Pāli, he follows it with a translation or paraphrase. If I were to render the original Pāli text in English and then follow it with Dharmasēna's paraphrase, which I would also have to translate into English, the effect would not only be clumsy but repetitive and inelegant. By keeping the Pāli stanza with a translation only in a footnote the reader can enjoy Dharmasēna's sometimes elaborate, sometimes terse paraphrases and compare them with their Pāli originals. The English translation then reads more smoothly.

Endnotes

INTRODUCTION

1. This identification has been subsequently contested. See Burlingame's Introduction to the *Dhammapada Commentary* Harvard Oriental Series, 1979, Vol. 28, p. 59.

2. E. W. Burlingame 1979, p. 145.

3. Ibid., p. 145.

4. *Saddharmaratnāvaliya*, 1985, Vol. I, p. 2. (Colombo: Government Publications Bureau, 1985).

5. Burlingame, 1979, p. 26

6. *Saddharmaratnāvaliya*, vol. I p. 75.

7. Ibid., p. 74.

8. Burlingame, 1979, p. 170.

9. Ibid., Vol. 28, p. 146.

10. *Saddharmaratnāvaliya*, p. 24.

11. In Sinhala the distinction between the two forms is quite marked. The written language differs in grammar, style and often also vocabulary.

12. *Saddharmaratnāvaliya*, p. 43.

13. Burlingame, 1979, p. 160.

14. *Saddharmaratnāvaliya*, p. 44.

15. Burlingame, 1979, p. 169.

16. *Saddharmaratnāvaliya*, p. 72.

17. *Saddharmaratnāvaliya*, p. 94.

18. Ibid., *Nāgasēna*, p. 65.

19. Ibid., p. 64.

20. Ibid., p. 78.

21. Burlingame, 1979, p. 174.

22. A Summarized translation from the Introduction to the *Saddharmaratnāvaliya*, 1985, pp. x–xii.

23. The *Saddharmaratnāvaliya*, 1971, p. 1246.

24. The *Nikāyasaṅgrahaya* by Jayabāhau Dēvarakṣita, ed. by M. de Z Wickramasinghe, 1890 and translated by C. M. Fernando, 1908, p. 24.

25. The date is given as 'one thousand eight hundred and fifty four years after the *prathambōdhi*' (the first enlightenment of the Buddha). Godakumbura (1955) makes the calculation to be 1266 A.D.

26. Godakumbura 1955, p. 82.

Saddharmaratnāvaliya
(The Jewel Garland of the True Doctrine)

Extract from the *Sūvisi Vivaraṇa kathā* (The Stories of the Twenty-Four Prophetic Reveleations)

namo tassa bhagavato arahato sammāsambuddhassa
(I salute the exalted, the noble, the All-Enlightened One)

Like the earth, which supports the Three Worlds, as deep as the ocean, limitless as the sky, as steadfast as Mount Meru, as majestic as the sun and gentle as the moon, our Lord Buddha, Teacher of the Three Worlds, his mind cooled by compassion, about four incalculables and one hundred thousand eons ago,[1] during the time of the Buddha Dīpaṅkara, on hearing just a mere part of a four lined Doctrinal stanza, destroyed all Defilements and acquired sufficient merit to become a Buddha. However, because of his compassion for all beings, he thought that to do so would be as if, during a time of famine, he were to consume alone a meal he had obtained, while others looked on hungrily. So he decided, "It is not fit that I should attain *nirvāṇa* while not just one or two, but twenty-four incalculables of beings are sinking in the ocean of *saṃsāra* as the ship of their meritorious deeds founders for lack of the strong planks of Wisdom. Therefore, like this kingly Sage (the Buddha Dīpaṅkara), Teacher of the Three Worlds, I, too, will become a Buddha in order to help them cross the sea of *saṃsāra*. I will lead them on to the great port of Enlightenment in a ship constructed of the Thirty-Seven Factors of Enlightenment with planks and sails of Wisdom and a mast of Contemplation; a ship that I will build throughout an entirety[2] of four incalculables and one hundred thousand eons. Then, using the hand of my sermons I will row them across to the shore of *nirvāṇa*. Thus, he resolved to be a Buddha.

For earlier, in the time of the Buddha Brahmadeva, he had made the resolve mentally, and in the time of the Buddha Gautama the Senior he had made the resolve verbally, and so he already had the requisite prior *karmic* foundations. Thereafter, born a man not a woman, he had become an ascetic and attained Higher Knowledge. Greatly meritorious, and with the firm resolve to become a Buddha, he sacrificed his life to the then living Buddha Dīpaṅkara, who then made a prophetic declaration.[3] Just as those with Understanding of the Path refrain from all sinful acts and are established in the land of the Noble Ones, so he engaged in meritorious acts intent on fulfilling the Thirty Perfections. And just as those with Understanding wash off the dirt of Defilements and make their minds pure, so he purified his mind. With his pure mind he advised others, like righteous parents who discipline their children so they become righteous like themselves. Thus, he refrained from all acts of Demerit, did only what was good and purified his mind in order to attain the blessings of this world as well as Spiritual Attainments.

Therefore follow his advice, refrain from all sinful acts, engage in good acts, and purify the mind. As in times of rain there is prosperity and in times of drought there is hardship and both prosperity and hardship are dependent on rainfall, so engagement in the Doctrine is essential for those who hope to attain the Teachings of *nirvāṇa*.

Engagement in the Doctrine comes from a study of the Teachings with a mind intent on renunciation. Just as an ant cannot pierce through a crystal mountain or as one, who has become a Stream-Enterer, cannot indulge in sinful acts that lead to hell, so without good actions, without knowing the true nature of phenomena and understanding its characteristics, one of little intelligence cannot achieve that goal, as a man, blind from birth, cannot find his way without a cane. Only a being of great merit can.

Therefore, if there be one who, though lacking in intellect, has a desire to do good, in order that such a faithful one may obtain advice, understand the Teachings, engage in meritorious acts, and finally achieve *nirvāṇa*, for the benefit of such good men do we compose this treatise named the "*Saddharmaratnāvaliya*."[4]

We have abandoned the Pāli method and taken only the themes in composing this work. It may have faults and stylistic shortcomings, but (you the reader should) ignore them. Be like the swans who separate milk from water even though the milk and water be mixed together, or like those who acquire learning and skills even from a teacher of low caste, because it is only the acquisition of knowledge not the teacher's status with which they are concerned. So, consider only its usefulness, and those who have their Eye of Wisdom clouded in a hazy film of Delusion and lost in the great forest of misdeeds do not see the road leading to the city of *nirvāṇa*, apply the healing salve of the *Saddharmaratnāvaliya* to remove the film of Delusion that blinds the Eye of Wisdom, and go happily with clear Vision along the highway of Right Actions to the city of *nirvāṇa*.

Just as one protects one's herds of oxen and, when they stray toward dangerous marshlands, directs them to the grassy pastures, so one should control the mind that veers always toward sinful acts. There is no being superior to one's own mind. Therefore, to keep oneself from sinful deeds, establish oneself in what is good, and avoid such sins as the harming of living creatures, one should discipline one's own mind.

A woman bears all the pains of childbirth thinking, "What greater pleasure is there than to look on the face of the child one has borne." Similarly, think only of the flavor of *nirvāṇa* one is about to savor. Thus, beginning with the story of the Senior Monk Cakkhupāla, who disregarded the pain in his eyes, we have decorated the highway to the city of *nirvāṇa* with the festive banners of three hundred stories, and constructed a great hall named the *Saddharmaratnāvaliya*, so that you can rest there in the company of those who now proceed to the city of *nirvāṇa*.

As it is said: Our Buddha, Teacher of the Three Worlds, about four incalculables and eighty thousand eons ago, in the land of Daṁbadiva . . . (The text then relates the *Sūvisi Vivaraṇa* or stories of the twenty-four occasions when, in past lives, the Bōdhisatva made supreme sacrifices and fulfilled the Perfections, each time making a Rebirth-Wish to become a Buddha. On each occasion, he obtained a "prophetic declaration" or guarantee from the Buddha living at the time, that he, too, would become a Buddha. This is followed by an account of his final birth as prince Siddartha and of his life and teachings as the Buddha. The stories of the *Buddhacarita,* as they are called, are a standard introduction to much of Buddhist literature and therefore familiar. I have not translated these sections of the text. I have, however, translated the concluding paragraphs of this lengthy preamble, because there, the monk Dharmasēna, in his inimitable, faintly ironic style, seems to provide a rationale for the telling of stories.)

... Of the two (the disciples Visākhā and Anēpiḍu) the nobleman Anēpiḍu, never asked the Buddha a single question on any occasion. Why did he not do so? Not because he believed the Buddha was incapable of preaching, but that he thought, "The Revered Buddha is delicate. As becomes a king, he is delicate. It would tire him to preach to me, feeling obliged to do so because he thinks 'This nobleman has been very helpful to me.' "

Meanwhile the Buddha on his part, thought, "This nobleman seeks to protect me where I do not need protection. I have fulfilled the Perfections and gifted my head, my eyes, my flesh, and blood for no other reason but to become a Buddha and show others the path to *nirvāṇa.* One cannot show the path to *nirvāṇa* without preaching the Doctrine. Apart from Buddhas and Pasē Buddhas, who is there who can do without words of admonition from another?

For it is said:

> gaṇḍuppādō kikīceva kunto brāhmaṇa dhammiko
> ete abhāyā bhāyanti sammūḷhā caturo janā.*

Just like the earthworm who eats very little, in the wrong belief that were he to fill his stomach with vast quantities of mud there would be no room left in the earth for him to hide, or like the Kirala bird, who lies on his back with his feet up, in the wrong belief that if the sky were to fall he would be safe in that position, or like the Kosvālihiṇi bird, who shakes his tail continuously, in the belief that the earth could not bear him if he were to stop, so this man's misconceptions are great." So

*The earthworm, the kikī bird, the kunta bird and he who engages in brahmanic practices these four, deluded, are beset with fear when there is no reason to fear.

thought the Buddha. Therefore whenever the nobleman came, even if he was not asked, he told a story from the Teachings.

Endnotes

SÜVISI VIVARAṆA KATHĀ

1. . . . , about four incaculables and one hundred thousand eons ago . . .

The word *asankya* means uncountable or incalculable. Instead of using a term like "countless," Buddhist writers, who must deal with concepts of vast spans of time, use the term "uncountables" as units of time that can in turn be counted. Thus, phrases such as "four uncountables and five hundred thousand eons ago" help make the intangibles of vast extents of time *seem* more comprehensible to the readers' imagination.

2. . . . a ship that I will build throughout an entirety . . .

Refers to the period of time he spent fulfilling the Perfections *(p. pāramitā)* in order to become a Buddha and teach the Doctrine to his fellowmen.

3. . . . then living Buddha Dīpankara, who then made a prophetic declaration.

The Sinhala word is *"vivaraṇa"* and means a declaration or formal statement to the effect: "Such a thing will one day, come to pass." I have translated it as 'prophetic declaration' which I think combines the two meanings instead of the commonly used translation "warrant."

4. . . . we compose this treatise named the *"Saddharmaratnāvaliya."*

The author sees his work to be a kind of "intermediate text," of benefit to those without the intellectual capacity to comprehend the Doctrine in all its complexity. Thus, while it is not just a commentarial text on doctrinal philosophy, it is also more than a mere collection of stories.

The Stories

The Monk Cakkhupāla (Guardian of the Eyes)

In those days, there lived in the city of Sävät a rich nobleman named Mahāsumana. Though blessed with much wealth, he had no offspring to enjoy its benefits. Trees that bear fruit do so only in due season. Perhaps the good deeds of his past lives had not sufficiently matured to provide him with the gift of a son.

One day when the nobleman was returning from the river after his bath, he saw amidst the forest foliage a certain Ficus tree, its trunk white, as if the earth goddess had poured over her head a cascade of clear water from an upturned, sapphire-blue, jeweled, waterpot. Perhaps because it was taller than the other trees and looked as if the earth goddess held an umbrella of peacock feathers over her head, or perhaps because it bore fruits without first flowering, the tree was called "Vanaspati" (King of the Forest). The nobleman saw the tree and thought, "This is most beautiful. A powerful spirit must surely reside in such a tree. I might obtain the gift of a child by invoking this deity." Therefore, he cleared the grass and weeds[1] and built a wall around the tree, similar to that built around a Bodhi tree. Within the wall he spread a pearl-like covering of sand, hung flags and square banners, decorated the trunk with silk cloth, and strung garlands of flowers on its branches. He then said, "O goddess, this is not all I will do. If with your blessings I get a child, I will pay back my debt by rendering even greater services." Thus, praying for a child he proceeded on to the city.

A tree that is not watered delays bearing fruit. Once watered, it flourishes, grows big, and becomes fruitful. Similarly, not long after the invocation the nobleman's wife conceived. Ceremonies for the protection of the fetus were performed and ten months[2] later the child was born. Since children born with the intervention of a spirit are of no little merit, this, too, was a child of great merit.

The nobleman named the child "Pālita" (which means he who is protected or guarded), because he was born as a consequence of protective services rendered to a tree deity. Sometimes a tree does not bear fruit at first, but once it starts, it then continues to bear. The nobleman's wife, too, bore another son. They called him "Culla-pālita," which means Junior Pālita. To avoid confusion they called the older son "Mahā-pālita" or "Senior Pālita," identifying him with the epithet *mahā*. Thus, they were named and when they grew to be men, suitable brides were found for them; they were set up in different households.

In the city of Sävät, there were about seventy million people, of whom fifty million had achieved Enlightenment and twenty million had not. No matter what those who had not achieved Enlightenment did, those who had, maintained a distinctive way of life. Since their faith was unshakeable and they were firmly walking on the Path, during the morning they offered alms. Later in the day, carrying scented flowers and votive offerings, they went to visit the great Buddha, King of the Universe. They presented to him what they had brought, listened to his sermons, and strove for the various stages of Enlightenment that they still lacked.

One afternoon the young man Mahāpālita saw the devotees all dressed up; they were going to hear the Buddha's sermons. They carried offerings of sugar cane, honey, cane sugar, palm sugar, and eight different kinds of drinks. They gave what they had but it was nothing in comparison to the taste of *nirvāṇa* on which they feasted. Mahāpālita asked, "Where are they going all decked out as if for a wedding or a religious festival?"

"The Fully Enlightened One, King of the Universe, has defeated the five Māra demons of death by the power of his jeweled wheel; he has attained mastery over a hundred thousand crores of *Sakvaḷa* universes. The treasures of those universes, like pearls, precious gems, conches, shells, and coral, are, however, subject to change and decay. But as in the *Vedabbha Jātaka* story,[3] where the Brahmin knew the magical *Vedabbha* formula and by the power of that formula caused seven kinds of gems to rain down and destroy one thousand five hundred and one men, such treasures are full of danger. The Buddha, to protect us from such dangers, has brought forth from the ocean of the *Tripiṭaka*, that Casket of the Doctrine, gems of the nine states of Spiritual Attainments. We go to seek that," they said.

"If that is so, I will go too. The Buddha, Teacher of the Three Worlds, will not say 'I do not know you and so I will not preach to you.' It makes sense then to hear his sermon and obtain the wealth of Spiritual Attainments. Worldly wealth, after all, is not hard to come by. If his word is true, it will be a blessing just to enter the faith, even if Spiritual Attainments are to be experienced only later." So saying, he went and saluted the Buddha. Since he was new, he stood at the very back of the group, even though the Buddha himself made no such distinctions.

The Buddha, when he preached, looked into the mind of each of his listeners and assessing each one's capacity to understand the path to Spiritual Attainments, preached his sermon to suit their individual characters and abilities. On that particular day, he sensed the potential of young Mahāpālita to achieve Enlightenment. However, he saw also that though old enough in years, he had still not matured sufficiently in intellect, and so had come for his heritage, bearing a foolish notion of the purity of his birth. Therefore, like a father who portions out his wealth so that his children, who are still too young, may enjoy it at the appropriate time, the Buddha made him a gift of the Doctrine in such a manner as to be of use to him later. He preached in orderly sequence the following sermon.

"*Dāna*, Generosity, or the act of giving,[4] is a sure means of obtaining heavenly joys. It is the source of all blessings. It is like a close kinsman who stands by those who suffer and helps assuage their grief. *Dāna* is like a ship that ferries one over the ocean of suffering. Like a well-guarded fortified city, it protects one from pressing fears. For the miserly, it is as unapproachable as a venomous snake. Like a lotus that does not mingle with the water, it does not associate with the niggardly. There is no blessing greater than generosity, other than *nirvāṇa* itself. Therefore, what intelligent man will not give generously? One who gives unsparingly will long enjoy the pleasures of heaven and be surrounded by thousands of heavenly maidens. He has no regrets and so is always happy. He is well-respected, well-known, and well-spoken of by all men. Generosity is wealth that can be possessed only by the individual concerned and cannot be shared with thieves, enemies, or kings. It prepares a person according to his capacity for one of the Three Forms of Enlightenment." Thus, he spoke on the value of giving.

"Furthermore, as armor worn in times of war protects a man from enemy arrows, so one should wear the armor of Morality to ward off the arrows of enemy Defilements that obstruct Generosity. But those who give should not restrict themselves only to giving; they should also observe at least the Five Precepts of Moral Conduct.

"*Sīla,* Moral Conduct, is the most important basis for all blessings both in this world and beyond. Whatever adornments one may wear there is none more beautiful than Moral Conduct. There is no perfume more pervasive, no purer water for washing away the impurities of Defilements, no cooler breeze to calm the heat of passion. There is nothing like Morality to bring one fame. If one requires a ladder to climb to heaven, morality is that ladder. It is the gateway to the city of Enlightenment. Those who seek their own welfare should practice, either the Five Precepts on a daily basis, or the Eight Precepts on full moon days, or, if one has the potential, become a novice and observe the Ten Precepts with their forty categories, or the complete rules of discipline for a monk with the higher ordination as laid down in the *Vinaya Piṭaka.*"

Having thus illustrated the rewards of Moral Conduct he continued, "Furthermore, if one acts morally, one achieves Moral Purity and can enjoy either the worldly rewards of Trance States or the other-worldly rewards of Spiritual Attainments such as the Path and the Fruits.[5] Failing that one can be born in the heaven called the "Caturmahārājikā,"[6] and in the five other heavens and enjoy those pleasures till the end of one's life-span there.

Bhāvanā or Contemplation can be cultivated even in these heavens because they have there the aids to meditation such as the *kasiṇa* of colors. Thus, one can attain to Trance States there and then be born in the world of Brahmas[7] and enjoy its pleasures. There, if one meditates more and becomes an *anāgāmin*, a Non-Returner, one will be reborn into the pure abodes reserved for Non-Returners and will experience the joys of the Brahma world mixed with the taste of *nirvāṇa* for one thousand, two thousand, four, eight, or sixteen thousand eons. Therefore the comforts of heaven are desirable," he said. However, lest there be those who wished only for heavenly joys and so did not attain *nirvāṇa*, in order to turn them away (from such transient pleasures) the Buddha continued thus:

"Heaven, unlike *nirvāṇa* is not eternal, not permanent. When the eon ends in flame, the entire universe below the *Ābhassara Brahma* heaven will be destroyed. When it ends by floods, the entire universe below *Subhakīrṇa* will be destroyed. When it is destroyed by wind, the entire universe below *Brahappala* will also perish. Even those Brahma worlds that are not destroyed at the end of the eon will, however, not outlast the natural process of decay. Therefore, do not be attached even to heaven." Such were the sermons he preached.

The nobleman Pālita listened to the whole sermon preached in orderly sequence and a wise thought surfaced in his mind, "When creatures die, they take nothing with them; neither the wealth they have acquired, nor their kinsmen. Even this body that one guards as one's own does not accompany one. It holds back, reluctant, as if postponing the journey. The Doctrine of the Buddha, Teacher of the Three Worlds, is clear and gleaming white like a conch shell. It cannot be correctly practiced by remaining in this impure secular world. The benefits of wealth can be best obtained by acts of giving. The edification of self, however, cannot be realized except by Moral Conduct. If one fails to realize the true essence of self, then wealth alone cannot bring one *nirvāṇa*. There is thus no point in continuing this lay life. I will become a monk." So deciding, he came up to the Buddha at the end of the sermon and asked to be ordained.

"Don't you have any close relative[8] whose permission you should seek?" the Buddha inquired. He answered that he no longer had parents, however, he had a younger brother as his next of kin. "If that is the case inform at least him," the Buddha said.

As a man with a deadly disease will make every effort to get a prescribed medicine in order to cure himself, so, to be freed of the disease of Defilements, Mahāpālita decided to find the medicine of permission. Thus, he saluted the Buddha and went home. There, he called his brother and said, "I leave to you whatever wealth there is in this house. You can enjoy its benefits." Instead of thinking I should try to take whatever I can for myself, his brother replied, "Why should I do that when you are still around?"

"I want to enter the order of the Buddha and become a monk. A monk only needs his three robes and a begging bowl. He has no use for the comforts of the lay life. That is my reason."

"Brother what are you saying? Our parents may no longer be alive but you are my older brother and so stand in their place for me. If you are reluctant to use this wealth jointly, there is so much of it we could easily divide it. And since you are a man of such great merit, then like Cullantevāsika in the *Cullaseṭṭhi Jātaka* story,[9] who with one dead mouse earned two hundred thousand gold coins and enjoyed the life of a nobleman, you, too, can obtain riches. Moreover you can remain in the lay world and still do a great deal of good. I certainly don't wish you to become a monk," said the younger brother.

The nobleman Mahāpālita replied, "Brother, when I went to the temple I heard the Buddha preach. Only a golden bowl is a fitting receptacle for the oil of a lion. So for the lion-oil of the Doctrine of that lion-king the Omniscient One, only the bowl of the monastic order of his disciples is suitable, not the life of a householder. I cannot fully practice his teachings as a layman. I must therefore become a monk."

The nobleman Cullapālita persisted however, "You are still young. If, in spite of our entreaties you wish to be ordained, then enjoy the lay life now, while young, and take to the robes in your old age."

To that the nobleman Mahāpālita responded, "Listen my brother. One cannot observe ascetic practices when old. A monk must adhere to certain rules and practice austerities. If he does not, he cannot acquire moral discipline. He is like a merchant who does no business and so acquires no riches. Without discipline, the journey through *saṃsāra* becomes long. When the journey is long, *nirvāṇa* recedes further and further away. If that were to happen, it would be a great loss. Weakened by age and decrepitude, unable even to perform the ascetic practice of begging, what further feats of asceticism could one perform? It is best to become a monk while one is still strong and able to do everything. The Buddha did not take to teaching in old age. Even though Vasavarti Māra (the god of death) tried to stop him, he did not stop but became a monk at the age of twenty-nine and a Buddha at thirty-five. Thus, he was young when he was ordained. I, too, will go to him while I'm still young, be ordained, and become an *arahat*." So saying he joined the Order.

He joined the Order, became a monk, received the higher ordination and lived for five years under the advice and guidance of his teacher and preceptor. By the sixth year, he had qualified to be on his own.

He went to the Buddha and said, "Lord, how many categories of religious practice are there in your Order?"[10]

"Two," the Buddha replied, "*Granthadhura*, or the Practice of Scholarship and *Vidarśanādhura*, or the Practice of Contemplation."

Since Mahāpālita was still a beginner, he said he did not understand fully what those categories were. The Buddha explained that the Practice of Scholarship involved mastery of the texts or the words of the Buddha. This was the foundation of both Practice and Realization. The Practice of Contemplation took one through the six stages of progressive spiritual purification leading to the purification of Philosophical Insight.

On hearing that the monk Pālita said, "Lord, since I was ordained at a late stage in my life, I do not have the quickness of mind or the retentive powers necessary for scholarship. Even if I were to undertake that practice I would still have to learn the Practice of Contemplation in order to end this sojourn in *saṃsāra*. I will therefore undertake the Practice of Contemplation, cultivate Insight and serve both ends at once. Give me a formula for meditation." The Buddha then instructed him on suitable formulas of meditative practices that would lead him to the point of attaining *nirvāṇa*.

He learned these meditative practices, but since he was unable to meditate where he was, he wanted to go elsewhere. So he went to the Buddha, saluted him and said, "I will go away to meditate." Now it is true that to go away alone may be conducive to the practice of meditation,[11] but it was contrary to the rules of doctrinal practice. Therefore he looked for monks to accompany him. He gathered together sixty monks, performed the duties obligatory for monks leaving their monastery of residence, and set out to seek a suitable place for meditation.

He and his monks walked four hundred and eighty leagues and arrived at a rural village. The sixty monks arranged their robes in the proper manner, slung their begging bowls into their cloth coverings and with measured steps, not looking beyond the length of a plough-yoke, they went from house to house begging for alms in the manner of monks.

The villagers were very pleased when they saw these monks, moving with restrained gait,[12] adorned with their nine thousand one hundred and eighty crores, five hundred thousand and thirty-six ornaments of virtue, and more radiant than kings wearing sixty-four royal ornaments such as crowns.

For it is said:

Sobhantevaṃ na rājāno—muttāmaṇivibhūsitā
Yathā sobhanti yatino—sīlabhūsanabhūsitā.*

---

*Kings bedecked in pearls and gems[13] shine not as bright
As an ascetic adorned in resplendent morality.

They invited them into the village, relieved them of their begging bowls, arranged seating for them, and in order to partake of the sweetness of *nirvāna*, offered them delicious foods. When the monks had eaten the villagers inquired, "Where do you go Reverend monks?"

"We are going to spend the rainy season[14] of *vas* in a suitable retreat," they answered. Being intelligent, the villagers realized that the monks were looking for a suitable dwelling place in which to conduct the rites of the rainy season, so they said, "Your Reverence, if you were to spend the three months here with us, we would have an opportunity to make offerings and perform our worship. We will provide food for you as best as we can. On full moon days we will observe the Eight Precepts. We will have a chance to listen to sermons, something so rare for us who live in rural areas. We will observe the Five Precepts daily. Indeed we shall be most pleased if you will spend the rainy months right here." They invited them in this manner.

The monks said to each other, "These lay devotees have invited us so we should stay. Let us turn the channels of their ears to the ambrosial river of the True Doctrine and direct its waters to moisten the fields of their minds. The seeds of faith can then be sown there and a harvest of worldly blessings as well as Spiritual Attainments be reaped. The four kinds of offerings they make will be the sails on the boat of our Insight. The Psychic States will be its mast. Guided by the rudder of Knowledge of the Path, we shall thus cross the sea of *saṃsāra*, which normally takes endless years to cross. Thus, in the short space of three months, the duration of this rainy season, we shall arrive at the shore of *nirvāṇa*." They accepted the invitation.

The devotees, too, knowing that they had accepted the invitation, constructed a dwelling place with appropriate space in which they could spend their days and nights, and gave it to them. Thereafter, the monks went begging for alms in that village. Just as they observed their ascetic practices flawlessly, so the devotees attended on them equally flawlessly.

A lay devotee in that village, a physician, was particularly inspired by the Senior Monk and, desiring to be of some service, said to him one day, "When many people live together it is likely that illness will occur. If such a thing happens, call on me for whatever help you need." They accepted his offer.

On the first day of the rainy season, the monk Pālita called the sixty others together and said, "Friends, today is the beginning of the monsoon. During the course of the next three months, which of the four meditative postures will you practice? The monks not understanding quite what he meant, said they would observe the four meditative postures of sitting, standing, lying down, and pacing back and forth.

To that the Senior Monk responded, "Friends, when one lies down one becomes sleepy. What kind of asceticism can be practiced in one's sleep? Let us not be indolent. We have given the matter serious thought, have come a long way, and were instructed by the Buddha himself on the objects of meditation. The Buddha, though he is in one place, has the power to know all we say, do, or think. We would be caught like thieves with all their stolen goods on them. If the Bodhisatva, by the power of an incantation known as "*Cintāmaṇi*" (Thought Jewel), could track the footsteps of a thief who had committed a robbery twelve years before, as we are told in the *Padamāṇavaka Jātaka* story, now that he is a Buddha with all-knowing powers, how can he be ignorant of our shortcomings? If you want to please the Buddha, you can do so only by observing the correct rules of conduct of a monk. Those who live heedless, make the four hells their abode. Vigilence will block your path to those hells."

The monks responded, "Master, what will you do?"

"I intend to spend my time in meditation, sitting, standing, and pacing up and down. I will not lie down. When we lie down, we allow the maiden Sleep, our constant companion, to argue with the maiden Concentration. When the two dispute, those thieves, the Five Impediments or besetting sins, ever alert for a chance to seize a careless moment, seeing us distracted by their conflict, steal the gold of Discipline and Contemplation from the house of our mind. To prevent this from happening, I will not lie down or stretch my limbs," he said.

The others agreed saying, "Good. It is necessary that we be Vigilent." Then they began their meditative practices.

In order to perform in its highest form the ascetic practice of *Nesajjika* or not lying down, the monk Pālita would sit, stand, and walk, but he would not lie down and sleep. Those three forms of concentration were more rigorous than the body could stand. Thus, he became exhausted. One month after the start of the *vas* (rainy) season commenced, his eyes began to trouble him. Tears gushed forth like water pouring out of a perforated pot, almost as if the substances of lust and sin were being pressed out by the power of Insight. But, just as Insight shrivels if the oil of commitment to Meditative Trance dries up,[15] so the body, too, withers if its moisture spills out. Tears gushed forth as if to dry out his body, but the monk continued his meditation throughout the three watches of that night. At dawn he went to his room and remained there.

When it was time to go on their begging rounds the other monks came to the monk Pālita and said, "Sir, it is time to go out and beg."

"If so, friends, bring me my double robe and bowl." He got them to bring him his robes and set out on his rounds in spite of the pain in his eyes. The other monks seeing the tears pouring out of his eyes inquired why it was so. He told them of the pain in his eyes that was causing them to tear. Then the monks asked, "Shall we call in the lay devotee, that physician who offered to treat us? It is true that it is against the rules of our Order to allow a person to treat the ailment unless he belongs to the category of those permitted to do so, but it is not wrong to ask for advice. Should you not tell the physician of the pain in your eyes?" When he agreed, they did so. The physician made a medicinal oil of ingredients that he himself provided and sent it to the monk.

The oil had to be inhaled while lying down. However, since that would involve breaking his meditative resolve, the monk Pālita inhaled the medicine in a sitting posture and thereafter set off on his begging rounds to the village center.

The physician saw him and asked, "Master do your eyes still pain you?"

"Yes, devotee," he answered.

"I prepared a medicinal oil and sent it. Did you inhale it?"

"Yes, I did," he answered.

"What benefit did you have from the inhalation?" he asked again.

"There is no noticeable improvement," replied the monk.

At that the physician thought, "In order that my eye of Wisdom will not be afflicted with the pain of Defilements, I prepared a herbal oil that at a single inhalation would cure him of the pain. Why has the pain not abated? If he inhaled it sitting up, it would surely not have reached his head. One cannot blame the efficacy of the medicine if it is administered incorrectly." Thinking thus he asked, "Master did you inhale it seated or lying down?"

The monk realized that if he were to admit he had done so while sitting up, the physician, who probably knew the requirements of religious practices as well as he knew his medicine, would know that he was observing the austere practices of Sleepless Meditation. On the other hand, as he had already decided not to veer away from his determination no matter what was said, and perhaps because the physician might get annoyed that his instructions were not being followed and so lose all interest in the cure, he remained silent.

"Why bother to question one who does not answer? I will go to the monastery, examine his sleeping quarters and set my doubts at rest" thought the physician. Since he was well versed both in the symptoms of the disease as well as its hidden causes, he said to the monk, "Reverend Sir, proceed to your cell," and sent him on ahead to the monastery. He then followed the monk, examined the living quarters and saw only an area where the monk paced up and down and where he sat, but no place for sleeping. Thinking that the monk would speak now that the physician had seen there was no sleeping area, he asked again, "Did you inhale the oil while seated or lying down?" Once again the monk said nothing.

The physician now had no doubt it had been inhaled seated. He said, "Master, do not use a medicine wrongly. Just as you cannot adopt a wrong meditative practice and hope to cure Defilements and attain the eye of Knowledge of the Path, so you cannot regain the use of your eyes if you use the medicine incorrectly. If you use it correctly and regain your eyesight, you can also attain to the Path and acquire the Divine Eye of Higher Knowledge. But if you practice only your meditation and that, too assiduously, then you will only acquire the eye of Knowledge of the Path." So he advised and exhorted him.

The monk replied, "Lay devotee, please go away now. There is someone else I must consult. I will talk to that person and do what I must."

With whom did he discuss it? Not with the monks who accompanied him, not with his kinsmen, since there were none around. Whom then did he consult? He talked to his own body.

"Tell me Monk Pālita," he said, "What is it that you want to achieve? Must you have eyes to see that which is desirable and arouses lust and desire, and what is undesirable and provokes anger? Or do you yearn for the Buddha's *sāsana?* In this *saṃsāra,* which has no beginning or end, how many countless times have you been born without eyes? Countless are the occasions when you have lost the eyes you were born with. Within this period of four incalculables and one hundred thousand eons, twenty-seven Buddhas have achieved Enlightenment and passed away. This Buddha has been born to complete the twenty-eighth cycle. Many Buddhas have achieved Enlightenment in the past and you have had no special benefit from them. If now you think only of your eyes, you will have no benefit from this one either. You resolved not to stretch out your limbs or lie down for the duration of this rainy season. Thus, whether you keep your sight or lose it, seek only the vision of the Buddha's teaching in accordance with your earlier pledge." So he spoke, admonishing himself.

Since his body could say nothing to the contrary, he continued to inhale the medicine from a sitting position and again set out for the village. The physician saw the monk and questioned him as before. When he was told that the medicine had been inhaled, he inquired about its good or ill effects. The monk announced that there was no noticeable improvement as yet. Once again the physician inquired how it had been administered. The suitable discourse when in the company of a gathering of monks was a sermon on Doctrinal teachings. The alternative was to remain silent. So the monk said nothing.

The physician, since he got no answer to his repeated questioning said, "Master, the practice of your religious discipline is one thing. Our method of cure is another. Since you do not follow your instructions, I cannot undertake to involve myself in your cure. Henceforth, do not put the blame on me and say, 'The medicinal oils prepared by such and such a physician failed to cure the pain in my eyes.' I, on my part, will not have to walk around proclaiming my incompetence." At that the monk Pālita returned to the monastery, and seemed to advise himself saying

Paṭikkhitto tikicchāya—vejjenāsi vivajjito
Niyato maccurājassa—kiṃ pālita pamajjasi*

"The physician has given up on the treatment of your eyes. When one tries to cure two ailments at once, what is used as a remedy for one often aggravates the other, and it only leaves one in discomfort. Might it not be better to concentrate on curing just one ailment? Therefore, cultivate Meditative Insight that is the remedy for Defilements." Thus, admonishing himself, he began to cultivate Meditative Insight.

For it is said:

Cakkhūni hāyanti mamāyitāni
Sotāni hāyanti tatheva deho
Sabbampi'daṃ hāyati kāyanissitaṃ
Kiṃ kāraṇā pālita tvaṃ pamajjasi**

"Much as I may claim these eyes as mine, one day they will die. Not just my eyes but my ears and my whole body will perish. Before this happens I should try to help myself." He began then to pursue his meditative practices with even greater intensity. About twenty hours into the night, after he had begun his intense concentration, the power of his past sins destroyed his two eyes, those friends that had enabled him to see the Buddha in his physical form. At that very instant, his friend, Knowledge of the Path, destroyed his enemy, Past Sins, together with all the other enemies and their chief, the Fetters that bind one to *saṃsāra*. They were all destroyed in such a manner as to cause no further trouble.

---

*You have been refused treatment, the physician gives up on you,
Destined now for the King of death, O Pālita, why do you delay?[16]

**Eyes that one claims as one's own soon perish,
so do the ears and the body,
all that is associated with it perish.
O Pālita, why then do you delay?

Thus, the monk Pālita vanquished the Impediments of sin by the power of Meditative Insight. Since he would no longer be reborn in this or any other life and never again take lodging in a mother's womb, he remained instead in the womb of the monastery.

Next day when it was time for the monks to go on their begging rounds they came to him and said, "It is time to go begging." The monk Pālita answered, "You had better go without me." When they inquired why he did not go with them, he told them he was now blind and so could not make the journey.

The monks saw his dead eyes and with tears pouring from their own replied, "Master, do not be sad. You may have lost your two eyes but you have the eyes of the sixty of us that amount to one hundred and twenty eyes. We will remain with you always and serve you hand and foot." So they consoled him. They cleaned his room and living quarters and saw to all his needs. They then attended to everything that had to be done regarding their own dwelling places, and set off for the village.

Since the monk Pālita was the chief of all the monks and since the villagers held him in high esteem, they asked the monks, "Where is our other monk?" They were told that he had not come because he had lost his eyesight. They then sent gruel and sweets to the monastery for him and took gifts of food to him for the noonday meal. When they saw his sightless eyes, they wept and said, "Master though you cannot go out and beg we will provide for all your needs. Though you have suffered a great loss in losing your sight we have made a great gain in terms of our after-life. We now have the chance to acquire much merit because of your presence here. Therefore, do not be sad that you have lost your eyes." So they comforted him and left.

From then on they sent rice and gruel to the monastery for him. The monk Pālita, since he did not need the use of his eyes, only his powers of speech to be able to advise his fellow monks, admonished them continuously. The monks, too, followed his advice and by the end of the rainy season escaped the deadly whirlpool of *saṃsāra* and donned the crown of the *arahats*.

In the story of the *Suppāraka Jātaka,*[17] those who heeded the advice of a blind Bosat escaped the whirlpool of the ocean and reached the shore. Similarly, heeding the far-seeing advice of the monk Pālita, who though blind had the vision of Wisdom, they obtained the crown of the *arahat* to indicate their conquest of that land beyond the *Sakvaḷa* universes, *nirvāṇa,* with its four islands, the four Fields of Analytic Knowledge.

They spent the rainy season thus, as *arahats,* maintaining great spiritual purity. Thereafter, they performed the conclusion ceremonies for the season, and since it was customary at the end of these ceremonies to visit the Buddha, they informed the monk Pālita that they would like to do that. The monk said to himself, "I have lost my sight. The way is dangerous, the forest full of demonic hazards. If I go along with the others, I will be an inconvenience to all. They will not be able to go on their begging rounds. I will therefore send them on ahead. They need not be burdened with me and can then avoid the dangerous paths and happily beg along the way." So he thought and advised them to go ahead.

"What about you, Reverend Sir?" they asked. He told them what he had thought. The monks listened but replied they did not like the idea. They argued that they had all come with him, not ahead of him, and so should not go back without him. When they insisted the Senior Monk answered, "That will be difficult for us to do. However, our younger brother, who is a devotee, will ask you for news of us. Tell him we are blind. He will send someone to fetch us. We will come with that person. All of you go on ahead and worship the Buddha, Teacher of the Three Worlds, on my behalf. Salute him and his eighty great disciples." So he commanded them.

Their minds, like that of the Senior Monk Pālita, were tranquil, free of hatred, like water drops on a lotus leaf. It had been so since the time they had become *anāgāmins* or Non-Returners. Thus, though no one harbored any anger, they begged for pardon as was the custom on departure.

It was now time for their begging rounds so they set out for the inner village. The villagers welcomed them, served them alms and, realizing from their manner that they were leaving, asked if they were setting forth on a journey.

"Yes, lay devotees. It is a long time since we have seen the Buddha. We wish now to see him," they said. The villagers wanted to ask them to stay but knew they would not. They accompanied them for part of the way, weeping and sorrowful, and then returned to the village.

The monks travelled about four hundred and eighty miles and finally arrived at the Devramvehera monastery. They saluted the Buddha and his eighty disciples on behalf of the Senior Monk. The next day they went for alms to the street where the monk's younger brother lived, with the intention of meeting him. The nobleman recognized them as the monks who had accompanied his brother. Since it was not fit to question them in the street,[18] he invited them to his home, respectfully seated them, and engaged in pleasant conversation until the meal was over. Only afterwards did he ask about his brother. The monks informed the nobleman of his brother's blindness. The younger brother wept at the news and asked, "What should be done now?" The monks said "Though he did not accompany us he said he would come if someone were sent to bring him."

"In that case let us send our nephew, the younger Pālita" said the brother. Because the road was dangerous,[19] the monks advised that it would be safer if the young man were to travel as a monk. "Once ordained a monk he need remain in the order only if he so desires. If not he may give up the robes when he returns." So they explained, knowing his vacillating mind.

The monks ordained the younger Pālita so as to ease his journey across the desert. Then, after about a fortnight of instruction in the conduct and behavior of a monk, they told him the route and sent him on his way.

The novice reached the village where his uncle begged for alms. There he met a friendly lay devotee at the entrance to the village and inquired, "Is there an ascetic monk living around here?" When the man replied that there was one, he asked again, "What is the name of that monk?"

"The Senior Monk Pālita" was the reply. Realising it was his uncle, the novice asked the villagers for directions to find him.

"Who are you?" they inquired. He told them he was the monk's nephew. The lay devotees then led him to the temple.

The novice Pālita greeted his uncle and spent the next fortnight or so observing the monastic rules and attending on him. Then he said to him, "Master, our uncle the lay devotee at home, wishes to see you. Let us set forth."

"In that case hold on to one end of this stick." said the Senior Monk. When the novice had done so, he followed his nephew into the village to beg.

The villagers sat him down, offered him alms and then said, "Master, all these days you remained inside the temple. Have you come out today because you intend to travel?" Thus, they inquired, having doubts also about the arrival of the novice.

"Yes, it is indeed so. I go to see the Buddha," the monk replied.

At that the villagers begged him to stay, making all manner of appeals. But when he was determined to leave, they followed him for a distance of two hundred and forty leagues because it was a joy for them to see him. Unfortunately, they lacked the vision to drag themselves the other two hundred and forty leagues in order to look on the face of the Buddha himself, Teacher of the Three Worlds. True, they had had the ears with which to hear his sermons and so were already ensnared, unable to tear themselves loose from the True Doctrine. They returned to their village saying, "What use is there in further talk?"

The novice held one end of the blind monk's cane and led him through the forest. Along the way they came to a friendly village. As flies that feed on scents also settle on excrement, so, though he was accompanying a saintly monk and even holding one end of his cane, when he heard the song of a woman, who had come from that village to gather firewood, he was enthralled, as if he had heard a command from Klēśa Māra, the death-demon of lust. Perhaps it was because he had not yet taken up a form of meditation and so had not put down roots in the Buddha's teachings, or perhaps it was because there is no sound more seductive and apt to arouse a man[20] than the voice of a woman singing. Anyway, enchanted by the song, he let go the end of the cane and said, "Master, sit down here awhile. I have something to do." He then went to her.

As a pile of garbage attracts more dirt, so she, too, approached him, as if to support those lustful Impurities and rebirth in hell. He on his part, though he had not joined the Order from any real conviction, now chose to ignore the rules of conduct suited to a monk and forgot that he had left the Senior Monk helpless and stranded by the roadside.

As it is said:

Balavanto dubbalā honti—thāmavanto'pi hāyare
Cakkūma andhitā honti—mātugāmavasaṃ gatā*

So devoid of wisdom, destroyed for a woman's sake, he gave away the goods of morality to the thieves of lust and was left destitute.

"I heard a female voice singing somewhere nearby," mused the Senior Monk. The novice, too, has been gone for quite some time now. What could have happened? Has he met with some disaster?" He had no occult powers to divine what had happened, but he began to have his suspicions.

That sinner, the novice, stuck like a post in the stream of *saṃsāra*, though he had been born a man with rational powers, failed to see the sinful ways of women. The Bosat by contrast had perceived them so clearly, even when he was born as a cuckoo bird in one of his less fortunate births, as related in the *Kuṇāla Jātaka* story.[21] The young novice followed his instincts and came to great harm because of a woman. A man who cultivates a rice-field expects to harvest grain from it, not just straw. But, this man, even though he had joined the Order, was unable to obtain the rewards of Discipline.

[After a while] he returned to where the Senior Monk was and said, "Master, come, let us be on our way." The Senior Monk did not pick up his end of the cane. He said, "Novice, did you meet the robbers of Lust and hand over the goods of Virtue?" The novice said nothing, lest his

*Bewitched by women even the strong become weak
The powerful perish. Those with eyes no longer see.

weakness be exposed. The Senior Monk realized from his silence that veils of Delusion had indeed shrouded the eye of the novice's intelligence. So he continued, "Only a man who can see can help a man who is blind. You have your physical eyes but have lost the Eye of Wisdom. You cannot see the path to the heavenly worlds or to Emancipation. Therefore, it is not fitting that you should take the end of my cane or walk one step further with me."

The novice was greatly upset at these words. Since he had no lay clothes to wear, he draped his monks robes in the manner of a layman and said, "Master, I now wear my robe like a layman's white garb. Therefore, I am no longer a monk but a layman. In fact, I became a monk not from any conviction but for fear of highway robbers. I intended to give up my robes as soon as I returned home. Let us now proceed."

"Young man, a layman who sins is no different from a monk who sins. Like a man who steps into a pond to bathe and ends up with mud on his body so you broke the rules of the Order, while you were still a monk. What then will you not do as a layman? It is far better not to do an evil act than to do one. Therefore, it is better for me to die in this forest than to have you to lead me."

At that, like a man burned by fire and exposed to the noonday sun, the ex-monk suffered great remorse and wept. Ashamed to stand before his uncle, since he had done something he should not have, he left by another path.

Three hundred and forty thousand leagues above the earth, in the Tusī heaven, is god Sakra's stone seat.[22] It is about two hundred and forty leagues long, two hundred leagues wide, and about sixty leagues thick. It is so soft that, like a heap of red hibiscus flowers, it comes up to his navel when he sits down in it, and flattens when he stands up. This seat became uncomfortably hot because of the power of the monk Pālita's goodness.

Sakra cast his divine eye over the earth to find out why his seat was heating and he saw that it was caused by the rays of the monk's goodness. He said, "There must be a reason for this. Should I not find out what it is? To do nothing in such a situation would be wrong. If I am indifferent, my head will split into seven pieces."

For it is said,

> Sahassanetto devindo—devarajjasirīdharo
> Khaṇena upagantvāna—cakkhupālamupāgami.*

---

*Sakra of a thousand eyes, King of heaven,
Instantly appeared before the monk Cakkhupāla.

Sakra went up to the monk and shuffled his feet to indicate that he was there. The monk heard him and asked, "Who is it?"

"It is I master, a traveller."

"Which way are you headed, lay devotee?"

"I go to the city of Sävät," he replied.

The monk thought, "If the man is travelling fast then I would only delay him," so he merely said, "If so go on your way."

"I go, but where are you headed, Your Reverence?" the man asked.

"We, too, are going to the city of Sävät," the monk replied.

"In that case let us travel together."

"Lay devotee, I am blind. If we travel together, you are likely to be delayed."

"Master, I have no urgent business. If I go with you and, if in the process I accomplish even one of the Ten Acts of Merit, I will be happy. Therefore I will gladly go with you," he replied.

The monk thought to himself, "This is indeed a kind man."

"If that be your wish, take hold of the end of my cane," he said. The god Sakra then picked up the end of the cane and they proceeded.

As it is said:

> Saṃkhipiṃsu pathaṃ yakkhā—anukampāya dārake
> Nikkhantadivase yeva—cetiraṭṭhamupāgami."**

When King Vessantara of the *Vessantara Jātaka* story,[23] went to the Vakgal cave in the Himalayas, the gods' compassion for his children was so great that they made their one hundred and twenty league journey between the city of Jayaturā and the city of Maili in the land of the Cē-tiyas belonging to the Vajji princes, so short, that they were able to get there by evening. So also for the monk Pālita and his guide, the two hundred and forty leagues still left to go were so compressed that by evening they arrived near the Devramvehera monastery.

The monk heard the sound of conch shells and other music. He asked, "Where does that sound come from?"

"The city of Sävät" replied the guide.

"Our outward journey took a long time. Today it was short." said the monk.

Sakra, disguised as the traveller said, "I knew a short route."

**The compassion of the gods made the children's journey short.
That very day they came to the land of the Cētiyas.

The monk who knew the short route to *nirvāṇa* thought, "This man is surely some deity come to help me."

God Sakra then conducted the monk to the dwelling endowed by his younger brother. He seated him there and went to meet the brother. He called out to him by name as if he were a friend and said, "Don't you know that your brother has arrived. He is here. I saw him seated in the monstery that you built."

The monk's younger brother, the nobleman, went to the temple, saw his brother and wept loudly.

"Even though I told you not to join the Order you insisted on doing so. Now see what has happened" he lamented. Then he added "What good is it now to weep? I should do something to help you." So saying he had two young slave boys freed and he had them ordained so that they could stay with the monk, look after his needs and get him his rice and gruel from the inner city. Thus, he assigned the two freed boys to the monk who was himself freed from the bondage of craving. The two ordained slaves attended to all the monk's needs.

One day, monks came from many different regions to worship the Buddha. They first came to the Devramvehera monastery, greeted the Buddha, then the senior disciples, and afterwards wandered around looking at the individual residences of monks. They hastened also to visit the temple residence of the blind monk who was now called "Cakkhupāla," Guardian of the Eyes, since the story of his blindness was well-known.

It was already evening, and a thunderstorm was brewing. Because it was dark and raining, the visiting monks decided they would stay the night and return in the morning. Rain fell during the early part of the night and then ceased. Now the monk Cakkhupāla was a person of great determination, and since pacing up and down was an exercise he had undertaken for a long time now, he got up at dawn for his walk. It had rained the previous evening and many small red-bugs had emerged. Because no one had yet swept the walkway for meditation, as was customary, and because he was blind, he trampled many bugs and squashed them as he paced up and down. The monks, who had come to visit and stayed on because of the rain, noticed the squashed insects where the monk Cakkhupāla had walked and asked, "Which monk walks here?" The two ordained servants replied, "It is our teacher who walks here."

"This monk does great harm. While young and in possession of his sight he slept and did not observe the rules of austerity. Now that he is old and blind he does so, and destroys many lives in the process. He thereby sins. Why can't he ask around and find a place to walk in that does not contain living insects? We should report this to the Buddha."

They went to the Buddha and said, "Master, the monk Cakkhupāla while pacing up and down kills many living creatures."

"How is that so? Have you seen him kill these creatures?" the Buddha inquired.

"No we have not seen him do it" they replied.

The Buddha then said to them, "Just as you did not see him do it, so also he did not see the creatures he stepped on. *Arahats* harbor no thoughts of violence." He then informed them that the monk was now an *arahat*.

The monks then asked the Buddha, "Master, if he had enough merit to become an *arahat*, why then is he blind? If his good *karma* could win for him *arahatship*, how could it not avert that calamity?" They spoke thus since the workings of *karma* were known only to the Buddha and beyond their understanding.

The Buddha said, "O monks, although he had acquired enough merit to become an *arahat*, he committed a heinous act in the past and its consequences were inescapable." Then, in order to prevent these monks, too, from doing such deeds the Buddha told them the story of the monk Cakkhupāla's sinful past *karma*.

"In the past, O Monks, in the city of Benares, during the time of King Baṃbadat, a certain eye doctor was wandering through villages, provinces, and principalities, treating people. In one place he saw a blind woman and asked, 'What is your trouble?'

'I am blind,' she replied.

'I can cure you,' he said to her.

"Since that was what she had wanted she readily agreed to be treated. The physician, however, was not doing this out of charity. 'What will you pay?' he asked wanting to know how much she would give him once he cured her blindness. The woman wished to be cured and also wanted the physician to be keenly interested in the treatment so she said, 'If you cure me of my blindness what more do I want? I will put myself, my children, my wealth, and all I possess in your service.'

"The physician thought to himself, 'If that is what she promises it should be very useful to me.' He therefore prepared some medication and gave it to her. One dose of the medicine and her eyes regained their normal vision. Her blindness was cured. Though her sight improved, unfortunately, the woman's greedy nature did not change. Reluctant to give away what she had promised, she thought, 'I contracted to be his slave as payment because of my desire to regain my sight. Once I am bound to him he will have no regard for me. There is only one course left, to get out of it by some ruse.'

"Thus, when the physician inquired if her condition had improved or worsened she answered, 'In the past I could see a little, but ever since I used your medicine I cannot see at all.' The physician was fully aware of the efficacy of his medicine so he thought, 'The woman says this because she is reluctant to make the promised payment. I don't care about the money. If I wanted wealth I could easily acquire it since I know good cures and can treat many patients. However, it is clear this woman has no intention of paying, so I, in turn, will destroy her sight.' Thus, ignoring the consequences of his deed for his next life, he went into the house and told his wife about his decision. She on her part did not stop him. Nor did she say, 'Do it,' and acquire Demerit herself.

The physician then prepared a deadly compound and gave it to the woman, saying, 'If your blindness is increasing then apply this medicine.'

"She, thinking 'This is a harmless medicine given in the belief that my blindness is increasing' and perhaps also because the blackness of her *karma* was great even though darkness had not yet taken hold of her vision, she applied the poisonous medication to her eyes. It was a medicine well-suited to her dark black *karma*. The moment she applied it both eyes were instantly blinded like two lamps extinguished. But that very moment, the darkness of her past black *karma* in turn, lightened and disappeared.

"The physician, as if taking on a burden that someone else had discarded, took on the Demerit that she had just shed. O monks, that physician is now the Senior Monk Cakkhupāla who, though he no longer cures diseases of the eyes, is now firmly engaged in curing the disease of Defilements and has gained the Eye of Knowledge of the Path. That sinful act, which my son committed, has pursued him until now, waiting for an opportunity to overtake him, like a runner pursuing a runner. If a person does not distance himself from such sinful acts that occur through the Three Doorways (of action, speech, and thought), that sinful act will follow him as inexorably as the cartwheel follows close on the heels of oxen. So the consequences of the *karmic* acts of human oxen ever follow at their hoofs as they move yoked to the cart of *saṃsāra*, which provides the time frame for those sinful deeds to bear fruit.

As it is said:

> Sandhimekantu kammekaṃ janeti na tato paraṃ
> Anekāni vipākāni sañjaneti pavattiyaṃ.*

"[There are two kinds of *karma*.] *Paṭisandhi vipāka karma* has a single consequence. Its effects are felṭ just once. *Pavatti vipāka karma* however, follows close behind one, can occur many times, and take effect in sev-

*A single *patisandhi karma* brings about only one result and nothing thereafter. But a *pavatti karma* generates multiple results.

eral subsequent births right up to the time *nirvāṇa* is achieved. But since my son is now an *arahat*, it has stopped here." Thus, he preached.

The Buddha, King of the Three Worlds, with the medicine of this sermon cured thirty thousand monks of the disease of continued rebirth. He led them to the Fruits of *arahatship* and calmed their minds. Similarly, good men can be cured of the sickness of sinful acts with the medicine of this our work, the *Jewel Garland of the True Doctrine*. Even if they cannot attain release through the subjugation and total annihilation of Defilements at this point in time, they may subdue some of the constituents of those Defilements, and cultivate goodness. Thus, they may purify their minds and in the future, obtain the blessings of this world as well as Spiritual Attainments.

Endnotes

THE MONK CAKKHUPĀLA

(In the Notes, the *Saddharmaratnāvaliya* will be referred to as SR. All references to the *Dhammapadaṭṭhakatha* will be to E. W. Burlingame's English translation and will be shortened to DA.)

This story illustrates the first verse of the *Dhammapada* stanzas, which is as follows:

> Mano pubbaṃgamā dhammā—mano setthā mano mayā
> Manasā ce paduṭṭhena—bhāsati vā karoti vā
> Tato naṃ dukkhamanveti—cakkaṃ'va vahato padaṃ.
>
> Mind is the forerunner of all conditions, mind is foremost
> and they are mind made,
> If one speaks or acts with an impure mind
> Then pain follows one even as the wheel [follows] the
> hoof of an ox.

In the DA, the story is introduced with this stanza followed by the characteristic introduction, "Where was this religious instruction given? At Sāvatthi. With reference to whom? Cakkhupāla, the Elder." The story then follows. The same verse is again recited by the Buddha at the conclusion of the story. One wonders whether this introductory material, which appears at the beginning of each story in the DA (creating a formal repetitive pattern), was not the work of a later scribe or editor. In the SR by contrast, the stanzas of the *Dhammapada* are seldom quoted but rather expanded and explained in prose often as a sermon by the Buddha who, in turn, is contexualized as a character in the story.

1. Therefore, he cleared the grass and weeds . . .

The ceremonies performed for the Ficus tree described here by the monk Dharmasēna are similar to those performed in Buddhist temples in Sri Lanka for the Bōdhi tree or tree of Enlightenment (also a variety of Ficus). A wall is constructed round the tree, fine sand is stewn in the enclosure, and the tree is decorated with strings of banners or cloth flags. The best example of the continuity of this tradition can be seen in the temple premises of the sacred Bōdhi tree in Anuradhapura. This particular passage of description appears also in the fifth century DA text. One might infer, therefore, that the later Buddhist tradition was a continuation of much older forms of tree worship.

2. The counting is probably in terms of lunar months. Sinhala works always refer to a pregnancy as lasting ten and not nine months.

3. *Vedabbha Jātaka* story,

Captured by robbers, a Brahmin makes treasure rain from the sky. A second band kills him because he cannot repeat the miracle. Mutual slaughter leaves only two robbers with the treasure. One poisons the other's food and is himself slain by his fellow.

4. "*Dana*," Generosity, or the act of giving,

This sermon preached by the Buddha is an elaborate interpolation by the author of the SR. The monk Dharmasēna expands the outline provided in the original, "He preached in orderly sequence . . . [on] Almsgiving, the Moral Precepts, Heaven, the evil consequences and defilements of Sensual Pleasures and the blessings of Retirement from the World . . . " [DA, 148] into a full-scale sermon incorporated into the body of the text. The tone and style of this section is very much that of an oration, the sentences short, the images sharp, and the phrases rhetorically patterned.

5. . . . the Path and the Fruits . . .

Refers to the Eightfold Path and the Four Stages on the way to *nirvāṇa.* As a Buddhist concept, the term *mārga-phala* is often used to denote the Spiritual Attainments of Buddhism. For more detailed comments see Glossary.

6. Failing that one can be born in the heaven called the "Caturmahārājikā," . . .

Heaven for a Buddhist is a lesser good. Though pleasurable and something that laymen can aspire to, it is not eternal. Here the monk Dharmasēna interpolates a long discourse on Buddhist cosmology, making it very clear to his lay audience that the ultimate goal for a Buddhist should be the cessation of all attachments including the desire for heaven. For a Buddhist, the pleasures of heaven are finite and can only last as long as his/her good *karma* lasts. It is not the final salvation.

7. Here the distinction is between the sensuous heavens of the gods of the *dēvaloka* and the Brahma heavens of a higher order of divine beings, who are free from sensual passions.

8. "Don't you have any close relative . . . "

Obtaining the permission of one's parents or close kinsmen is an important condition to be fulfilled by anyone wishing to join the Order. Like so many of the *Vinaya* rules, it was laid down in response to a particular incident that is related in the story of Prince Nanda (p. 180). The Buddha's father, King Suddhodhana, was deeply grieved that both his sons and grandson had left home and become monks without informing him. He then obtained a promise from the Buddha, that in the future, a parent's or a kinsman's permission must be obtained before such a serious step was taken.

9. *Cullaseṭṭhi Jātaka* story,

A young man picks up a dead mouse, which he sells; he works this capital until he becomes rich.

10. "Lord, how many categories of religious practice are there in your Order?"

The two categories of practice for a monk are kept distinct. Most monks choose one or the other. The *granthadhura* monks, who engage in scholarship, are those who live in monasteries and interact closely with laymen in teaching and spreading the Doctrine. The *vidarśanādhura* monks, who are concerned with meditation, are often the forest dwellers or *vanavāsins*. The laity even today tend to regard the latter group as closer to the ideal of the *arahat*.

11. . . . to go away alone may be conducive to the practice of meditation, . . .

The reference here is possibly to the stipulation in Buddhist texts that monks should not engage in rigorous meditative practices entirely on their own. Stressful psychological situations could arise that in turn could endanger mental stability. Therefore instruction and monitoring by another, often a Senior Monk or a teacher, is considered important.

12. The seemingly precise recording of these numbers creates an effect that is much more overwhelming than if vaguer terms like "countless" or "infinite" were used. The same technique is used for describing eons of time that are counted in units termed "uncountables."

13. Kings bedecked in pearls and gems . . .

Several Pāli stanzas are interpolated into the SR text. They do not, however, always coincide with the stanzas in the DA. In some cases, new stanzas are included and in others stanzas found in the DA are summarized in prose or eliminated altogether. In this story, only the two stanzas recited by the monk Pālita in his debate with himself and the verse describing Sakra are identical with those found in the DA text. The author of the SR clearly did not feel constrained to give a verbatim translation even of the Pāli stanzas of his original text.

14. "We are going to spend the rainy season . . .

The period of *vas (p: vassa)* refers to the season of the rains when monks are enjoined to take up residence in a monastery. During this time lay devotees see to all their needs. In turn the monks preach the Doctrine to the laymen and provide them with opportunities for meritorious action. (It was no doubt initially a pragmatic necessity that soon became a vital part of Buddhist practice.) Even today, lay devotees invite a monk (especially those known for their preaching skills or learning) to spend the period of *vas* in their particular temple. The period ends with a celebratory and purificatory ritual *(vas piṇkama)* in which the laymen participate.

15. But, just as Insight shrivels if the oil of commitment to Meditative Trance dries up, . . .

The constant use of medical metaphors is very much a feature of the SR and does not appear in the DA. The reference here to medical lore gives us an insight into the thirteenth century medical practice in Sri Lanka. The DA text refers to "an ointment prepared for the nose." In translating this phrase as an "oil for inhalation," the monk Dharmasēna was no doubt describing medicines and methods that were familiar to him. Such inhalations happen to be still a part of traditional *(ayurvedic)* medical treatment in Sri Lanka. Many monks did, and still do, have a good knowledge of the ayurvedic medical system. Several, like the author of the *Pūjāvaliya,* the monk Mayurapāda, who was a contemporary of the monk Dharmasēna, were practitioners of medicine. From the internal evidence in the text, the medical metaphors, medical lore and familiarity with the theory and practice of diagnosis and cure, one can assume that even if not a practitioner himself, the monk Dharmasēna was very familiar with both the medical literature, and how it was practiced.

The text also indicates that there were several categories of medicine men at the time. There were itinerant physicians, who traveled from village to village looking for patients who needed help, and there were also resident physicians, as in the Maṭṭakuṇḍalī story, who had to be invited to the home and given board and lodgings for the duration of the treatment. Then as now, payment was important and could be in goods or services. Note that while the monk Dharmasēna reveals considerable familiarity with medical practice, the medicine men in the stories are *not* monks. The practice of monks becoming medical practitioners was possibly a later (post-fifth century) development.

Padamānavaka Jātaka story

In the Jātaka Collections this particular story is listed as the *Padakusala māṇavaka Jātaka* (See Fausboll Vol. 3, pg. 501–514)

16. Note that the author summarizes and expands on the verse in the course of the narrative, for the benefit of readers who would not understand the Pāli.

17. *Suppāraka Jātaka* story,

The Bōdhisatva is born as the son of a mariner. By sixteen he had gained complete mastery of the art of seamanship. When his father died he became head of the mariners. Wise, and full of intelligence, no ship ever came to harm with him aboard. Later he was blinded with salt water in his eyes; he retired to become a king's assessor and valuer. The king however, was miserly and did not pay him as his skill and wisdom warranted.

18. Since it was not fit to question them in the street, . . .

The formalities involved in the interaction between monks and laymen are underlined in these comments. Such polite formalities are still customary in Sri Lanka and can be seen in the interaction between monks and laity especially when monks are invited to lay homes for ceremonial feasts or *dāna*.

19. Because the road was dangerous, . . .

There were specific advantages to traveling as a monk. As ascetics who had no possessions, they were not targets for highway robbers and brigands when traveling through lonely regions. Note, however, the young Pālita does not merely don the robes of a monk but must "become" a novice. This, too, is part of Buddhist practice. The robe is revered and only a member of the Order can wear it. While a monk must conform to the rules of the Order when he is in robes, he is free to leave the Order and give up his robe any time he so wishes. Note the gesture of the younger Pālita in refashioning the *style* of wearing his robes, hoping thereby to be treated as a layman.

20. . . . there is no sound more seductive and apt to arouse a man . . .

The monk Dharmasēna's comments about women are often negative. Such an attitude is not uncommon in Buddhist texts written by celibate monks for whom the female symbolized seduction away from ascetic practices. In this case, however, the monk Dharmasēna happens to be echoing sentiments already present in the original DA text that introduces the following quotation from the *Aṅguttara Nikāya* at this point. "Therefore said the Exalted One, 'Monks, I know of no other single sound which so completely takes possession of the heart of a man as this, monks, namely, a woman's voice.' "

21. *Kuṇāla Jātaka story,*

A king of birds, for the instruction of his friend, a royal cuckoo, relates many instances he had known to illustrate the deceitfulness, ingratitude, and immorality of womankind.

22. . . . in the *Tusī* heaven, is god Sakra's stone seat.

God Sakra's heavenly seat named "*Paṇḍukambala śailāsanaya*" (literally stone seat covered with a pale blanket) warms to the power of goodness on earth. He is then moved to intervene on behalf of the good person who may happen to be in distress.

23. *Vessantara Jātaka* story,

A prince devoted to giving gifts falls into disrepute through giving a magical elephant. He is banished with his family into the forest where he gives away everything he has left including his two children. The children are taken away by a Brahmin and forced to walk a long distance. But Sakra intervenes, makes the distance short, and brings them to the city of their kinsmen, who ultimately set them free.

Maṭṭakuṇḍalī (Flat-Earring)

Further, in order to increase the faith of the believers we will tell another story.

The monk Cakkhupāla, in his birth as a physician, had the Eye of his Wisdom clouded with a film of Delusion. Blind to the straight road of Right Actions, he walked the sinful road of Wrong Deeds. What he did may seem insignificant, but it was an ill deed. As a consequence he became blind and suffered his fate even in the very birth in which he became an *Arahat*.

It is not so with those who look on the world with the clear Eye of Wisdom and walk the road of Right Actions. I will illustrate with the story of Maṭṭakuṇḍalī how, when one does a good deed however insignificant, one obtains the blessings of this world as well as the blessings of Spiritual Attainments.

How is that so?

In the city of Sävät, there once lived a Brahmin named "Adinnapubbaka," which means Non-Giver. Like the father in the *Sudhābhōjana Jātaka* story,[1] who had millions, but was reluctant to give anything to anyone, until the god Sakra finally taught him to give alms; or like the nobleman Illisa, who could not part with anything he possessed, until the god Sakra took on the guise of Illisa and generously gave away all his wealth; so this Adinnapubbaka, until he heard the Buddha's sermon, abandoned his miserly ways and attained *nirvāṇa*, he did not give away so much as a drop of oil from the tip of a blade of grass. The name Adinnapubbaka was therefore appropriate.

This man had one son and loved him as his life. One day, he wished to give his beloved child a piece of jewelry. However, just as a banyan tree though it is enormous produces a very small fruit, so this man who had millions thought small. He realized that if he hired a craftsman to make the ornament, he would have to feed the man for several days till the work was completed.[2] This would mean spending money on rice and other foods. In addition, when the work was finished, he would have to pay him a fee. When this was all added up it would amount to a good deal. He calculated that it would cost much less if he were to make it himself, even though he knew nothing about jewelry-making. He mulled it over, bought the gold himself, and just as a man who cannot write scribbles lines on a page, so he beat up the piece of gold to look like an ear ornament. The earrings had none of the fine work that denotes good craftsmanship. They were just pieces of flattened metal. Thus, the son acquired the name Maṭṭakuṇḍalī,[3] which means Flat-Earring.

When the young man was sixteen years old, he was stricken with anaemia.[4] The mother realized her son's condition was bad, and even though she knew the Brahmin had no interest in anything other than his wealth, she said to him, "Your son's condition is serious. Though he says nothing, he looks very sick. Get someone who knows medicine to treat him." She spoke thus as if she did not know how his mind worked, even after it was so clearly demonstrated by the ear ornament he had made.

The Brahmin replied, "Good wife, what are you saying? If we call in a physician for this illness, we will have to pay for his travel, feed him until the illness is cured, as well as pay him a fee when the work is done. Moreover, since the illness is likely to be serious, the fee will not be small. If one removes even one arrow from a bundle of arrows, the loss is noticeable. Similarly, whatever the amount of one's wealth, when one spends some of it, even for a day, the total is diminished. We know it from the story of the squirrel in the *Kalandaka Jātaka*,[5] who shook a few drops of water off his tail and as a result the waters of the ocean were lessened."

By talking like this, he displayed his ignorance and, though not stated in so many words, showed what a simpleton he was.

The wife replied, "Brahmin, so you say, but what then should we do?"

"We shall do whatever will not lessen my wealth."

He then went to various physicians and asked them what remedies should be used to cure one who was suffering from anaemia. The physicians thought "Instead of taking us to the patient,[6] so we can treat him after examining him and finding the specific cause of the illness, this man leaves the patient at some place far away, and makes general inquiries about the illness. He does not even mention who the patient is. Therefore, we, for our part, will prescribe a general remedy." From the way in which the Brahmin spoke they figured, "This man's son is suffering from anaemia. The father is making these inquiries because he is stingy and does not want to pay a physician's fee."

Just as the medicine prescribed by the monk Cakkhupāla,[7] when he was born a physician, caused blindness in his patient, so without saying that this was a remedy for various other diseases too, they prescribed a medicine that could aggravate the anaemia. The Brahmin listened carefully, purchased the various ingredients such as the bark of certain trees and so forth, boiled and strained them, and administered the medicine to his son.

Like a man who applies medicine to the palm of his hand when he is suffering from elephantiasis,[8] or like one who rubs sandalwood on the lips in order to adorn the eyes, so the miser administered the wrong medicine. It was not one prescribed after careful consideration of the context and the cause of a disease. Specific poisons require specific magical charms to counteract them. If the wrong incantation is used, the poison spreads even as the patient is being treated. So the young man's illness worsened to the point where only death could cure it.

At that point, like a man who lets go of an eel but holds on to its tail, so, more afraid of the damage to his purse than of the illness, the Brahmin called in a physician only when the disease had reached a point beyond treatment.

The physician arrived, examined the patient, and realized that the disease could not be cured. "I cannot spare the time. Find another physician to treat him," he said and left. The moment he left, the Brahmin knew that his son's death was imminent. He thought, "When the boy dies, those coming to the funeral will see all the wealth that fills the inner rooms and think me stingy. They will say, 'This man has all this wealth and he acts like a pauper. He did not treat his sick son but left him to die. What a miser!' " So the Brahmin moved his child even before he died; he put him out on the porch under the eaves.

That very day the Buddha, in the course of his meditation, entered into the Trance of Great Compassion. He cast his Omniscient Eye over the world in order to see who had performed acts of merit in the times of past Buddhas. Thus, he cast the net of his Wisdom[9] over the great ocean of the ten thousand Universes and caught the little fish, Maṭṭakuṇḍalī, hiding on the shore of the outer porch. It was fortunate to get caught in the net of the Buddha's Wisdom, so Maṭṭakuṇḍalī remained quite still, without the slightest movement, and was easily netted.

The Buddha asked himself, "What benefits will come from my going to the boy? When I appear before him,[10] his mind will be made tranquil by my presence and even if he has done no other meritorious act, this tranquility alone will result in his being reborn in the Tavtisā heaven. He will live in a golden pavillion about one hundred and twenty leagues high, attended by one thousand divine maidens.

"The Brahmin then will cremate his dead son and walk about the graveyard weeping. Maṭṭakuṇḍalī, now a divine being four leagues tall (he himself will be three leagues but his crown will be a league high), attended by one thousand heavenly maidens decked in ornaments that could fill sixty carts, will contemplate his extremely joyous life and think, 'Such heavenly pleasures could not have come from doing nothing. I must have done some good deed. What was it that I did?' He will then reflect on his past actions and realize that he had done nothing more than to evoke a tranquil state of mind towards me at the moment of dying.[11] He will then think, 'Alas Adinnpubbaka, my father, because of his miserly anxieties about the loss of his wealth, failed to treat my illness and left me to die. Now he goes to the graveside and weeps as if for the rag in which my corpse was wrapped. I will make him weep all the harder, like a runner being pursued.' Annoyed with his father, he will then come in the guise of the dead Maṭṭakuṇḍalī and stand weeping not far from his own grave.

"The Brahmin will see him, but knowing his son to be dead will ask, 'Who are you?'

'I am your son Maṭṭakuṇḍalī.'

'Where are you now?'

'I have been reborn in the Tavtisā heaven.'

"Since the Brahmin had not seen his son perform any act of special merit, and because he did not have the power to look back on past lives, and also since he did not know about the state of tranquility that his son had achieved just by looking at me, and because there is nothing in the *vēdas* to suggest that by a single meritorious act one can be born in heaven, he will ask, 'What act of merit did you do to be born in heaven?' The Brahmin will not believe Maṭṭakuṇḍalī when he says it was simply a result of tranquil state of mind he had achieved.

"The Brahmin will then come to me and ask, 'Can one be born in heaven even if one does nothing more than achieve a tranquil state of mind at the sight of you?' I will then reply, 'O Brahmin, there are hundreds, thousands, and even hundreds of thousands, uncountable numbers who have been born in heaven merely by doing so.' As an illustration, I shall recite a verse from the *Dhammapada*. At the end of the recitation, eighty-four thousand people will reach the city of *nirvāṇa*—some having destroyed the enemy Defilements, others having humbled them. Once having entered the city, they will later completely vanquish those Defilements.

"The god Maṭṭakuṇḍalī will gain heavenly joys for his tranquil mind that was attained on his deathbed. But like one who, no matter how much rice he eats, cannot assuage his thirst unless he drinks, so he will not be satisfied until he reaches *nirvāṇa*. He will become a Stream-Enterer, endowed with one thousand facets of wisdom. His place in heaven will be established, and he will be ensured freedom from future births in hell.

"The miserly Brahmin will also become a Stream-Enterer and, as if using acid to burnish copper, he will clean out his miserly thoughts. He will dig up his hidden wealth, and in order to preserve it forever, he will enshrine it in the Buddha's *sāsana*, that place free of all fears."

Thus, on the dawn of the second day, the Buddha rose from his meditative trance and knew that much benefit would come from this child. He put on his robe, which was like a garland of *kobōlīla* flowers dipped in lacquer; he glowed like a coral embedded in a piece of red lacquer. He draped his robe from the navel to the kneecap so as to cover three parts of the body[12] and emerged like a full moon partly hidden by rosy clouds. Over the robe he tied a belt, glistening with pearls strung on a golden chain; it looked like a lightening bolt. Over that he wore the outer robe, which was like a spread of Red Hibiscus flowers, or Ficus fruits, or like a red carpet thrown over the forehead of an elephant, or a net of pearls encasing a golden lampstand, or a red carpet covering a golden *stūpa,* or a red cloud covering a full moon, or molten lacquer flowing down a golden mountain, or like the mountain Sithulpauva in the Himalayas encircled with a garland of Hibiscus flowers. So, draping and adjusting his robe, the Buddha left the temple and, like a lion emerging out of a golden cave, he set forth, emanating rays of light from his whole body. They scattered like servants sent ahead in ten directions. He was attended by his disciples, headed by the Senior monk, the Great Kaśyapa. Thus, he entered the city of Sävät, begged from house to house, and came finally to the house of Adinnapubbaka, though not to beg for alms there.

At the time, Maṭṭakuṇḍalī was sleeping with his face turned to the wall. The Buddha, knowing that the boy had not seen him, sent forth a ray from his body. That ray of light struck the wall. Maṭṭakuṇḍalī, as he lay dying, saw the ray and as if seeing an image of the Buddha and paying obeisance to it, he turned toward the yard. He recognized that the person who had arrived had the thirty-two or so marks of a Great Being, the eighty lesser marks, as well as the glow that emanated for a depth of a fathom around a Buddha. The visitor also had a halo about a metre high with light rays spreading in ten directions like golden Mount Mēru, burning in flames at the end of the eon.

Maṭṭakuṇḍalī saw the Buddha, who soothes the eye of those who look upon him, calms the minds of those who think of him, soothes the ear of those who hear him, whose goodness, acquired through one hundred million eons, was as if moulded together and sculpted into a single form. Then he thought, "Alas, because of the unfortunate association with my foolish father, for eight of the past sixteen years, I was unable to go to the Buddha, or worship him, or offer alms, or listen to a sermon. Now my legs are too weak even to walk up to him and greet him. Even if I were to get to him, my hand is already too stiff to lift in the gesture of worship. What else is there to do? At this point, since it is not too much effort to activate one's thoughts, I can at least make my mind tranquil. I will therefore do so." Thus, he made his decision and, though he was not destined to cure himself, he was destined to see the Buddha. He looked up, made his mind tranquil, and the purpose of the Buddha's visit was achieved.

For one who cannot carry heavy loads just the weight of his body is a heavy enough load, so the Buddha felt that this one act should suffice for Maṭṭakuṇḍalī. Therefore, in order that he, who was dying of the bodily sickness of anaemia should be free of all disease and pain in his next life, the Buddha provided him with the balm of a tranquil mind and left.

Maṭṭakuṇḍalī maintained his tranquil state of mind even after the

Buddha was long out of sight. He died and though he did not cross this Ocean of Suffering completely, in all its aspects, he did so in one area. Like a man waking from sleep, he was born as a god in the Tavtisā heaven, in a golden pavillion one hundred and twenty leagues high.

The Brahmin cremated his dead son. Unlike the great Bōsat in the *Uraga Jātaka* story,[13] he was unaware that he should not grieve for his son. So he went daily to the graveyard and wept saying, "Alas my only son is dead." Now the god Maṭṭakuṇḍalī, contemplating his heavenly pleasures and pondering over what meritorious act he had performed that entitled him to enjoy his present pleasures, finally realized that it was because he had made his mind tranquil at the sight of the Buddha. So he thought, "This Brahmin, afraid of losing his wealth, did not treat my illness and let me die. Like the man who does not cultivate his rice field when he should and then weeps for a harvest he can never get, so he now walks around the graveyard mourning for his only son. This is hardly enough punishment for one who did me such harm. I will make him suffer even more."

Thus, he took on the form of his earlier self, Maṭṭakuṇḍalī, went to the graveyard and sat holding his head in his hands, weeping, like a kinsman at a funeral. The Brahmin saw him and thought, "I weep for the loss of a son. For what does this man weep?"

In the *Culladhanuggaha Jātaka* story,[14] the woman, who was given in marriage by her parents, fell in love with a brigand and had him kill her husband. Then, when she was abandoned by the thief and robbed of all her clothes and jewelry, she went unashamedly to the god Sakra (who had come in the guise of a jackal) to ask what was the cause of her misfortune. Similarly, the Brahmin, who imagined he had a reason to grieve, went up to Maṭṭakuṇḍalī and asked, "You have sandalwood paste annointed on your body, you are decked in all the seven ornaments, wear garlands of flowers, and you look just like Maṭṭakuṇḍalī. You weep with your hand to your brow. What do you cry about?"

Maṭṭakuṇḍalī replied, "I have a carriage and it is of pure gold. But I do not have two wheels that are good enough for it. If I find what I want, I will live. Otherwise I shall kill myself." Thus, he related the cause of his grief, hoping thereby to dispel it.

The Brahmin's feelings of generosity had been aroused by the death of his son, so he said, "Child, I will give you the wheels you desire. I am a wealthy man. I can have them made of gold, silver, pearls, or gems. However you want it, I will provide it. Tell me, which do you want?" This man who had been unwilling to pay for food or the trivial cost of a workman to make earrings for his son, and instead had made them himself, now said, "I will make you a pair of wheels of the seven precious metals."

The god Maṭṭakuṇḍalī thought, "This man did not provide medicine for his own sick son. Instead, like one who pours hot water on a plant that desperately needs watering, he gave the wrong medicine and killed his son. Now he is willing to do anything for one who happens to resemble his son. I will give him a jolt."

"How big a pair of wheels will you make for me?" he asked.

"Whatever size you request" replied the Brahmin.

"My chariot is of solid gold. To match it, I must have the sun and the moon. If I get them, then my chariot will be so powerful I could travel faster than anyone, except perhaps the Bōsat, who was born as a swan, in the story related in the *Javanahaṃsa Jātaka*.[15] Only the sun and moon can match my chariot. I have no use for anything else.

The Brahmin replied, "Child, you are very foolish. You desire things you can never have. It is like wishing for a coconut palm tree to produce Talipot-palm nuts, or expecting a fire to be cool, or hoping for heavenly joys after sinful deeds. Even if you die weeping, you can never get those two things you ask for."

Maṭṭakuṇḍalī replied, "You call me a fool but in our weeping you and I are alike. Which of us two is the more foolish, or the more wise? If a man sees something and weeps for it, is he stupid? Are those who weep for what they do not see, wise? Tell me, which of us two is the fool? If you can't grasp such a simple fact, then continue to weep."

Upon reflection, the Brahmin realized the argument was irrefutable. So he said, "Child, what you say is true. You ask for the sun and moon that you see. There is nothing foolish in asking for what you see. I weep for a son who is dead and gone to the other world. When I weep I only see my own tears,[16] not my son. There is no one more foolish than me, indulging in useless tears." Then he thought, "This fellow has said this to distract me from my grief. I will stop mourning and speak of his goodness.

For it is said:

> "Ādhittaṃ[17] vata maṃ santaṃ—ghatasittaṃ va pāvakaṃ
> Vārinā viya osiñcaṃ—sabbaṃ nibbāpaye daraṃ
> Abbahī vata me sallaṃ—sokaṃ hadayanissitaṃ,
> Yo me sokaparetassa—puttasokaṃ apānudi.
> Svāhaṃ abbūḷhasallosmi—sītubhūthosmi nibbuto
> Na socāmi na rodāmi—tava sutvāna māṇava."*

*I was aflame with grief, like butter spattered on fire
Now you have quenched that sorrow as if water were sprinkled on it.
You plucked out the dart of my sorrow, lodged deep in the heart
I was overcome with grief for my son, now it has been assuaged.
I have removed the dart, I am tranquil, cooled,
I hear you O youth, and now, I neither grieve nor weep.

"Child, you are kind. You see a fiercely burning fire rush toward a village to burn up the houses, and instead of merely looking on or walking away, you spray water and put it out. The fire of my grief over the loss of my child has scorched all thoughts out of my head. It has been put out by the water of your words. With the hand of your wisdom you have gently pulled out the arrow of my grief and with your medicinal advice stopped the flow of my thoughts and cured me of the wound. I acknowledge your maturity and from now on will not grieve for my dead child. We are parted it is true, but since he does not weep, my doing so only causes my own body to dry out. One may ignore good advice when it is given, but a wise man later realizes that it is a blessing. I have learned from your advice and have taken good note of all you said. Now, when a stranger does one a special favor it is good to get to know him. Therefore, tell me, who are you?"

The god Maṭṭakuṇḍalī replied, "If you weep for a dead son, then I was that son. I left this world and was born in heaven."

The Brahmin was surprised. "You lived in my house until you died. In all that time I never saw you perform any special act of merit such as giving offerings to monks. How then did you get to heaven? If you got to heaven that easily, then everyone must be up there!"

The god thought, "If, after coming all this way and after all this talk this Brahmin is still not inspired to have faith in the Buddha, his Teachings, and his Order of Monks, and if he does not perform acts of merit, then all my effort would have been in vain. It would be like rain water falling on the outside of a waterpot! I must therefore speak in such a manner so that he, too, will achieve a state of tranquility and thereby enjoy the pleasures of heaven."

Thus, he said, "O Brahmin, it is true I did not perform any meritorious act like making offerings. But it was because you gave me no instruction even though you were ripe in years. However, if even an owl, unfortunate enough to be born as a bird, can arrive at a state of tranquility by merely looking on the Buddha and his monks, and by that act alone can escape being born in hell for over one hundred thousand years, and can finally become the *Pasē Buddha* Somanassa, then will not that same tranquility of mind benefit us? When I had been put outside under the eaves of the house to await my death, I saw the Buddha, who had come out of compassion for me alone, as if to present to a single individual, gifts that are meant for many. Gazing at one so tranquil, it was impossible not to achieve a state of tranquility myself, and, so by means of that ladder of tranquility, I climbed to heaven."

The Brahmin did not have the courtesy even to thank the person who had helped him so much. Instead, like a man stuffing himself on heavenly food expecting to digest it later, he began to think even as the god was speaking, "How wonderful is the power of the Buddha. Without doing a single other act of merit, by only making his mind tranquil, this man has obtained such celestial comforts. Merit such as that cannot be harmful to others. So with a tranquil mind I, too, will take refuge in Buddha." He then informed the god Maṭṭakuṇḍalī of these thoughts.

As if offering a chew of betel nut[18] to those who have just finished a hearty meal in order to complete the feast, so the god decided to offer a final word of advice[19] to one who had now assuaged his grief and taken refuge in the Buddha. He said, "Go take refuge in Buddha. In addition take refuge in the Teachings honored by the Buddhas. Take refuge also in the Order of Monks that helped to preserve it. Establish yourself in these Three Refuges that impede the threefold factors of Actions, Defilements, and the Consequences of Action that result in the continuous Cycle of Existence. Be compassionate, avoid killing, take only what is given, avoid sexual misconduct, lying, and the taking of intoxicating drinks as if avoiding a poisonous snake, and live in tranquility doing good."

The Brahmin accepted the god's advice as a preliminary to his acceptance of the Buddha's advice. Having thus admonished him, the god Maṭṭakuṇḍalī returned to his heavenly abode. The Brahmin went home and said to his wife, "Good woman, I will invite this Gōtama-monk, give him food, and question him. Prepare an offering of food." So saying he went to the temple and without greeting the Buddha or engaging in pleasant talk,[20] he stood on a side and said, "Exalted Gautama, will you come with your monks today and partake of food at our house?" Even though the invitation was not anything special, the Buddha accepted it silently, considering the future benefits that would come of it.

Knowing that the Buddha by his silence had accepted the invitation, the Brahmin returned home quickly and prepared a very special feast. He was not in the habit of giving alms, so it was as if a great rain was soaking the ground after a long drought.

Like the moon attended by its auspicious planets, the Buddha arrived at the Brahmin's palace. He sat in a seat prepared for him and shone like the sun rising over the Yugandhara mountain. The monks sat around him like an expanse of red lotuses blossoming and swaying around a golden boat. The Brahmin with his own hands offered the food to the Buddha and to the monks.

Many had gathered there that day, believers of erroneous faiths as well as believers of the right faith. Of the two groups, the unbelievers thought, "This Brahmin has invited the medicant Monk Gautama[21] to his house not just to offer him food. He has done so to vex him with questions. Let us go there to watch the discomfiture of the medicant Monk Gautama and see what a hard time he gets." Those holding the right beliefs thought, "This sun, the All-Knowing Buddha, with his brilliant discourse and the radiance of his person is going to dispel the darkness of Ignorance of the unbelieving Brahmin. Just as an artist mixes his paints to obtain the right color, so he will combine his two kinds of brilliance. Let us go, too, and with that same radiance dispel our own dark Defilements. Let us apply to our eyes the pleasing collyrium of his face."

The Brahmin approached the Buddha when the meal was over, sat on a low seat, and began to question him. What did he ask?

"Ascetic Gautama, are there those who enjoy the pleasures of heaven without ever giving alms to you or to your monks, not even a ladleful of gruel or a spoonful of rice? Can they get to heaven without observing religious practices? Can they do so without listening to sermons? Can they enjoy such pleasures merely by evoking a tranquil mind at the sight of you?" he asked.

The Buddha replied, "O Brahmin, why do you ask that? You are like a man who knows where he is going and still asks the way. Did your son Maṭṭakuṇḍalī not tell you how, by merely evoking a tranquil mind at the sight of me, he obtained the pleasures of heaven?" The Buddha then repeated to the Brahmin the conversation he had overheard with his Divine Ear.

Although the god had appeared in the guise of Maṭṭakuṇḍalī, the Brahmin had thought him to be someone else. So he said, "O Exalted Gautama, when did my son come and where did he talk to me?" The Buddha explained, "One particular day, when you were weeping at the cemetary, you saw someone who looked like Maṭṭakuṇḍalī, decked in ornaments and flowers. He was standing weeping and you asked him why he wept. That was your son Maṭṭakuṇḍalī." To convince him of that the Buddha told the story of Maṭṭakuṇḍalī.

Just as a piece of paper,[22] on which a scribe writes is transformed by a King's signature into a royal deed of gift, so this story has now become the word of Buddha.

"Listen O Brahmin," the Buddha continued. "What one sees is more convincing than what one hears. Yet, inspite of what you have already seen you want to hear about it also now from me, like a man who has experienced the efficacy of a medicine and still goes asking around for other remedies. I will say only this. Yes, there are hundreds, thousands, in fact countless people who have made their minds tranquil when they saw me and have thereby been reborn in the world of the gods."

All but the enlightened few refused to believe him since they did not know the power of a Buddha. To turn them from their disbelief and to give even the critics the gift of a share[23] in the blessings of Spiritual Attainments, the Buddha willed that the god Maṭṭakuṇḍalī descend together with his heavenly palace, filled with the luxuries of heaven. Instantly, the god, with his arms three leagues long, decked in jewelry, stepped forth from his heavenly abode, saluted the Buddha, and stood respectfully on a side.

As if asking for proof in order to quell people's doubts about the wealth the god was enjoying, the Buddha asked, "God, what act of goodness did you do to obtain these heavenly pleasures?"

The god replied, "I can not think of anything I did except that I evoked a tranquil mind when I saw you. That is only a small act of merit to record but I certainly obtained all these blessings from that one deed." He spoke clearly for all to hear.

A large section of those present, seeing the deity and his riches thought, "Indeed the Buddha is a wondrous field for us to cultivate merit,[24] because even Maṭṭakuṇḍalī, who did nothing else, has obtained such great wealth merely by evoking a tranquil mind." Thus, they were delighted and inspired to do good deeds. Just as a king when showering great wealth on a person, draws up a list of what he gives, and displays his magnanimity by announcing, "These are the gifts I give you," so the Buddha preached the Doctrine in order to confer the blessing of *nirvāṇa* on the gathering, on the Brahmin, as well as on the deity.

He preached thus: "O Brahmin, when hundreds of people get together and commit a robbery, though they participate equally in the act of stealing, one of them is called "robber-chief." In the same way, an evil mind is what leads one to evil actions.

Similarly, when many do a good deed together, one of them becomes the leader in this action. A wholesome mind leads one to good actions in much the same way. Sinful deeds inevitably follow sinful thoughts as the wheel constantly follows the hoof of the ox wherever he goes. So does a good act done with a tranquil mind follow like a shadow that never leaves. It will never abandon you. The result will be rebirth in heavenly abodes, unless one has already attained the state of enlightenment of an *arahat* and the *karmic* consequences of such deeds have thereby been rendered inactive. Continuous good actions take effect in this very life. Like a fertile seed that will not die until it has attained its full growth, it will stop only after it has worked itself out. Thus, make your mind tranquil, it is the source of all good deeds, and perform meritorious deeds."

At the end of this sermon, eighty-four thousand people achieved the ultimate release of *nirvāṇa*. Maṭṭakuṇḍalī, the god, decked himself in the jewelled ornament of a Stream-Enterer. Gem-studded, he now had the ability to understand the Teachings in one thousand ways. The Brahmin Addhinnapubbaka, who, up to that point had not the slightest trace of generosity, became also a Stream-Enterer and began to give freely. In the story of the *Naḷapāna Jātaka*,[25] the waters of the demon-infested lake became available to eighty thousand monkeys, so also the wealth of Adinnapubbaka became beneficial to the Buddha's *sāsana*.

Similarly, good men should use the stories of this book the *Jewel Garland of the True Doctrine* as a mirror to study the reflections of the Teachings. They should deck themselves in the ornaments of Virtue, such as Discipline and Contemplation, and shine with the radiance of those jewels.

Endnotes

This story illustrates verse 2 of the Yamaka Vagga stanzas:

> Manopubbaṃgamā dhammā . . . chayāva anapāyini
>
> Mind is the forerunner of all conditions, mind is foremost and
> they are mind made
> If with a pure mind one speaks and acts,
> Then happiness follows like a shadow that never leaves.

The introduction of link passages into the SR text is a device used by the monk Dharmasēna in order to give his work an overall unity. He conceives of his work as a garland *(āvaliya)* so connections between the stories, though tenuous, do exist. This is specially true of the stories of the first section that illustrate the "Yamaka Vagga" (Twin Verses) stanzas. The Yamaka Vagga stanzas are "yoked" or "coupled," this thematic balance is emphasized by the link passages in the stories.

Such link passages are not a feature of the original DA text. They indicate the author's sense of the work as being more than a collection of stories and of having some kind of overarching unity.

1. *Sudhābhōjana Jātaka* story,

A rich miser is seized with a great longing to have some rice porridge and to avoid having to give any of it to anyone else. He retires into a forest to cook it for himself. Sakka and other gods appear and claim a share of the porridge. The miser is converted by their admonitions, gives away all his money, and becomes an ascetic.

2. . . . , he would have to feed the man for several days till the work was completed.

In traditional Sri Lankan households, even as late as the 1940s, gold and silver craftsmen were invited to "live in" while working on an order. All their meals were provided during this period and, when the work was completed, a further payment was made. This was probably a continuation of the medieval patron-client relationships referred to in this story, which no doubt existed in thirteenth century feudal Sri Lanka. The DA version makes no such reference. It merely states: "Knowing that if he gave the commission to a goldsmith he should have to pay him a fee, he beat out the gold himself."

3. Thus, the son acquired the name Maṭṭakuṇḍalī . . .

The giving of nicknames or identifying people by some special characteristic, is a popular practice. This text is full of such names as Addinnapubbaka (Non-giver), Maṭṭakuṇḍalī (Flat-Earring), Thūlatissa (Fat-Tissa). In the villages of Sri Lanka, even today, such names are common. In many cases, the names stick with the individuals through life and often become the name by which they are best known.

4. When the young man . . . , he was stricken with anaemia.

The name of the disease in the text is *pāndu rōgaya,* an anaemia or jaundice that results from malnutrition. The implication is that this rich man did not spend money even on food for his own family.

5. *Kalandaka Jātaka story*

There is no reference in the E. B. Cowell edition to a *Kalandaka Jātaka* story. There is a *Kalanduka Jataka* which tells a different story. The *Kalandaka Jātaka* referred to here, is about a squirrel who tried to empty the ocean by bailing out the water with its tail. It was an attempt to save its young when the nest fell into the sea. It is possible that this Jātaka story existed in the collection because it is mentioned in other Sinhala literary works such as the *Buduguṇālaṅkāraya*.

6. . . . Instead of taking us to the patient, . . .

Another commentary on medical practice, the diagnosis and treatment of disease and the underpinnings of the medical approach.

7. Just as the medicine prescribed by the monk Cakkhupāla . . .

Another cross reference—this time internal to the story and adding a further link to the author's "garland."

8. A disease that causes extreme swelling of the legs.

9. Thus, he cast the net of his Wisdom . . .

The image here brilliantly illustrates the all-encompassing nature of the Buddha's compassion: that in the vast undifferentiated ocean of human suffering, it can zero in on the little fish Maṭṭakuṇḍalī, a helpless child left out to die.

10. When I appear before him, . . .

This entire section is a projection into the future, an anticipation of events that *are* to happen if the Buddha *were* to go to Maṭṭakuṇḍalī. It is the use of a kind of flash-forward technique. The identical events then are repeated when they actually occur. The text tends to be confusing and repetitive even in the original. Though none of the editors have remarked on it, there is the possibility that it was originally a scribal error that was subsequently incorporated into the text.

11. . . . evoke a tranquil state of mind toward me at the moment of dying.

This is more than just becoming tranquil. In Buddhism, it is regarded as a conscious act of acceptance or conviction that sets the mind at rest. The phrase is *pahan sit ätikalā* which means, "he created or generated a tranquil state of mind.

12. He draped his robe from the navel to the kneecap . . . to cover three parts of the body . . .

Buddhist monks wore their robes according to certain rules that were laid down in the *Vinaya Piṭaka.*

13. *Uraga Jātaka* story,

Refers to the story of a Brahmin who lost his son but neither he nor any of his family lamented or wept. Sakra asks each one in turn, why they do not grieve? Each utters a stanza. The wife of the dead man recites the following verses:

> As children cry in vain to grasp the moon above
> So mortals idly mourn the loss of those they love.
> No friend's lament can touch the ashes of the dead
> why should I grieve, he fares, the way he had to tread.

14. *Culladhunuggaha Jātaka* story,

A woman, who betrayed her husband to death and was afterward deserted by her lover, has her folly brought home to her by witnessing the fate of a greedy jackal.

15. *Javanahaṃsa Jātaka* story,

The story of a royal goose and a human king who became fast friends. The goose saved two foolish geese who raced with the sun.

16. When I weep I only see my own tears, . . .

Interesting psychological insight into the nature of tears. One weeps out of self-pity not for the person lost.

17. "Ādhittaṃ . . .

Here again the author's explanation of the Pāli stanza is more than just a translation. It is an expansive version of the text and context.

18. As if offering a chew of betel nut . . .

Betel leaves and arecanut are passed around at the end of a meal; small amounts of it are chewed. The "chew," like coffee, serves to round off a meal.

19. . . . to offer a final word of advice . . .

Here Addhinnapubbaka is given a brief summary of Buddhist ethics for the lay life. In so doing, the author also instructs his lay readers and listeners.

20. The Brahmin in his eagerness, greedy for gain, ignores the formalities of good manners. Such formalities are very much part of Buddhist practice and are observed in Sri Lauka even today.

21. "This Brahmin has invited the medicant monk Gautama . . .

Note that nonbelievers always refer to the Buddha as the mendicant monk Gautama, sometimes even more informally as Gōtama-monk, just another mendicant teacher. The believers refer to him as the "Buddha."

22. Just as a piece of paper, . . .

Deeds or royal gifts of land were often inscribed on copper (sometimes other, more precious) metal sheets. Here the image underlines the belief in the transforming power of the written word such as a royal signature. Similarly, the monk Dharmasēna's story, in the telling, is transformed into the word of the Buddha.

23. . . . to give even the critics the gift of a share . . .

The limitless nature of the Buddha's compassion is underlined and the lengths to which he is prepared to take it in order to be of benefit even to his critics.

24. . . . "Indeed the Buddha is a wondrous Field of Merit, for us to cultivate . . .

The Buddha and his monks individually and collectively are referred to by this agrarian metaphor. They provide "a Field of Merit" where laymen can sow the seed of good deeds and reap the rewards of such good actions in this and other lives. In providing this opportunity they perform an important function.

25. *Naḷapāna Jātaka* story,

Thirsty monkeys come to a pool haunted by an ogre. Their leader miraculously blows the knots out of some bamboo canes and using these as straws the monkeys safely quench their thirst.

The Senior Monk Nāgasēṇa

To increase the faith of the faithful, we related the story of Maṭṭakuṇḍalī, describing what joys and blessings he obtained merely by the power of his serene thoughts. Now, in order to encourage those same good men in the practice of the Doctrine, we shall relate the story of the Senior Monk Nāgasēna. By a simple act of merit, the monk Nāgasēna acquired such intellectual powers that he could unravel the complexities of the Buddha's teachings and answer all questions.

Very long ago, at a time when the Buddha Kasub (who was prior to our Buddha Gōtama) was already dead, but while his teachings still prevailed,[1] there was a certain temple located on a river bank where many monks lived and practiced their monastic discipline. Vigilant in the performance of their customary duties, these monks woke early, and without indulging in talk that might diminish their prospects of heaven and Enlightenment, concentrating continuously on the Buddha's great qualities, they took up brooms and swept the yard. However, instead of each one disposing of his sweepings individually, they would collect it all and, since it was not against monastic practice, get another person to dispose of it.

One day a certain monk called up a young novice and said, "Novice, throw out these sweepings." The novice heard him but acted as if the words had fallen on deaf ears. Disobedient, he did not do it even when told twice and thrice. The Senior Monk was angry that he had not come when called. "This novice is disobedient," he thought and spoke sharply to him, and struck him with the broom handle. One should learn from this incident that in anger one acts rashly.

The novice took the beating and began to cry. However, perhaps afraid that, if he did not do as he was told he might be beaten some more, he collected the sweepings with an air of indifference and threw them out. They were only sweepings, but the act of throwing them out was meritorious even though done at the bidding of another, so he decided to make a Fervent Rebirth-Wish.[2] His first wish was that, by the merit gained from this action, in every future life until he attained *nirvāṇa,* wherever he was born, he would have power and glory like the midday sun, for it was lack of power that had caused him to be beaten. When he stepped down into the river to wash his hands after throwing out the sweepings, he saw the lapping of the waves and thought, "From this birth through future births, until I attain *nirvāṇa,* just as this river has countless waves, so may the endless waves of questions generated by the river of my wisdom move to the shore of my mouth — in other words, may I be a great debater." Triggered by pride he made his second wish.

The monk who struck him put the broom back in the broomshed and went down to the river to bathe. He overheard the novice make his wish and thought, "By the mere fact that he threw out dirt which I swept up, and which he did indifferently, at my bidding, he now makes a Fervent Rebirth-Wish. If his wish comes to pass, then I, who first swept the yard must also have my wishes granted." So he, too, made a Fervent Rebirth-Wish. "From this birth, until I achieve *nirvāṇa,* in whatever world I am born, may I have unlimited understanding to counter without hesitation whatever argument this man presents in debate. Further, as the waves of this river constantly break against this shore, so may his arguments be demolished when brought to me. May my counter reasoning dry up the waters of his discourse in the ocean of his mouth as the sun dries the ocean at the end of the eon." They each wished thus. Thereafter, from the time of the Buddha Kasub until the dispensation of our Buddha (Gōtama), both of them spent time in the worlds of gods and of men.

In the past, when our Buddha destroyed the pride of the unbelieving sects the Tīrthakas by performing the two miracles in the city of Sävät, and when he went to Tavtisā heaven in three victorious steps, while he was preaching the *Abhidhamma* texts to the gods there, headed by his mother, he said, "I will preach the *Abhidhamma* and its various divisions.[3] When I am no more the Senior Monk Moggaliputtha Tissa, with the help of the great king Dharmāśōka, will select a thousand powerful *arahats* and hold a Council at the monastary of Aśōkārāmaya.

For it is said,

Yā saṭṭhi titthiyasahassa nisāgatantaṃ
Dullaḍdhighoratimiraṃ vinihacca sammā
Sā tissa theraravinā gamitā vikāsaṃ
Saṅgīti cāru naḷinī api dassitā me.*

The monk Mogalliputtatissa will preach the *Kathāvatthu* embroidered with one thousand arguments, five hundred from my doctrine, and five hundred from other doctrines, in order to still the controversies of sixty thousand Tirthakas." In the same way, the Buddha predicted for the two rival monks, "Five hundred years after my death these two people will be born again in the world of men. That part of my doctrine, which I expounded in such a manner as to be comprehensible only to men of sharp intellect, not the dull witted, these two with their keen

*The night of the sixty thousand wrong believers ends
The Monk Tissa, like a sun, illumines their night
Destroys the black darkness of erroneous beliefs.
The Council of Monks, that lovely lotus, blooms.

minds will unravel, using the method of questions and answers, similes and illustrations. Thus, they will eliminate confusion and misunderstandings. As a man strengthens and repairs a dilapidated house so that it can remain standing for a long time, in the same fashion, will they strengthen my teachings to make them last five thousand years."

As it was predicted, so of the two who made Rebirth-Wishes, the novice died and was born in India in the city of Sāgala. Just as an ascetic, after twenty thousand years of austerities, which entitle him to attain whatever heights he wishes, then lapses and so ends up in a lowly situation, or as women lacking in virtue,[4] even though they attain Trance States, can only be born in the lower Brahma worlds, so the novice was born as the Yon King, Miliňdu.[5] As a result of his Fervent Rebirth-Wish, he had a mind that was as sharp as a diamond. A man with money acquires much goods. Similarly he, too, acquired knowledge in many branches of learning. He was skilled in nineteen areas of study such as mathematics and music. He had an abundance of royal wealth and splendor. In power, strength, intelligence, and manly beauty there was no other king in India to compare with him.

One day King Miliňdu thought, "In the event of a war, I should know the strength of my army." Thus, in order to review his forces, he set forth in a great procession, gorgeously arrayed as when the gods gathered in heaven to defeat the Asura demons. Accompanied by his fourfold army, he left his city whose splendor seemed an insult to the heavenly city of Tavtisā. He amassed his forces on the outskirts of the city, took a count, and learned how many soldiers he had.

The king was fond of discussion and debate. He now looked at the sun and thought, "The sun is yet high in the sky. There is still time to return to the city. What should we gain by marching back there so early. I should ask my ministers if there is anyone around knowledgeable enough to coverse with me. If there is, I will go talk to him." He inquired whether they knew of anyone fit to discourse with him.

As men who, when asked to describe a lion describe a jackal, merely because it, too, is an animal and fourfooted, so the five hundred Yon ministers believing all men to be the same, said, "O King, in the time of the Buddha there were scholars such as Pūrṇa Kāśyapa. In the same tradition now, there are six ascetics named Makkhali Gosāla, Nigaṇṭanātha Putra, Sanjaya Bellaṭṭiya, Ajita Keśakambalī, and Kukudha Kāthyāna, who all walk around in the garb in which they were born.[6] Go debate with them. If your highness has any doubts or questions they, with their theories derived from their tradition of scholarship, will answer them.

Thereupon King Miliňdu, accompanied by about five hundred ministers, climbed into a chariot of white horses that surpassed the chariot of the god Sakra. With the bearing of a Sakra entering his pleasure garden, the king went first to Pūrṇa Kāśyapa. Even though no one teacher was superior to another, he went first to Pūrṇa Kāśyapa because he happened to be mentioned first. He saw the ascetic, naked, as if to proclaim to the world, "Know hereby that there is no such thing as fear or shame." The wise king realized that just as he lacked clothes so his doctrine, too, might lack virtue and did not worship him. Instead he thought, "This man may not be virtuous, but he could be wise and may have answers to my questions. As with rice, where only the grain free of the husk and cleaned of broken pieces is of any use, so the core content of his words may be useful." Thus, just as one pacifies, with a flick of one's thumb, snapping dogs that are about to attack, so the king spoke to him pleasantly and stood respectfully on a side. Then drawing him into conversation the king asked, "Pūrṇa Kāśyapa, Your Reverence, who is the protector of this world?"

Pūrṇa Kāśyapa, whose name means Kāśyapa the Full, but who was full only in name, not in goodness, said, "O King, who but the earth protects this world?" He gave this answer perhaps because there was such a belief in his particular doctrine, or perhaps he thought that any hesitation when questioned might result in a loss of honor.

The king replied, "Your Reverence, if the earth protects humanity, and if hell is located below the earth, then how do men pass through it and get born in hell? Does the earth, located in between, not protect them? One could understand if they were going to a place of blessing. But headed for a place of suffering as they are, and besides, passing right through the earth, not any great distance away from it, how is it that this earth does not protect them? Like a mother, who watches her son about to fall into a pit and does nothing to hold him back, why does the earth, which is there to protect humans, do nothing to stop them who are headed for hell? One might say the child is not hers. But the earth as a whole must protect humanity. I did not understand you to say that only half-humankind will have protection from half the earth. Did you answer as you did merely because the words came to your lips, and not because it was true? Or did you not know who really protects the earth, just as you seem not to know that going about without clothes is a sign of depravity? Only young children wear no clothes. You may be old in years but you act like a child."

Thus, like a superior warrior, who, though unarmed, snatches a weapon from the hand of an unskilled warrior and kills him with it, so the king took the very words of the ascetic and turned them against him, thereby defeating him in the debate. Pūrṇa Kāśyapa could neither substantiate his claim nor withdraw it. He had no further arguments, or perhaps they got stuck in his throat and he could not vomit them out.

Since he had nothing to say, he sat despondent, like a god that watches people eat but gets not even a grain for himself. Since Pūrṇa Kāśyapa could consume rice but had no answers to questions, King Miliňdu figured that the capacity of the others was not likely to be too different. However he thought, "Let me question them, too. As one removes the outer bark of a banana tree and exposes the lack of substance at the core, so I will show that their learning has no real substance."

He then went to Makkhali Gosāla and asked, "Reverend Sir, Makkhali Gosāla, do good and evil exist? Do good actions have beneficial effects and sinful actions ill effects?" Like Diktalayā and Dikpiṭiyā in the *Ummaga Jātaka* story,[7] who, when each was asked the name of the other's parents, could not answer since neither knew it, so Makkhali Gosāla did not know what Merit and Demerit were or the true meaning of the words. Just as Diktalayā and Dikpiṭiya did not know one another's names, or who they were, so he did not know who he himself was. Such questions may seem to be about name and external form and make little sense except for those who seek after fundamental truths. Makkhali Gosāla answered the King like a man, who, when asked about a mango talks about a *Del* fruit,[8] describing something other than what was asked for.

"Great King, there are no such things as acts of Merit or Demerit. If there is no seed, then no plant can grow from it. Similarly, if Merit and Demerit do not exist, then their consequences are also nonexistent. The idea that *Dāna* (Generosity) is a meritorious act is something that ignorant men have told themselves. The wise do not think that way. I shall give an example to illustrate that there is no such thing as Merit, Demerit, or their consequences.

"Now if a man is born a king, since that is his destiny, he will continue to be a ruler even in the next life. That is in the nature of things. If a man is born a Brahmin, since that is his destiny, he will be a Brahmin in the next life, too. So with a merchant. A man born a farmer, since that has always been his occupation, will be born a farmer in the next life. Similarly, a low-caste person will be born low caste. One who is impure cannot become pure nor one who is pure become impure. If Merit and Demerit were to operate, then a king, who does sinful acts, should be born lowly as a consequence, and those of lowly birth, if they do good, should be born great because of such actions. But that is not the case. A king or Brahmin is born that way in this life and the next life. That is a fact of nature, not a result of good or sinful actions.

"Let me give you another example. By what Merit did *kiṇihira* flowers become golden-colored? Is it because they made offerings of golden hued flowers in a past life? Why did *kasa* flowers become black? It is the force of nature and not the result of good or bad actions."

Foxes may wish to roar like lions but they emit only fox sounds. So Makkhali Gosāla thought he was answering questions but he was merely mouthing empty words.

The king replied, "Your Reverence, if those born as kings or Brahmins are reborn always the same, then an armless man must be born armless in his next life, one who is lame here will be lame in the next life, one without a nose will have no nose in the next life, too. But the next life is not just an extension of this one. The world of the gods and the Brahma heavens are also part of the next life. According to what you say, there must be the lame and handicapped in the heavenly worlds of the gods and Brahma!"

At that Makkhali Gosāla had nothing to say. He was speechless like one born mute because of the sin of indulging in empty prattle. King Milińdu thought, "Alas, the land of Daṁbadiva is empty. I have not found anyone who can debate with me, answer my questions, and dispel my doubts."

He called up his ministers and said, "I took your suggestion and went out to debate with wise men, but like a merchant who returns from a business trip empty-handed, I have learned nothing. This night, free of the bane of darkness is most pleasant. On such a night what wise Brahmin should I seek in order to hear words that soothe my ears? Who can meet my arguments and tell me what I seek to know?"

The Yon ministers knew no one other than Pūrṇa Kāśyapa. Even if there were others they were sure they would meet the same fate when confronted by the powerful king. They therefore remained silent, staring at the king's face, like men who, though they can hear, are mute and cannot speak.

At that time, the city of Sāgala quickly emptied of its wise men who were afraid of having to debate with the king. It was like a threshing floor emptied of grain, left only with the chaff. Those who happened to be left, for lack of a place to disappear to, refused to confront him in debate. Many monks took to the Himalayas.

Around that time, about one hundred crores of *arahats* lived in the Red-Rock plateau in the Himalayas. Among them was the Senior Monk Assagutta. He heard with his Divine Ear[9] the King saying to the ministers, "Tell me is there any wise monk who can debate with me?" Assagutta then called up the one hundred crores of *arahats* from the Red-Rock to the top of the Yugandhara mountain, one of the seven Himalayan peaks, and said, "King Milińdu has asked if there is any monk here competent to debate with him?" Not one responded. The question was repeated twice and thrice but since they were not competent, they remained silent. Getting no reply the Senior Monk Assagutta addressed the monks thus:

"If all of you remain silent when only five hundred years have passed out of the five thousand,[10] then what will be the fate of the Buddha's Teachings after two thousand years? If right now, there are about one hundred crores of *arahats* and not one to meet his challenge, does it not suggest that the power of the Buddha's *sāsana* is ending?

"In Tavtisā heaven, east of Sakra's palace Vijayantha, there is a heavenly abode, named Khetumatī. There the god Mahāsēn lives. He can debate King Miliňdu and, as if passing a fine thread through the eye of a needle, convince him with his similes and images."

Thereupon the one hundred crores of *arahats* vanished from the Yugandhara mountain and appeared in the Tavtisā heaven. God Sakra saw them approaching from afar and evoking a serene mind toward them went to their leader, the Senior Monk Assagutta, and said, "Your Reverence, why have you come? Please tell us."

In order to obtain the god Sakra's support for the protection of the *sāsana,* the Senior Monk Assagutta said, "Listen Sakra, I came intending to speak, even if you had not asked me. Now that you ask I will speak. You may not be aware of it because of the divine luxury in which you live,[11] but at this time, in the city of Sāgala, there is a Yon king named Miliňdu, who comes up to scholar monks, confronts them in debate, and causes much discomfiture. There is no one in the world at present smart enough to debate with him. Though what he threw out, in a past life was mere unclean sweepings, the intelligence he has been blessed with is keen and clear. In the past, he had neither status nor power and so had to throw away sweepings. Now he has both power and status and can influence men's minds. Inquire and let me know if there is anyone in heaven who can debate with this king." He spoke thus to enlist Sakra's support.

Thereupon god Sakra replied, "Your Reverence, that King Miliňdu went to earth from no less a place than this very heaven. There is another god named Mahāsēna, presently living in that other heaven, Khetumatī, which you can see out there. He is a match for King Miliňdu as one wrestler is for another, or as fire that can soften iron. Let us plead with him to be born a human and engage the King in debate." Thereafter, accompanied by Sakra they went to the heavenly abode, Khetumatī, and sent Sakra first, to urge him to be born on earth.

A hundred years after the death of the Buddha, ten thousand Aladivādins, who held wrong views, had lived in the city of Visal and preached false doctrines as true. They had proclaimed ten erroneous doctrines, and had contaminated with the poison of false beliefs, the waters of the True Doctrine that filled the lake of the *sāsana*. At that time, the Senior Monk Yasa and his followers had resided in the Vāluka monastery. With the help of King Kālāśōka, they had rid the *sāsana* of sinful monks and set up the second Council of Monks so that the True Doctrine could prevail for another five thousand years.

It was said thus:

> Ettāvatā dasasahassa supāpabhikkhū
> Niddhūya dhūtadasavatthumalā akaṃsu,
> Yaṃ te sunimmala yasena yasena saddhiṃ
> Saṅgītimujjitamalā api dassitā sā.*

Thereafter, casting their Divine Eyes to see what further dangers might undermine the work they had just completed in establishing the Order, they foresaw that in the time of King Dharmāśōka, son of Bindusāra, sixty thousand Tīrthakas would don monks robes, not because they were fit to do so but merely for profit. Like jackals in lion skins, or men who pick up white quartz pebbles imagining they are gems, their concern for personal gain would result in the likely ruin of the True Doctrine. The monks, who had participated in the second Council,[12] then went to the Brahma land, knowing that until the monk Tissa set up the third Council of the Buddhist Order and restored Buddhism, not only in the middle kingdom, but also in the countryside, there would be no one on earth, or in the seven heavens, other than Great Brahma himself, capable of resolving these conflicts. Similarly, now, the one hundred crores of *arahats* accompanied by the god Sakra went to the Khetumatī heaven to the god Mahāsēna and pleaded with him to enter the human world.

Just as one has no attachment for that which one considers valueless, so the god Mahāsēna, hearing their plea but not knowing the full significance of the task, was reluctant to be born a human purely on the basis of Sakra's pleadings.

Sensing his reluctance, the Senior monk Assagutta said, "O you who are free from suffering, do not hesitate. Your action will be of great benefit to the *sāsana*. We have looked over all the worlds and there is no one as suited as you for this task. Therefore at the request of so many *arahats* and on the invitation of the gods and Brahmas, and because the action is in itself meritorious, consent to be born on earth. You may already be engaged in practices leading to Enlightenment but like a Bod-

---

*Ten thousand sinful monks contaminated the *sāsana*.
They introduced ten ascetic practices.
The renowned monk Yasa and his followers held a Council
And cleansed it of such Defilements.

hisatva born to serve humanity, be born on earth and put an end to King Miliňdu's harassassment[13] of the monks."

Thus, they appealed to him having consulted everyone's opinions. At that point, the god Mahāsēna thought, "They say that I will debate King Miliňdu and be able to defeat him. They say that because of me the waters of Truth that fill the lake of Buddhism will be cleansed of the Defilements of wrong views. They say I could be of great benefit to the *sāsana.*" He was pleased and said, "If the religion can benefit from my action, then I agree to be born a human." He accepted the invitation of the *arahats.* The *arahats,* having obtained the pledge that god Mahāsēna would be born a man, left heaven and set up their residence again in the Red-Rock plateau of the Himalayas.

While they lived thus, the Senior Monk Assagutta called them one day and said, "Brothers, is there anyone here who did not involve himself in these activities?" He was told that the Senior Monk Rohaṇa had not participated because he was already enjoying the Trance State of the Attainment of Cessation. Assagutta, seated in the assembly, sent for him. It was not yet time to arise out of the trance, for a week had not yet passed, but because of the importance of the request, the Senior Monk Rohaṇa arose and went to the Red-Rock plateau.

When he arrived, the Senior Monk Assagutta said, "Brother, don't you see that the Buddha's religion is declining because no one can successfully refute King Miliňdu? Is this a time for indifference? The *sāsana* needs your support."

The Senior Monk Rohaṇa replied, "I could not participate in the journey to the heavens, but aside from that, is there anything else that I can do?"

"Brother, before going into the Trance State of the Attainment of Cessation, you were not unaware of the decline of the *sāsana,* which we had all seen happening. However, you chose to remain indifferent and did nothing. Therefore you should be punished."

"What is the punishment?" the Senior Monk Rohaṇa asked.

"Brother, the punishment is this. Near the Himalayas is a Brahmin village called "Kajaṃgala." In that village lives a Brahmin whose lineage is pure on both his mother's and his father's side. A son named Nāgasēna will be born to him. You, O monk, must go begging to that house for the next seven years and ten months, whether they give you any food or not. When the said period is over, take young Nāgasēna with you and ordain him. An enormous service will be rendered by him to the *sāsana.* Since you will be a contributor to that, your punishment will then be over."

Thus, on the grounds of it being a punishment, he ordered that Nāgasēna be ordained. Just as the blow with the broom handle, struck in a past life, had to have its *karmic* consequences, so this was a fitting retribution. The Senior Monk Rohaṇa listened and agreed. He had not been a party to the earlier act of Merit, but by this act he was able to contribute to it.

The god Mahāsēna left heaven and was conceived in the womb of the wife of the Brahmin Soṇuttara. The moment he was born all the weapons in the village began to shine as a portent of his prowess. Special first rice[14] sprouted for him as a mark of the primacy of his intellectual powers. To quench the drought of hardship a great rain fell.

From the day god Mahāsēna was conceived in the Brahmin mother's womb, the Senior Monk Rohaṇa went daily to that house for a period of seven years and ten months. During all that time, he got neither a spoonful of rice nor even a ladleful of gruel. Let alone food he did not even get respectful greetings. What did he get when he went for alms? Only abuse and harsh words.

One day when the Senior Monk Rohaṇa was at that house on his usual begging rounds, for the first time he heard the words of polite refusal, "Please go away." So he moved on. The Brahmin, who was head of the house, happened to meet the monk on the road and asked him, "Did you go begging to our house, too, O monk of great merit?" The monk replied that he had.

"Did you get anything there?" he asked again.

"Yes, I did." replied the monk, referring not to any food but to the first polite words he had received. The Brahmin, devoid of generosity, became enraged, as if he had suffered a great loss. He stormed into the house and inquired, "Did you give anything to that monk who came begging for alms to this house?" When he heard them say they had not, he thought, "If he got nothing, then he has lied to me. I will catch him in his lies." He cancelled all his business the next day and remained at home.

On the following day again, the monk went begging to that house. What he hoped to get was not just the words, "Please go away," but something far more valuable. The Brahmin saw him and said, "Yesterday though you got nothing from our house you lied, saying that you had. Is lying a good thing?"

"Listen O Brahmin, all these days I got nothing from your house, but yesterday I got at least the words, "Please go away." Though that was all, it was at least something. Therefore I said I had received something from your house."

The Brahmin thought to himself, "This monk is happy with so little. He is like the she-stork, who thrills at the mere sound of thunder, as if enjoying the pleasures of motherhood. Now if he were to get something to eat and drink he would be truly joyful." The Brahmin was pleased with the monk and requested that a spoonful of rice and a little curry, taken from what had been prepared for him, be given to the monk. "Do this daily," he ordered.

Thereafter, on the excuse of a spoonful of rice, the Senior Monk went daily to the house, until such time as the boy was of an age to be ordained. As the tip of a wick is quick to absorb oil the moment it touches it, the Brahmin, seeing the calm demeanor of the monk, who was now a regular visitor, was greatly pleased and invited him to eat at the house regularly. The Senior Monk accepted his invitation, partook daily of a meal and, as if paying for the food he ate,[15] he always preached a short sermon.

Seven years and ten days passed in this way. During that time, the Brahmin's wife had given birth to a son and had named him "Nāgasēna." The child Nāgasēna grew like the moon that fills out from quarter to quarter. When he was seven years old, the Brahmin called his son and said, "Son Nāgasēna, learning is something that can only be acquired at this stage, not when you are grown-up and your thoughts turn to other things. Therefore, you should now learn all the skills that one born a Brahmin should know. The boy asked what he should learn and the father replied, "You must learn the *Three Vēdas*, as well as other skills, just as one who eats rice must also have curries to go with it." The son replied, "Good. Why should I be lacking in anything? I will certainly learn everything."

Soṇuttara, the father, invited a Brahmin scholar who was competent to teach Nāgasēna; he made the necessary offering of one thousand gold coins, which was the teacher's due. Since he was reluctant to send his son away from home, the father arranged for a couch in a room in the palace itself and told the Brahmin scholar, "Sit here and teach my son."

The Brahmin teacher taught young Nāgasēna the *Vēda mantras* that were central to the Brahmin faith. The boy Nāgasēna did not need to recite anything twice. Like the Senior Monk Anaňda, who learned fifteen thousand stanzas by hearing them just once, so Nāgasēna at a single reading, learned the four *Vēdas* including the *Atharvavēda*,[16] all the lexical works and so forth, and all the books on prosody.

When he had been living as a monk in the time of the Buddha Kasub, he had swept the yard meticulously, so now he had all his knowledge ready at the tip of his tongue and could draw on it without hesitation or doubts. Although then he had to twice request that the sweepings be removed, now he could at a single reading comprehend hundreds of thousands of works.

When he had committed all these books to memory he went up to his father and said, "Is this all a Brahmin has to learn? Is there nothing more?"

"There is no more," the Brahmin replied, as if all the food in the stores and barns had been consumed and there was no more left. "We do not know anything else. This is all." Nāgasēna then recited to his teacher all that he had committed to memory and left the house.

In order to satisfy the pleadings of the young woman, his former Rebirth-Wish for Knowledge, he made the maiden of Wisdom sweep out the entire house of his learning. But he found nothing useful in there and so could not win the favor of the young woman, his Rebirth-Wish. Thus dissatisfied, he thought, "These *Vēdas* that I have learned are empty of substance like grain that has no kernal, only the husk. They are like empty chairs or beds."

Around this time the Senior Monk Rohaṇa happened to be living in the hermitage of Vattaniya. With his power to see into the minds of men, he realized that Nāgasēna, living in Kajaṃgala, was dissatisfied. He therefore took his robes, left Vattaniya, where he was residing and arrived at the Brahmin village of Kajaṃgala. Young Nāgasēna, standing at the doorway of his house, saw from a distance, the monk approach. He thought, "My predicament is such that I would have gone even to the place where he resides, to ask him about the true meaning of what I have learned. But now, as if one suddenly finds the medicinal herbs one is searching for growing right here by the roadside, he comes to me." Thus, he was most pleased at the prospect of a meeting.

Like a thirsty man who sees a watercarrier from afar and goes up to him to ask for a drink, he went up to the Senior Monk Rohaṇa. Since he had not seen an ordained monk like him before he asked, "Who are you, shaven and in robes?"

"We are members of a certain order of ascetic monks,"[17] he replied.

"Why did you seek ordination as a monk?"

"To rid ourselves of lust and such like Defilements."

"If that be so, why don't you grow your hair long like the other ascetics?"[18] The monk did not say, "Because we cut it." Instead he thought, "I should speak in a way that will attract him to our Order. If I merely say that I cut it every fortnight or every month and therefore it does not grow beyond a knuckle's length, he will not gain an understanding of the hardships and travails of the lay life. I will therefore use his question to make him comprehend the truth of the sufferings of lay life."

Thinking thus, he answered, "Look young man, those who grow their hair have sixteen chores to perform. What are they? A man must wash his hair regularly, then dry it without leaving any dampness. He must groom it and tie it, oil it, and shape it. When it is washed, it must be decked with flowers. Perfumes must be bought, even at a price; the hair must be scented. The tangles must be combed out and the hair deloused. When grey hairs appear they must be dyed. When the hair begins to fall, it is an annoyance. As for me I have none of those chores.[19] That is why I shave my head."

Nāgasēna said, "True, that is all true, I agree. However, your clothes, too, are unlike those of others." In order to attract him to the robes, the monk Rohaṇa replied,

"Listen young man, these robes, if uncut, have their value undiminished. If they are not dyed,[20] their colors remain brilliant. They then become much desired items of wealth. The danger from thieves and robbers is great. When lost, one grieves over them. One has the chore of carefully laundering them. But our robes are cut up, resewn, and so are valueless. By dying them ochre, their original colors are dimmed. No one desires them or envies us for having them. That is why our robes are different."

Young Nāgasēna thought, "His answer to my questions regarding the difference in dress and hair is satisfactory. But such practices must derive from some philosophy. I will ask him about that." So he asked,

"Do you subscribe to a particular philosophy?"

"Yes, young man" the monk replied and thought, "This young man is himself learned so he will not be attracted by anything ordinary." To stimulate the young man's interest, the monk said,

"We have a most profound philosophy that has to be guarded and held in the palm of one's hands."

"I would like to know what you know. Only misers hide something sweet and consume it alone. That is selfish. A man, who is not base but generous, shares with others. You should teach me whatever profound philosophies and doctrines you know," Nāgasēna said, eager for knowledge.

The monk thought, "The Fervent Rebirth-Wish this man made gives him the ability to understand everything. His thoughts and ideas are noble, and like a Bōdhisatva, he is fit to hear the Doctrine." Then, in order to free himself, too, from his own punishment, the monk spoke thus, "If you wish to learn we can teach you."

The young man, unaware of what kind of philosophy it was and in what manner it would be taught, replied, "Good. Tell me what you know."

"I have no time now. It is my turn to beg for alms so I must go," said the monk.

Young Nāgasēna then took the monk's begging bowl and led him to his own home, and invited him in. There he offered him food with his own hands and when the monk had finished eating Nāgasēna said, "Now that you have leisure will you teach me your philosophy?"

"If you so wish young man. However, I cannot teach it to you as you are now. If you will get permission from your parents,[21] come to us, and be ordained like us, then I can teach you," he replied.

Young Nāgasēna went to his parents and said, "O parents, this ascetic has told me he knows a profound philosophy. I asked to learn it but he has refused to teach me unless I, too, become a monk. If I don't become one, I will not get to learn about this Doctrine. I cannot forego this extraordinary knowledge because of so ordinary a matter as ordination. Permit me therefore to become a monk and learn about this Doctrine."

The parents thought, "This child has questioned the limits of our learning. There is nothing more that he can learn from us. Once he has mastered this other philosophy there is nothing to prevent him from abandoning the robes and returning to us." They therefore agreed and granted him permission to become a monk.

The monk Rohaṇa led Nāgasēna to the hermitage of Vattaniya and, having spent the night there, they then went on to the Red-Rock plateau in the Himalayas. There in the midst of a crore of *arahats,* he ordained the young man. Upon ordination the young man thought, "I became a monk because of my desire for knowledge. What is the use of delaying? I must learn it soon." So he said, "Now that I have taken on your garb, teach me your philosophy."

The Senior Monk Rohaṇa thought, "I cannot teach him the Rules of Discipline, the *Vinaya Piṭaka,* as he is still a novice. However, this young man has a keen mind. Just as a finely sharpened instrument is needed to cut something fine, so his sharp mind calls for a profoundly penetrating sermon. I will teach him the *Abhidhamma Piṭaka*[22] in its complexity."

So he said, "In the beginning, a monk studies the *Vinaya Piṭaka.* It is best suited for the cultivation of Discipline. Next he studies the *Sutta Piṭaka,* which is suited for the attaining of Trance States. The last is the *Abhidhamma Piṭaka,* which is best suited for the acquisition of Wisdom. Thus, in our philosophy there is a beginning, a middle, and an end. All three are good. If the wisdom you have acquired up to now is of this nature, then let it suffice. If not, take up the three that we have mentioned and study them. By following the Rules of the *Vinaya Piṭaka,* you keep the precepts and purify yourself like gold that is burnished. By learning the *Sutta* texts, you attain to Trance States. By studying the *Abhidamma Piṭaka,* you develop Insightful Concentration and obtain the Wisdom of the Path. Thus, by studying the Three Books of the *Tripiṭaka,* you will understand this Doctrine. By adhering to its rules, you will accomplish its practices. Then by attaining the Path and the Fruits you will achieve full Realization or Supreme Enlightenment. When you complete the practices of Discipline, you will realize the Discipline of Supreme Practices; by fulfilling the Trance States, you will realize the Discipline of the Supreme Mind, and by attaining the Path and the Fruits, you will realize the Discipline of Supreme Wisdom.

"You, however, are still a novice, so you have not reached the point when you can learn the *Vinaya Piṭaka*, the Rules for fully ordained monks. The *Sutta Piṭaka*, which contains the Stanzas of texts, has little in it to sharpen your intellect. I will therefore go beyond them and teach you the *Abhidhamma Piṭaka*, the philosophical texts."

Like a stream of water channeled into a viaduct, the novice Nāgasēna, whose mind was channeled toward learning, heard the Senior Monk preach the *Dhammasangani*,[23] which comprises groups in threes, such as the Threefold Wholesome Deeds; and the group of two such as the Twofold Causes; and the *Vibhaṅga*, comprising the eighteen divisions such as that of the Aggregates; the *Dhātukathā*, comprising the fourteen ways of analysis such as *Saṅgraha;* the *Pudgalaprajñapti*, comprising the Sixfold Nomenclatures, and the *Kathāvatthu*, comprising one thousand sermons — five hundred from one's own doctrine and five hundred from the doctrines of others; the *Yamakas*, comprising the ten expositions such as the *Yamaka* of Root and that of Aggregate; the *Paṭṭhāna*, which comprises twenty-four ways of exposition such as the basis of Cause, the basis of Support, the basis of Supremacy, the basis of Continuity, the basis of Immediate Presence, the basis of Latent Impression, the basis of Arising Before, the basis of Arising After, the basis of Association, the basis of Karma, the basis of Result, the basis of Attachment, the basis of Detachment, the basis of Being, the basis of Non-Being, the basis of Separation, the basis of Non-Separation."

All these categories of the *Abhidhamma Piṭaka* were taught to him and he learned them instantly. Just as a man with a mouth as big as the demon Rahu can swallow at a single mouthful a great many handfuls of rice, so he grasped it all without need to have it repeated even once. He then said, "Master I do not wish you to bother to repeat. I will now recite it all. He then went to the Red-Rock plateau where a hundred crores of *arahats* lived and said, "I have learned the entire *Abhidhamma Piṭaka* at one reading. As one packs a great deal into a single stanza, so I will recite it in its entirety, including the group of three such as the Threefold Wholesome Deeds."

The *arahats* said, "That is extraordinary. We would like to hear you. Please recite it."

Then the novice Nāgasēna recited the seven divisions of the *Abhidhamma* known as the *Prakaraṇas*. He did so in full detail and in the space of a seven month period. In other words, with the beak-tip of his intellect,[24] he wet the gullet of his mind and vomited out in seven months the waters of the *Abhidhamma Piṭaka*, which he had imbibed in a single mouthful, as if to show that it was not too much for him.

Since there was no one to applaud this great feat, the earth itself rumbled like a loud voiced man shouting his enthusiasm for the miraculous performance. That is, the earth goddess anticipated the applause of the other heavenly beings. She seemed to say, "Till now there has been no individual worthy to bear the weight of this teaching, therefore, hitherto I have not been overburdened. But now the weight is great," and the earth rumbled again to indicate this great weight. Thereafter, the gods of the Brahma, Naga, and Garuda worlds all shouted "Sadhu! Rejoice!"

Then the great Brahma applauded as if announcing to all around, "Let anyone come forth to debate with the monk Nāgasēna." Thereafter, one hundred crores of *arahats*, considering the benefits to the *sāsana* coming from this novice Nāgasēna, barely twenty years old, decided it was fitting he be granted the Higher Ordination[25] at the Red-Rock plateau and ordained him.

One day, after he had obtained his Higher Ordination, Nāgasēna went out begging with the Senior Monk Rohaṇa. He thought to himself, "Alas our preceptor does not seem to know too much. While there were the teachings of the *Sutta Piṭaka* still to learn he taught me the *Abhidhamma Piṭaka*. Why did he do that I wonder?"

The Senior Monk Rohaṇa perceived what was going on in Nāgasēna's mind and said, "Monk, you think wrong. Such thoughts are not worthy of one like you, just as female ornaments do not suit a man or male garments a woman."

At that the monk Nāgasēna thought, "Our preceptor is indeed very great. He knew what was going on in my mind as if clearly hearing words spoken at close range. I was like a thief caught red-handed with my loot. I was indeed wrong to think as I did about someone like him. I will beg his forgiveness. So he said, "Master, I will never even think such thoughts again. Forgive me for the wrong I did you."

The Senior Monk Rohaṇa said, "Listen, O monk. We do not forgive you by merely pronouncing the words, "We forgive You."[26] I do not forgive you for a very special reason. You did no wrong by speech or by bodily action but only in your thoughts, and though it was a serious wrong, you have now acknowledged it. Just as you have been concerned by what has happened, so there is a matter that touches us, too. It is this.

"There is a city in India called "Sāgala." A Yon King named Milin̆du rules there. Because he loves debate and controversy, he troubles the monks a great deal. You should go there, debate with him and split apart the great rock of his arguments with the sledgehammer of your counter arguments, and by doing so convert him to Buddhism. Just as a universal monarch (by his powers) attracts to one place, gems that lie scattered around, so by the power of your intellect gather together all the monks that are now dispersed in distant places. When you have done all this, then I will forgive you," he said.

Nāgasēna, as if to display his intellectual powers, said, "Your Reverence, it is nothing to confront the King Miliňdu. Were all the kings of India to come question me, I will not turn them away saying there are too many questions. I never complained before that the yard was too big to sweep, similarly, I will not complain about having too many questions. Like flower petals cut with a golden shears and scattered to the wind, so I will dispose of them. However, since my absolution is not tied up with that, please forgive me now."

Like a man who is not satisfied if he does not get exactly what he wants, irrespective of whatever else he may get, so the Senior Monk Rohaṇa said, "I cannot forgive you." Once he said that, it was not possible for Nāgasēna to remain any longer with him. However, as his five year period of apprenticeship in the monkhood was not yet complete, he could not live away from a preceptor. So he asked with humility and respect, "With whom then shall I spend the three months of the rainy season?"

The Senior Monk Rohaṇa replied, "Thus, it shall be. The Senior Monk Assagutta resides now in the hermitage at Vattaniya. Go to him and convey to him our greetings. Do not stop with that but pay him your respects, too. Tell him we inquired after his health. When he asks 'Why have you come?' say, 'I have been sent to spend the rainy season with you.' When he asks, 'Who is your preceptor?' reply, 'The Senior Monk Rohaṇa.' When he tests your training in discipline and your conduct towards your teachers by asking, 'Who am I then?' do not call him by his name while standing beside him. Say, 'Our preceptor knows your name.' " Thus, he advised him in the Rules of Conduct.[27]

Nāgasēna paid his respects to the Senior Monk Rohaṇa, bade him farewell, and heeding his advice, took up his robe and bowl and left for the Vattaniya hermitage. There he greeted the Senior Monk Assagutta and respectfully stood on a side. He informed the monk that he had been sent by his preceptor and conveyed his inquiries about the monk's health. Assagutta heard him and in turn asked after the Senior Monk Rohaṇa. He then asked, "Why has he sent you?"

"I was sent to spend the rainy season with you," replied Nāgasēna. The monk Assagutta did not say, "Good, do so." He asked instead, "Who are you?" He replied, "I am Nāgasēna." Since it was also necessary to know his preceptor's name he was asked, "Who then is your preceptor?"

"The Senior Monk Rohaṇa" Nāgasēna replied. Since that monk was not present, he could be referred to by name.

"Then who am I?" Assagutta asked again.

"It is impolite to refer to one's preceptor by name while in his presence, so how can I say yours? Our preceptor, however, knows your name."

"Good. You and your preceptor are no strangers to me. Take your bowl and robe and put them away in the appropriate place. There is no one else here to do it," he said.

Nāgasēna put his robes and bowl away, and slept the night there. Early the next day, he swept the inside and outside of the hermitage and brought clean water and tooth-cleaning twigs[28] for the older monk's morning toilet.

The Senior Monk Assagutta decided to test how disciplined Nāgasēna was. Therefore, though Nāgasēna was not inexpert at sweeping the yard—he had done so after all even in the time of the Buddha Kasub—yet the Senior Monk Assagutta took it upon himself to sweep the yard all over again, and instead of using the water and twigs brought for his toilet by Nāgasēna, he used fresh water and fresh twigs. Nāgasēna said nothing when the yard was reswept and the water he had brought remained unused, just as he, in turn, had seen a young monk remain silent when hit with a broom handle.

The Senior Monk tested him in this manner for almost a week to see how disciplined and controlled he was. Then knowing Nāgasēna to be obedient and willing to take advice, on the seventh day he questioned him again about Origins and Antecedents. As his Fervent Rebirth-Wish for intelligence had been granted, he could answer all the questions correctly. Then Assagutta said, "That is good. You can now spend the rainy season here," and gave him the formal permission.

About that time there was an old woman, a lay devotee, who for the past thirty years had looked after the Senior Monk Assagutta's needs. She attended on him for the three months of the rainy season, too. At the end of the period, she went to the Senior Monk Assagutta and said, "Reverend Sir, do you have other monks resident with you?"

"Yes, there is a guest, a monk named Nāgasēna" he replied.

"Will you both come to my home for the midday meal tomorrow?" she asked, inviting them. The Senior Monk accepted the invitation. The following day, together with Nāgasēna, he went to the house of the aged female devotee and sat down. The lay devotee herself served them. On the completion of the meal, the Senior Monk instructed Nāgasēna to preach the sermon for the devotee while he returned to the hermitage.

The devotee, inviting Nāgasēna to preach, said, "I am old. Simple little sermons are of not much use to me.[29] Preach to me a deep and profound one."

Nāgasēna then took what he considered a complex subject of deep meaning, the doctrine of "no-soul" from the *Abhidhamma Piṭaka*. The aged devotee heard the sermon and though she was old at the time, became a Stream-Enterer, a state in which one never grows old.

Like one who prepares a rice meal and while doing so thinks, "Why should one person have so much? I, too, will eat from it," and dips his hand into the pot, so Nāgasēna paid careful attention to what he was preaching, and he, too, developed Insight, attained to the state of a Stream-Enterer, and put down roots in the *sāsana*.

The Senior Monk Assagutta, who was in his temple, realized that both people had attained the state of the Stream-Enterer, and three times he praised them and rejoiced, repeating thrice the phrase, "Sadhu!"

"Just as Bandula, the soldier who shot down five hundred Liccavi kings with a single arrow, so with this single sermon many Defilements that lead to hell were vanquished for both of them simultaneously," So said the Senior Monk Assagutta, praising the monk Nāgasēna. Many gods, too, acclaimed him.

The monk Nāgasēna returned to the hermitage, greeted the Senior Monk, and stood respectfully on a side. The Senior Monk Assagutta addressed him thus.

"Monk, in the city of Pälalup at the monastery of Aśokārāmaya, there is a Senior Monk named "Dharmarakśita" (whose name means one who guards and preserves the Doctrine). An understanding of the Doctrine is the foundation for its Practice. Without understanding[30] there can be no Practice. Without Practice there can be no Realization. Without Realization there will be no one with lofty ideas, who attains the heights of Insight. If this happens the *sāsana* will be lost. If men of intellect such as you do not cultivate such understanding[31] of the Doctrine who will keep it alive for the future? Therefore go to him and study the word of the Buddha."

"How far is it from here?" Nāgasēna asked.

"Three hundred if measured in *yodun* and one thousand two hundred if measured in *gav*," he replied.

"Sir, that is very far. I am not familiar with the area and I will not be able to beg along the way as I travel. How will I survive the journey?" he asked.

"Do not worry about that. Along the way you will receive meals cooked from a very special rice. However, it is not just a single day's journey. You will have to take it slowly, resting along the way so that it will not be too tiring."

The monk Nāgasēna then respectfully took his leave of the Senior Monk Assagutta, took up his robe and bowl, and set off for the city of Pälalup.

About the same time, an important nobleman of Pälalup, having sold five hundred wagon loads of merchandise, happened to be returning home along the same road. When he saw the monk Nāgasēna, he stopped his wagon train, went up to him, and asked after his welfare.

"Where are you headed?" he inquired.

"I am going to the city of Pälalup," Nāgasēna replied. At the sight of Nāgasēna, affection as for a son sprang up in the nobleman, so he said, "It is good, my son. I, too, am going there. Accompany me and travel in comfort." Thereafter he himself prepared the meals and offered them. When the monk had eaten, he stood respectfully on a side and inquired, "What is your name?"

The monk answered, "I am Nāgasēna."

"Did you become a monk[32] only because of the exigencies of time and place or do you happen to know any sermons?" he inquired.

"Listen, O Nobleman, since I have not been able to study under a preceptor I do not know the *Sutta Piṭaka* or the *Vinaya Piṭaka*. However, I do know the *Abhidhamma Piṭaka*, since I heard it and studied it as a novice," replied Nāgasēna.

"That is indeed excellent because I, too, know the *Abhidhamma Piṭaka*," the nobleman replied.[33]

Just as one who speaks Tamil,[34] when addressed in Tamil, is excited at the chance to speak his language, so the nobleman said, "It is fortunate that we met. We may not be equal in learning, but it is always possible to learn from the one who knows more, so please preach to me from the *Abhidhamma*." Since the nobleman had said he knew the *Abhidhamma*, the monk wished to disclose his powers to the full, so like teaching an artisan who knows his craft, he preached from the *Abhidhamma*, keeping back nothing of the complexities of meaning. The nobleman heard the sermon and, in addition to his worldly wealth, he now also gained other-worldly wealth of Spiritual Attainments and became a Stream-Enterer.

When they had come almost to the city of Pälalup, at a point where two roads met, the nobleman sent the wagon loads of merchandise ahead, came up to the monk Nāgasēna and said, "This is the road to the Aśokārāma hermitage. It is the one you should take. You gave me the gift of Spiritual Attainments even though we had no prior acquaintance and you did not know me. I cannot adequately reciprocate such a gift. I have however a very valuable shawl. It is sixteen cubits long and eight cubits[35] wide. Dear son, accept it." He made the offering, paid his respects by circumambulating him[36] and left for the city of Pälalup.

The monk Nāgasēna went to the Aśokārāma hermitage, greeted the Senior Monk Dharmarakśita and told him that he came with the intention of studying the Doctrine. He then lived with him and in about three months mastered the Doctrinal texts by merely reading them once through, never having to go over them twice. In the next three months, he studied the deeper meanings of the texts he had learned. When he had heard and studied the words of the Buddha in this manner, he mastered the Scriptural texts that draw a man away from the worldly life.

At this point, lest Nāgasēna consider the texts of the Teachings as something quite separate from the Practice and the Realization of the religion, the Senior Monk Dharmarakśita advised him thus; "Listen, O monk. A cattle herder may look after herds of cattle but the benefit of the produce, the curd, goes entirely to someone else, the owner. Likewise, a golden dish may serve merely as a container for lion-oil. You, too, will have no claim on this religion if you merely guard your learning like the cattle herder guards his herd. Others will possess and enjoy its benefits."

Nāgasēna understood the implications of what was said, and thought, "That is sufficient for me. You do not need to say more." Just as a man who is expert at sweeping, sweeps the entire yard and street while others are still getting ready to start, so in a single day, using the ekel-broom[37] of Insight, he swept away the dirt of his Defilements, cleaned up all the paths and walks of the garden of his mind and attained full Enlightenment.

As he became an *arahat,* the gods applauded both his victory over his enemies, the Defilements, and the manner in which he conquered the entire city of *nirvāṇa* leaving nothing out. The earth rumbled as if blowing a conch shell announcing the victory. As soldiers going to serve a victorious king drop their shields at their sides, so Great Brahma applauded, too. As if to shower gifts on his victory, a soft rain fell.

At that time, the hundred crores of *arahats* living in the Himalayas at the Red-Rock plateau sent a message to Nāgasēna saying, "We would like to see you. Please come." The monk Nāgasēna then disappeared from the hermitage[38] and appeared amidst the hundred crores of *arahats* on the Red-Rock plateau. The *arahats* addressed Nāgasēna thus.

"Listen, O brother, King Miliňdu debates with monks and disturbs them greatly. Once when the snake-eating bird, the Garuda, was about to attack the snake, which was attending on the thirty thousand *arahats,* at that very instant, one of the *arahats* created a huge rock and led the snake youth to safety behind it. Thus, though they all have similar qualities, *arahats* may have different kinds of powers, just as water that is the same can taste different. Therefore, from among us all, you have the power to debate with him, demolish his arguments, and humble his pride."

The monk Nāgasēna responded, "Let all the kings of India, not just this one King Miliṅdu, come question me, I will answer them undauntedly. That shall be my task. The rest of you, do not worry about whether you can or cannot debate with him but accompany me to the city of Sāgala."

About the time that the monk Ayupāla lived in the monastery at Sankeya, King Miliṅdu called his ministers and said, "This night is most beautiful, free of the stain of darkness. On a night like this whom shall I engage in a debate? Who is there capable of discoursing with me?"

The Yon ministers answered, "There is an *arahat* named Ayupāla, who lives in the Sankeya monastery. He is learned in the *Tripiṭaka* and is wise. Please go and talk to him."

On the suggestion of his ministers, the King sent word, saying that he would like to meet the monk. The *arahat* Ayupāla, in turn, invited the king to visit him.[39] The King climbed into his chariot and escorted by his ministers went to the Sankeya monastery, exchanged greetings, and stood respectfully on a side.

"Reverend Sir, why did you become a monk?" asked the King. "What benefit do you get from it?"

"Great King, I became a monk so I could live according to the Doctrine."

"Reverend Sir, are there not laymen who also live according to the Doctrine?"

"Yes, O King. There are those who do. When the Buddha preached the *Damsak Pävatumsuta* sermon at Baranäs, sixteen crores of Brahmins attained the Path and the Fruits. There was among them only one monk, the Senior Monk Kondañña. Besides O King, when he preached the *Mahā Samaya* sermon from the *Dīgha Nikāya* text, and the *Mahāmaṅgala* sermon from the *Khuddaka Nikāya* text, and the *Samacittapariyāya* sermon from the *Majjhima Nikāya* text, and the *Rahulōvāda* sermon from the *Majjhima Nikāya* text, and the *Parābhava* sermon from the *Khuddaka Nikāya* text, an incalculable of people attained *nirvāṇa* on each occasion. All of these were laymen.

The King responded, "Reverend Sir, what then is the point of becoming a monk? If a sickness can be cured without medicine, why suffer taking unpleasant medicine? If one can reach a certain place without a ladder, why trouble to fix a ladder and then have to pay for it? If *nirvāṇa* can be obtained without becoming a monk, then becoming one and suffering hardships must be due to some past bad *karma*. Therefore, nothing is really gained by performing ascetic practices.

"A person who performs the penance of taking only a single meal, must be someone who, in a past life, stole what others ate and drank.

Therefore now, even though he wants to eat and drink he cannot get two meals.[40] One who practices penances must surely be paying for past bad *karma*, not for past good *karma*.

"If a person performs the penance of living under the open sky it must be because, in a past life, he robbed others of their homes. Thus, for forcing others out of their homes in the past, and causing them to sit under trees, now they sit under trees as penance. Those who perform the austerities of not sleeping are those who in the past plundered others. They must have tied up wayfarers, robbed them of their belongings so now they are robbed of sleep. Even if they have beds, they can only sit on them and stay awake till dawn. There is no point performing penances to achieve *nirvāṇa*, since *nirvāṇa* can be achieved even by lay people who perform no austerities. Performing austerities is therefore a totally useless activity."

Thus he argued, this man, who, in a past life, threw out the sweepings without bothering about its karmic consequences. He had no acquaintance with the Buddha's Teachings and so debated and argued as if attacking the *sāsana*.

The Senior Monk Ayupāla was unable to counter him with the reply that austerities were performed in order to discipline and control one's Defilements, so he remained silent. The ministers however realized, that just because he gave no response it did not mean that the *sāsana* was powerless. So they said, "O King, this monk is wise. He knows the answer but he has not the ability to state it in words. As a dumb mute who dreams but finds that he cannot relate his dream to others, so, though he has the knowledge, he does not have the power of words. He knows the answer but he cannot state it."

King Milin̆du replied, "You may say that but is it right that he should not utter a single word in reply? Alas, this land of Dam̆badiva is like a river run dry, or a kingdom without a ruler. It is emptied of wise men." Thus, the king spoke but the ministers sat looking on without accepting what he said. The king then looked at their faces and thought, "Perhaps they sit silent like this because there is yet another wise man around, just as in combat the strongest person is often kept behind to fight at the end." So he asked them, "Does your silence mean there is another, worthier one, to engage me in debate?"

At the time the monk Nāgasēna, a man of dazzling intellect and sparkling rhetoric, had gathered together forty thousand senior monks and forty thousand younger monks. As one cannot churn the ocean with a butter churning stick, so the sea of his intellect could not be disturbed by the churning stick of debate. As the mountain Mahāmēru cannot be shaken by a breeze, so he had a mind that could not be disturbed by the winds of contrary views. As the universe, Sakvaḷa, is filled with gems, so his mind was filled with the gems of virtue and knowledge. He had reached great heights of fame and gain, blockaded the path to hell and had shown many the road to heaven and *nirvāṇa.* Into the dark house of Delusion, he had brought the lamp of the Teachings. Since he had conquered the enemies of Defilements, he unfurled the flag of the Doctrine and blew the conch of the Law to call forth the Fourfold Retinue of monks, nuns, lay devotees both male and female. He beat the drum of the Buddha's Doctrine to alert them to the discipline of the Path. With the resonant voice of thunder and a sharp, lightning-like intellect that was suffused with the waters of Compassion, he poured forth Doctrinal rain. Thus, he wandered across towns and villages and came finally to the city of Sāgala and took up residence in the Sankeya monastery.

The Minister named Devamantiya, who had heard he was resident there said, "O King, be a little patient. Like an elephant in rut seeks another like himself, so this great monk Nāgasēna has come to pierce the tusk of controversy with the counter tusk of argument. He is a man whose intellect is as vast as the great earth, and attended by his train of monks, he has now arrived in this city. Please go to him and debate with him."

King Miliňdu when he heard the very name Nāgasēna was suddenly overcome with a great fear. However, summoning up all his kingly courage he hid his fears and questioned his minister again.

"Is his Reverence capable of debating with me? If so bring him to me."

Devamantiya replied, "He can debate not just with you, O King, but with any person of any stature whatsoever, be he a Brahma, a Sakra, or Mahiśvara himself. Were they to come, he would debate with them. Just as the sun when it rises melts the dew, so he has the power to defeat them in debate. Can a diamond that cuts through glass be stopped by a heap of chaff? Can a wind that shakes the mountain Mahāmēra be stopped by a fluff from the red-cotton tree? He may be young in reputation, but his powers of intellect are greater than the Mahāmēra mountain. Why then can he not debate with one like you?"

The king was very frightened, but to step back was not in keeping with the arrogance he had hitherto shown, so he said, "If that be so, send him word that I would like to see him."

The minister Devamantiya, who received the royal command, conveyed the message.

"Good, let him come" said Nāgasēna.

Then King Miliňdu, accompanied by about five hundred Yon ministers, climbed into a gorgeous chariot and went to the Sankeya hermitage to see the monk Nāgasēna.

The monk Nāgasēna, accompanied by eighty thousand monks, was seated in the outer courtyard of the hermitage. King Miliňdu saw the seated monks and asked, "Devamantiya, whose monks are those?"

"They are the monk Nāgasēna's retinue," he answered. More afraid than when he was hit with the broomstick, the king was terrified, like an elephant who comes upon a lion, or a snake a Garuda, or a fox a python, or a frog a snake, or a deer a leopard, or a rat a cat, or an evil spirit an exorcist, or the moon in the jaws of an eclipse, or a fish in a net, or a god at the point of death.[41]

However, the King hid his fear and said, "None of you need point out the Senior Monk Nāgasēna to me. I will find him myself from among those eighty thousand monks. He recognized the Senior Monk who was seated with forty thousand monks in front of him and forty thousand monks behind him. Just as he had known him then, when he had been struck with the broomstick, so he recognized him now and said, "Devamantiya, that must be Nāgasēna who sits there with forty thousand monks in front of him and forty thousand behind him."

Devamantiya replied, "You are right. It is he." The King, too, was glad he had recognized him without having to be told by another. As darkness disappears when a lamp is lit, so his fears disappeared. He mustered up his courage and said, "From the moment I started to debate, till now, I have met many great debaters, but I have never been as afraid as now, when I see before me the Reverend monk and his retinue of followers. Fear that should arise only after defeat, has come upon me already. Therefore I am already defeated. When at war, if one's forces break apart and flee at the mere sound of war drums, even before the enemy forces are sighted, then that indeed is defeat. The victory goes to the Reverend monk, just as the gem that was thrown at Kēvaṭṭa[42] ended up inevitably with the sage Mahauśadha. The monk Nāgasēna is indeed the winner." Thus spoke the king, conceding the victory to Nāgasēna even before the debate began.

One should therefore learn from this story, that King Miliňdu acquired fame and power by the mere act of collecting and throwing away the sweepings of others, and that done unwillingly and under compulsion. One should also realize that the Senior Monk Nāgasēna acquired great intellectual powers because of the simple meritorious act of sweeping the yard. Therefore, from these examples one should learn that the good consequences even of an insignificant act, can be very great.[43] Thus, avoid sinful acts by doing good and purify one's mind.

Endnotes

THE SENIOR MONK, NĀGASĒNA

This entire story does not exist in the DA. It is an interpolation by Dharmasēna. While the author of the SR introduces several passages of interpolations and additions into his translations of the DA stories, yet this is one place where he introduces a wholly new story into the text. As a result, it does not illustrate a specific stanza or stanzas from the *Dhammapada* as the other stories do, but is a further illustration of the far-reaching consequences of simple acts of Merit.

1. . . . but while his teachings still prevailed, . . .

It is believed that on the death of a Buddha his Doctrine and dispensation will continue for a specified period after him. Then, that Doctrine, too, will be lost and the religion will die out, until a new Buddha rediscovers those Truths eons later. The dispensation of the Buddha Gōtama is to last five thousand years.

2. . . . he decided to make a Fervent Rebirth-Wish.

Buddhism has no provision or place for prayer as the Buddha is not an all-powerful god. The nearest thing to a prayer is what is known as a *prārthanā* or Fervent Wish. The wish is usually made after the performance of a meritorious act and very often is a wish related to a future life. I have, therefore, translated it as a Fervent Rebirth-Wish or sometimes just as Rebirth-Wish.

3. The Senior Monk, Nāgasēna.

At this point, the text lists the six books of the *Abhidhamma Piṭaka*. (See the glossary.)

4. . . . or as women lacking in virtue, . . .

The text is ambiguous as to whether it is women who lack virtue who are therefore unable to achieve full Enlightenment, or that all women lack virtue and therefore can only be born in Brahma worlds. If it is the latter, then it is contrary to the Doctrinal position, for there are many accounts of women who achieve the Spiritual Attainments of the Path and the Fruits. (e.g. Samandēvi p. 223) The ambiguous and negative comments on women that surface in this text from time to time, seem rather to represent the views of the monk Dharmasēna and also perhaps of the Buddhist clergy of his time.

5. . . . so the novice was born as the Yon King, Miliňdu.

The term Yon is the Sinhala form of the word Yāvana. It is supposed to be derived from the word "Ionian" or Greek, and to refer to the Greco-Muslim communities that remained in India after Alexander the Great's expedition.

6. . . . , who all walk around in the garb in which they were born.

Those named here belonged to a sect of naked ascetics.

7. *Ummaga Jātaka* story,

This Jātaka is mainly about the feats performed by the Bōdhisatva born as the sage Mahauśadha, advisor to King Vēdeha. His opponent and rival is Kēvaṭṭa the advisor to King Cūlani Brahmadatta. The two advisors meet for a Battle of the Law. Kēvaṭṭa believes that, since he is senior to Mahauśadha, the latter will have to bow to him when they meet, acknowledging his superiority. However, Mahauśadha brings a priceless gem and offers it as a gift to Kēvaṭṭa. In giving it, he places it on the other's fingertips and, being too heavy to hold, it drops to the ground and rolls to the feet of the Bōdhisatva Mahauśadha. Kēvaṭṭa in his greed stoops to pick it up. At which point Mahauśadha exclaims, "Rise teacher, rise. I am young enough to be your grandson. Do no obeisance to me." The crowd hear him and shout, "Brahmin Kēvaṭṭa did obeisance to the Sage's feet." Kēvaṭṭa's supporters, seeing him bow to the sage Mahauśadha, take it as a sign of defeat and disperse.

There are innumerable branch stories within the main story. The tale of Diktalaya and Dikpitiya is yet another such story.

8. . . . , when asked about a mango talks about a *Del* fruit, . . .

The *del* fruit is as different in flavor from a mango as a potato from a peach. The *del* is a starchy, bland fruit that can only be eaten cooked. It is often used like a potato as a carbohydrate substitute. The mango by contrast is greatly valued for its sweetness and rich flavor. Hence the point of the contrast.

9. Enlightened Ones had the power to see into the minds of men and hear their thoughts. This was referred to metaphorically as "possessing a Divine Eye and Ear."

10. . . . when only five hundred years have passed out of the five thousand, . . .

A reference to the prediction made in the time of the Buddha that his Teachings (*sāsana*) would last five thousand years.

11. Note the ironic aside about the luxurious life of indulgence of the gods as contrasted with the ascetic life of the monks.

12. The monks, who had participated in the second Council, . . .

This detailed account of a similar situation in the past, when dangers beset the *sāsana* and a Council had to be held, emphasizes the inevitable process of deterioration, the schisms, and conflicts that take place even in the religious institutions and the constant need for revival and reaffirmation of the Teachings.

13. . . . , be born on earth and put an end to King Milin̆du's harassment of monks. . . .

Here the god Mahāsēna is specifically requested to do more than just attain his own personal salvation. He is asked in fact, to delay his personal quest for Enlightenment in order to help perpetuate the Doctrine, in the interests of the larger good of humankind. The point is made again and again throughout this story. For example the Monk Rohaṇa is "punished" for not coming out of his Trance State and thereby displaying indifference to the concerns of the *sāsana* (p. 62). This is in contrast to the doctrinal position (also accepted) that a Buddhist's first obligation is to seek his salvation and attain *nirvāṇa*. There seems to be an implicit debate here on this question and Dharmasēna supports the former position.

14. The first rice to be harvested from a field is considered special and set aside for rituals and offerings.

15. . . . as if paying for the food he ate . . .

Monks are expected to preach a sermon to the lay devotees who provide them with offerings. It is a gesture of thanks and reciprocity. This is specially so when a monk is invited into a lay household for a meal. The practice continues even today and there is always a sermon preached at the end of a *sāṅghīka dāna* or the ceremonial feeding of monks.

16. Nāgasēna . . . , learned the four *Vēdas* including the *Atharvavēda*, . . .

Dharmasēna appears to be familiar with the requirements of brahmanic scholarship. Since the study of Sanskrit and Pāli was very much part of a monk's scholarly education, such familiarity with Sanskrit texts was not unusual. His thorough and detailed knowledge of the complex categories, divisions, and nomenclatures of Buddhist texts is also displayed here.

17. "We are members of a certain order of ascetic monks," he replied.

The plural form is used by the monk both to indicate his identity as part of the Order, and as a mark of his status. It is much like the usage of royalty.

18. Most wandering ascetics and Brahmin mendicants at that time grew their hair long.

19. The monk Rohaṇa's detailed account of hair care gives us a glimpse of the sophistication of thirteenth century Sinhala fashions in hair care. Hair was washed, combed, oiled, shaped, perfumed, untangled, deloused, dyed, and so forth. This explanation could almost be an account of procedures in a modern beauty parlor!

20. Buddhist monks dye their robes a dull yellow or ochre, the color of dying leaves.

21. ". . . If you will get permission from your parents, . . .

No monk was permitted to join the Order without the permission of his parents or nearest kin. It is an important proviso. See note #8 in the Cakkhupāla story.

22. I will teach him the *Abhidhamma Piṭaka* . . .

The section that follows is a summarized account of some of the complex categorized formulations of Buddhist philosophy. The philosophical terms are used here without any explanations or simplification, as is usually the pattern. In presenting the content of this most complex and abstract text, the author Dharmasēna seems to be making a conscious display of his erudition for the benefit of his fellow monks and scholars. The passage would be incomprehensible to laymen, then, as now.

23. The texts listed in this paragraph are the seven texts of the *Abhidhamma Piṭaka*.

24. In other words, with the beak-tip of his intellect, . . .

The image provides a striking insight into the method of education so important for the perpetuation of texts in an oral tradition of scholarship. The texts were committed to memory and regularly "regurgitated."

25. . . . decided it was fitting he be granted the Higher Ordination . . .

The granting of Higher Ordination by which a novice or *sāmanēra* becomes a full fledged monk is an elaborate rite of passage undertaken after a period of rigorous training.

26. "We forgive you . . . "

A monk has the power to absolve a wrong done by a fellow monk with the phrase, "We forgive you." Here, however, the monk Rohaṇa decides not to do so for a specific purpose. See the story of the Monks of Kosaṁbä for another illustration of this practice.

27. Thus, he advised him in the Rules of Conduct.

Here the monk Rohaṇa gives his pupil a quick course in the Rules of Conduct for a monk. Since Nāgasēna had not yet studied the Book of the *Vinaya Piṭaka*, he was unfamiliar with those rules, which would otherwise have been a part of his initial study. Note that to address one's teacher (or an elder) by his name, in his presence, was considered disrespectful in the culture. It is still so, today, where kinship terms are often substituted.

28. . . . tooth-cleaning twigs . . .

Twigs of a certain plant, the ends of which when chewed form a kind of brush, were traditionally used in Sri Lanka as toothbrushes. They are sometimes still used by older monks and peasants in Sri Lankan villages.

29. Simple little sermons are of not much use to me.

A comment that provides insight into the place of women in the *sāsana*. Here the old woman asks to hear the complex Doctrines and Nāgasēna unpatronizingly preaches from the most complex and profound of the Abhidhamma texts. Note also that both Nāgasēna and the old woman hear the same text and simultaneously achieve the Spiritual Attainments of a Stream Enterer or Sōvān. Knowledge of the Doctrine and the achievements of Enlightenment were thus not confined to monks or males.

30. Without a study of the Theory . . .

There are three stages in the progress of a disciple. *Pariyatti* or the study of the Doctrinal texts to understand the Theory of the religion; *Paṭipatti* or the Practice; and *Paṭivedha* or the Realization of the goal.

31. If men of intellect such as you do not perpetuate the Scriptural texts . . .

This passage indicates the importance of study and scholarship in the Buddhist tradition, and describes how it was fostered and encouraged among men of ability and intellect. Nāgasēna had, up to that point, only studied the *Abhidhamma Piṭaka*. He is, therefore, sent to study the Doctrinal texts in their entirety and thereby to acquire the kind of scholarship considered essential for the preservation of the Teachings and the continuity of the tradition.

32. "Did you become a monk . . .

The implication is that people join the Order for a variety of reasons, as was seen in the case of the younger Pālita, who took on robes in order to make a safe journey through dangerous territory. See also the note on p. 34 (Cakkhupāla story).

33. " . . . I, too, know the *Abhidhamma Piṭaka*," the Nobleman replied.

Another illustration that the knowledge of abstract and complex philosophical texts was not confined to monks. Here a merchant, as earlier, an old woman, show familiarity with the complex *Abhidhamma* texts.

34. Just as one who speaks Tamil, . . .

The reference to the Tamil language in the metaphor suggests that it was not a language familiar to Sinhala speakers in thirteenth century Sri Lanka. However, it must have been sufficiently known and used in special contexts to make the image meaningful.

35. A cubit is an ancient unit of measure usually eighteen inches but sometimes twenty-one inches in length.

36. . . . , paid his respects by circumambulating him . . .

Circumambulation of *stupas*, shrines, and places of worship is a common Buddhist practice to indicate respect. Here it is done as a mark of respect to the greatness of the man.

37. A short broom made of the spines or *ekels* of the coconut leaf. It is used in every household even today.

38. The monk Nāgasēna then disappeared from the hermitage . . .

Arahats were believed to have supernormal powers such as the ability to fly through the air or appear instantly at whatever place they wished to be. The monk Nāgasēna, now an *arahat* can exercise such powers.

39. "Good let him come."

Note that in every case the king goes to the monk, never the other way around. Kingly power was subordinate to the *Saṅgha* or Buddhist monastic Order.

40. Buddhist monks eat only one meal a day.

41. For Buddhists, gods are not immortal. They may live in heavens for long years but they too are subject to the law of Karma and so must die. Death is thus feared by gods as by men.

42. . . . , just as the gem that was thrown at Kēvaṭṭa . . .

Refers to an incident from the *Ummaga Jātaka*. (See earlier note 7.)

43. . . . the good consequences even of an insignificant act, can be very great.

The better known Buddhist texts that deal with the story of Nāgasēna and King Miliňdu focus on the debate between the two (e.g. the *Miliňda Panna*). This story, however, seems much more a folk version, focusing on the life of Nāgasēna through several existences. King Miliňdu's fondness for debates and his encounters with other ascetics are briefly touched on, but the central debate with the monk Nāgasēna does not even take place. The king concedes defeat without asking a single question. Thus, the author seems to be concerned not with complex philosophical issues and debates on Buddhist doctrine, but rather with simple morality and the importance of meritorious actions in everyday life.

The Monk Tissa, the Fat

We have seen from King Miliṅdu's defeat,[1] the negative effects of disobedience. In a past life, he committed a disobedient act by refusing to throw out the sweepings when he was asked to do so. Though he finally did, it was only after he had been struck with a broom handle and made to do it. Because of that disobedient act he was rendered completely powerless—like a snake faced with a Garuda[2]—in the presence of the monk Nāgasēna. To illustrate this same fault even further, we shall tell the story of the monk Tissa the Fat.

How does it go?

The monk Tissa the Fat was King Suddhodhana's sister's son. Like a neglected rice field that is sown too late, he remained a layman all through his youth when he should have been practicing the austerities of a monk. Late in life, he joined the Order. But even then he avoided the harsher ascetic practices and happily partook of the tasty food offerings prepared for the Buddha. Though he was spare in his religious practices, he was generous in size and, because his head and belly were both enormous, he was known as "Tissa the Fat." His robes were always well-smoothed and of the finest cloth. To indicate his opulence, he often sat in a high place in the center of the temple where many gathered. Monks passing through (to the inner chamber) to pay their respects to the Buddha, when they saw this older monk, thought, "This must be one of the Senior monks." Unaware that he had taken ordination only late in life, they went to him and asked what they should do to pay him due respect and render service. When thus addressed he remained silent, for he knew that were he to speak his junior position in the order would be revealed.

One young monk, suspicious of his behavior, questioned him as to how many Rainy Seasons he had spent as a monk.

"I don't have too many to speak of. I took to the robes late in life," he replied.

"Why then, you undisciplined old man, aren't you aware that though old in years you are young in the monkhood? One should stand in the presence of one's seniors even if one happens to be seated on the ground. Instead of standing up like a firmly planted post to stop the flow of *saṃsāra,* you remain seated. Have you a right to remain silent when questioned, especially when you belong to an Order such as ours? Don't you see before your very eyes how the other monks behave? You are big in size and shape, but how is it that you are so small in your actions?" The young monk said many such things, and with good reason.

If the monk Tissa the Fat had had any real virtue, he would have been humbled. But puffed up with pride because of his royal lineage he replied, "Whom have you all come to see?"

"The Buddha," they replied.

"If so, how is it that you don't know who I am? I am a close kinsman of your Buddha. Can any of you claim such ties? Your Buddha's father and my mother were brother and sister. You will see if my relationship to the Buddha is not a fact when I tell him how all of you berated me with such scant respect for my standing."

Unaware of what the Buddha was going to say, he stormed up to him and lamented loudly like a sky thundering during a drought. The other monk, too, thought, "This man might go ahead and cause trouble." So the young monk accompanied him to the Buddha, saluted him, and stood by.

Now the senior monks, Nanda, Anuruddha, and Rahula, who were also close kinsmen of the Buddha, had achieved the heights of Spiritual Attainments such as the Path and the Fruits and had received recognition accordingly. If the monk Tissa was upset because he had not achieved that kind of recognition, it would be understandable. But it was not so. If he were a private individual, such an outburst might have been excused, but it was certainly not worthy of a respectable monk.

The Buddha knew well the reason for his outburst but asked, "Why, Tissa, what are you complaining about?"[3]

The monk Tissa answered the Buddha, "Master, without due respect for my connection to you, these people have scolded me. Whatever they may think of me, they should at least show some respect for your honor."

"Why, where were you seated when they scolded you?"

"I was seated in the room where many monks gather."

"Did you see these monks come there?"

"Yes, I did see them," he replied.

"When you saw them did you stand up and escort them in? Did you offer to relieve them of their bowls and robes? Did you arrange seating for them and wash their feet? Did you inquire if they needed anything to drink? Did you fan them and oil their feet?"

When he replied, "no" to all these questions, the Buddha continued, "Listen, Tissa. There is no place for birth, lineage,[4] age, or social standing, in my monastic order. Those were all duties you should have performed. It was wrong not to have done them. If you do not fulfill your duties, how can you practice Moral Conduct? If you do not practice Moral Conduct, how will you ever achieve *nirvāṇa?* Beg forgiveness from all these monks for the wrong you have done. Cultivate feelings of affection and respect towards these, your fellow monks, and perform your own duties and observances without any further delay."

"Master, they have scolded me enough and I have borne their abuse. Must I now beg their forgiveness, too?" Tissa asked, defying the Buddha himself.

The monks looked at each other and said, "How will this man obey us when he is disobedient even to the Buddha? Alas, this man's obstinacy is as great and weighty as his own fat self."

The Buddha heard them and said, "Listen, O Monks. It is not just today that this monk has been obstinate. In the past, too, he has been so."

At this the gathered monks said, "Master, even without your saying so we have just seen his obstinacy displayed before us. But it would be of benefit to us to hear[5] you tell the story of his disobedient actions in the past." Then the Buddha related a story of the past.

"Long ago, when King Bambadat was ruling in the city of Baranäs, there lived an ascetic named Devaḷa. He would spend the eight months of summer and winter in the Himalayas and in the Rainy Season would come down to live in the city of Baranäs in order to eat foods containing salt and lime.[6] When Devaḷa arrived at the city gate, he asked some small boys where he could find a place to sleep. They told him, 'The potter's shed is a convenient place.' He went there and asked permission from the potter. Since the potter's work was generally finished by night, and the shed was large enough, he replied, 'You are welcome to sleep in here.'

"While Devaḷa was inside, another ascetic named Nārada also came down from the Himalayas and asked permission to sleep in the shed. The potter, not knowing whether the two ascetics would agree to stay together, and in order to avoid being blamed for any later conflicts that might arise, said, 'Another ascetic came earlier and is already in the shed. On my part there is no objection, if you two agree, for I will acquire all the more merit.'

"The second ascetic Nārada said to the ascetic Devaḷa who was inside, 'If you have no objection, may I, too, sleep in here?'

'The potter's shed is not small. Sleep in one corner of it,' said the ascetic Devaḷa.

"The ascetic Nārada then sat down at a distance and engaged in pleasant conversation. When it was time, Devaḷa retired to sleep. Nārada was disciplined and restrained, so he first observed carefully where the ascetic Devaḷa was making his bed, as well as the location of the door. Nārada slept where he would not be stepped on, in case the other woke up at night and wanted to go out. The first ascetic, Devaḷa, though he had adopted the ascetic life, was quite unschooled in discipline and restraint. He rolled around [in his sleep], got up from where he had first rested, and stretched himself out across the entrance way.

"When the second ascetic Nārada got up in the night to go outside to relieve himself, he stepped on the ascetic Devaḷa's head, since he was lying in front of the doorway.

'Who stepped on my head?' Devaḷa asked.

'Teacher, it was I,' the other replied. He had been unaware that Devaḷa was lying across the doorway like a log placed to prevent it opening.

"Devaḷa, who was as unrestrained in his speech as he was in his actions, replied, 'You rogue with matted locks. Did you come from the forest to trample on my head?'

'Teacher, it is not something I did knowingly. Forgive me,' replied Nārada. While Devaḷa continued to scold, Nārada went outside.

"Devaḷa thought, 'It is bad enough he stepped on me when he was going out. It will be worse if he also steps on me when he returns.' So he put his feet where he had originally placed his head and slept with his head in the opposite position.

"Nārada returned and was about to step inside when he thought, 'The last time I came out on this side and stepped on his head. This time I will walk by his feet. Then even if I were to step on him it will be his feet I touch and feet can be massaged by touching. If I were to tread on his head again, he would be so angry that he would never forgive me. Let me pass by his feet.' Though he had intended to do everything right, the other's action defeated his purpose. This time he stepped on the throat of the ascetic, who was sleeping in the reverse position, as if he meant to silence him once and for all. When Devaḷa asked, 'Who is it?' Nārada answered, 'Teacher, it is I.'

'Why you rascal with matted locks! When you first went out, you trod on my head and now on your return, as if to put an end to me, you step on my throat. What wrong have I done you other than giving you permission to sleep here? I will curse you for your wicked act.'

"The ascetic Nārada replied, 'Teacher, it was not my fault. I did not know you had changed position. I was trying to pass by your feet. Forgive me, please. As ascetics we should forgive.'

'You kick me in the head and ask me to pardon you? I will not forgive you. I will curse you.'

'It is not something I did intentionally. Do not curse me,' Nārada pleaded.

"But Devaḷa was obstinate and did not know the extent of the other's spiritual power. Hence, in spite of the explanation that it was an accident, Devaḷa cursed him saying,

Sahassaraṃ sī satatejo suriyo tamavinodano
Pātodayante sūriye muddhā te phalatu sattadhā*

*The sun with its thousand rays and hundred majesties, dispels the darkness,
When that sun rises at dawn, may your head split in seven pieces.

That is to say, 'For twice treading on my head, may your head split into seven parts at sunrise tomorrow.'

"The ascetic Nārada replied, 'I have done nothing wrong. I explained but you refused to listen and now you have cursed me. If a wrong has been done by either one of us, just as calves run straight to their mothers, so may your curse fall on the guilty party.' Thus he, too, made his appeal.

"Since Nārada possessed the Fivefold Supernatural Powers, he was able to call to mind eighty eons of time, forty eons into the past, and forty eons into the future. Thus, he used his Divine Eye to see on whom his curse would fall. He saw that it would come back on the teacher like dirt flung against a headwind that blows back in one's face.

"Now the ascetic Nārada was a budding Bōdhisatva, and his compassion, like a divine medicine that cures all diseases, was directed not at any one person but to all creatures. Thus, out of compassion for Devaḷa, he did not allow the sun to rise when the thirty hours of that night were spent.[7]

"When the sun did not rise, the citizens of the town went to the king and said, 'Your Lordship, the sun that has risen every morning ever since the beginning of your reign has not risen today. Just as you regularly collect taxes[8] from all your provinces and the outer regions before the year is out, so before this day is over make the sun rise.'

"When he heard them, the king wondered at first if it could be because of some lapse on his part. He called to mind his own past actions but could think of nothing that he had done wrong. Then realizing that it could also be caused by some conflict among holy men, the king asked, 'Is there at present any ascetic in this city? If there is, he, by his magical powers may be preventing the sun from rising.' They told him of the two ascetics lodging in the potter's shed. The king immediately took up a lighted torch and went to the ascetic Nārada. He greeted him and stood respectfully on a side saying,

> Kammantā nappavattanti jambudīpassa nārada
> Kena loko tamobhūto—tamme akkhāhi pucchito*

That is to say, 'Reverend ascetic, the sun today did not rise at the usual time as it always does. People cannot plough or sow their fields. Darkness prevails. Why is this so? Tell us please.'

"Nārada related the recent happenings in all detail and said, 'I realize that the curse hurled at me, who am innocent, would, at sunrise,

*O Narada, in all of Jambudīpa no work gets done. Why is the world enveloped in darkness? Answer me please.

cause this ascetic's head to split into seven pieces. I, who in successive births have given away my own head, so many times, that if heaped up they would make a pile higher than Mount Mēru, decided to save this man whose head was about to split apart. Thus, out of compassion for him, I have forbidden the sun to rise.'

'One cannot always put out a fire one has started. Similarly, some people can destroy but cannot restore again. Can you now make the sun rise and at the same time prevent this ascetic's head from splitting?' the King inquired.

'Insults hurled at an *arahat* are no bar to heaven or even to achieveing *nirvāṇa,* provided the person acknowledges his faults[9] and begs the other's forgiveness. Therefore, if he asks forgiveness, the sun will rise and his head will not split.'

"Sometimes the very snake that bites a man is used to suck out the poison. So the King approached the ascetic Devaḷa and said, 'This conflict, since it centers on you, cannot be resolved except by you. Beg the holy man's forgiveness and end this darkness.'

"A pot of rice, once it burns, cannot be recooked, for rice does not revert to its former state. Similarly, this Devaḷa was so steeped in stubbornness that, even though he saw the problem, he would not ask forgiveness. He became all the more obstinate and even though his head was going to split into seven parts, his obstinacy remained intact.

"The king realized the ascetic was stubborn and would not ask forgiveness. He decided, 'This man does no work,[10] so it doesn't matter to him if the sun does not rise. But our lands will become barren and be devastated. We want the sun to rise.' He took hold of the unwilling ascetic, threw him on the ground, and forced him to worship the sage Nārada.

"Like the learned sage, Mahauśadha,[11] who on another occasion, when Kēvaṭṭa came to contest the Battle of Ethics threw a precious gem at his feet and, when he bent down to pick it up, held him by the nape of his neck, rubbed his forehead on the ground and said, "Arise, O teacher," so Nārada now told Devaḷa, 'Arise, O teacher, I forgive you.' He then added, 'Oh King, since this man did not ask forgiveness out of conviction, there is nothing to prevent his head from splitting when the sun rises. If you do not want his head to split, then take him to the pond nearby, stand him in the water up to his neck, and place a lump of kneaded clay on his head.' The King did as he was told.

"The ascetic Nārada said to Devaḷa 'When I withdraw my psychic powers and the sun begins to rise, dive under the water and surface at another point.'

"As he withdrew his powers, stars appeared and the sun rose. The rays struck the lump of clay and shattered it into seven pieces. Thus, the ascetic Nārada demonstrated how Devaḷa's head would have shattered. He also displayed how with his axe of Knowledge of the Path to Enlightenment, he could cleave the many heads of Ignorance. By so doing he dispelled the fears of the King and of many others, as well as the darkness of night."

The Buddha finished telling this story of a past life and continued, "Listen, O monks. The King at the time is now the Senior monk Anaňda.[12] That most stubborn man, who slept in the potter's shed and had to stand with a lump of clay on his head, that ascetic Devaḷa is now the monk Tissa the Fat. Though not made of clay, he is like a lump of hardened clay in his obstinacy. I was the ascetic Nārada, who thereafter practiced the thirty Perfections and became a Buddha. This man's stubbornness and disobedience is long-standing and goes back to that time."

He then called up the monk Tissa the Fat and said, "Listen, O monk. If one says, 'That man scolded me, abused me, tried to kill me, beat me, defeated me in argument, or stole what belonged to me,' and if, whatever the cause, one harbors thoughts of hatred and vengeance,[13] and deposits that treasure (vengeance), which is of significance only to oneself, inside the container of one's mind, and binds it tightly with the rope of one's thoughts, the result is fearful for the person concerned. Therefore in such a situation, wise men such as Buddhas do not undo that rope with a single tug. Instead they untie it slowly, take the pot in their hands, and place it where it cannot be reached. If they do not do so, since the ropes that bind it are strong, even if the ropes were to disintegrate and the pot to break, the person concerned will merely transfer his treasure (vengeance) into another pot and tie it still more tightly with rope. Thus, vengeance will never die.

"However, if one acts otherwise and says, 'Others may scold and berate me, beat me, retaliate against me, but it is probably because in the past I have done likewise to them. Thus, although the *karma* of the doer of such acts will continue to grow, my own *karma* will work itself out. It will die like a seed that withers away as the seedling grows.' Just as water poured into a cracked pot will leak out and finally be empty, so thoughts of vengeance against another will disappear, if they are subdued then and there."

On hearing this sermon, of the ten lakhs of monks gathered there,[14] some instantly killed the enemy Defilements of Illusion of Self and Doubt, two of the ten enemies, which lay coiled at the Stream-Enterer's *(sōvān)* gateway and so arrived at the city of *nirvāṇa* through the first gate. Others, while striving to kill them found that gateway not big enough and went to the next gateway of the Once-Returner *(sakadāgāmin)*. That entrance was blocked by the enemy Defilements of Lustful

Desire and Hatred. So they killed them in order to stop them escaping, and entered the city of *nirvāṇa* through that gateway. Still others, who had considerably weakened the hold of those enemies, realized that it was better not to have any enemies at all, and so killed them all off right there. But finding that particular gateway too small, they entered the city of *nirvāṇa* through the other gate of the Non-Returner *(anāgāmin)*. Those who were very clever, were victorious over all the Defilements at all the entrances and decided to enter through the gate of the *arahat*. That entrance, too, was blocked by enemy Defilements, but they completely exterminated them and entered the city of *nirvāṇa* through that gate.

The monk Tissa, though ripe in years and obstinacy, was green in wisdom[15] and so did not attain the spiritual heights of the Path and the Fruits on that occasion. He finally abandoned his disobedient ways, however, and at a later stage, became eligible to participate in both the blessings of the world and the blessings of Spiritual Attainments.

Therefore, just as the monk Tissa the Fat discarded disobedience, which one should avoid, learned obedience, and thus became eligible for future Enlightenment, so good men should give up sinful acts, do only good, and purify their minds and mental processes in order to achieve the blessings of the world as well as Spiritual Attainments.

Endnotes

THE MONK TISSA
Illustrates stanzas 3 and 4 of the Yamaka Vagga.

> Akkocchi maṃ avadhi maṃ . . . veraṃ tesaṃ na sammati
> Akkocchi maṃ avadhi maṃ . . . veraṃ tesūpasammati
>
> He abused me, he beat me, overcame me, robbed me,
> Hatred does not cease when one harbors such thoughts.
> He abused me, beat me, overcame me, robbed me,
> Hatred ceases when one does not harbor such thoughts.

1. We have seen from King Miliňdu's defeat, . . .

This is yet another link passage that does not occur in the DA text. It is a specific attempt by the author to tie this story with the one immediately before it, thereby, underlining contrasts, comparisons, and emphases.

2. A Garuda is a mythical bird that eats snakes.

3. "Why, Tissa, what are you complaining about?"

A comparison of this section with that of the fifth century DA will indicate the narrative skills of the monk Dharmasēna. He expands certain sections and cuts others in order to heighten the drama of the encounter. [See R. Obeyesekere 1989]

4. "Listen, Tissa. There is no place for birth, lineage, . . .

This is a specific statement of the Buddhist position regarding birth and social status. It underlines Buddhism's strongly anti-brahmanic position on the question of caste and birth. Not only is Tissa's kinship connection with the Buddha of no importance but he must also acknowledge and apologize to the other monks whom he has wronged by assuming such privilege.

5. " . . . But it would be of benefit to us to hear . . .

Note how a branch story is introduced into the main story. It is not merely an extension or flashback into a past birth. Rather, the introductory statement of the specific connection intricately links the two stories and makes them constantly reflect and refract on each other.

6. . . . to eat foods containing salt and lime.

Ascetics living in the forests, feeding on fruits and tubers, were supposed to come down to the city for their requirements of salty and sour foods. Lack of these could cause disease.

7. . . . the thirty hours of that night were spent.

According to the Asian system of calculation, hours were clearly of a different duration. I use the English word "hours" for lack of a better.

8. Just as you regularly collect taxes . . .

There is implicit here the idea of a tight bond of reciprocal duties and obligations on the part of both rulers and ruled, a concept central to the Buddhist notion of kingship. The image used underlines this fact. The attitude of the subjects to their king is thus not of begging for a kingly favor but rather that of a demand made on the basis of rights. The contrast with the passage in the DA is striking. See introduction p. xix.

Similarly large scale calamities and natural disasters were believed to be the result of a trangression on the part of the ruler (as also in the Oedipus myth), or to a conflict between ascetics with supernormal powers.

9. . . . , provided the person acknowledges his faults . . .

Note that in Buddhism there is no forgiveness of sins by an all-powerful God. There is, however, forgiveness at the human level. Monks can and should forgive each other's transgressions if the wrongdoer admits his fault and asks to be forgiven. See the story of Nagasēna and also the story of the priests of Kosaṁbä.

10. "This man does no work, . . .

A slightly ironic comment on the "unproductive" aspect of ascetics. It is a criticism that has constantly been made about monks and ascetics who do not labor for their living. Since the author is himself a monk, there is a level of self-irony implicit in the comment.

11. "Like the learned sage Mahauśadha . . .

A reference to an incident from the *Ummaga Jātaka*. (See note in Nāgasèna Story.)

12. The King at the time is now the Senior monk Anaňda.

Note how the branch stories are tied together and the reader brought back to the main story. This is a pattern common to most Buddhist stories as in the *Jātakas*. Buddhist stories are not only firmly contextualized at the beginning, with who said what and where, but they are always brought back to the main story and neatly tied together at the end.

13. . . . , one harbors thoughts of hatred and vengeance, . . .

The monk Dharmasēna's understanding of human nature and the workings of the human mind are revealed in this passage. What is even more striking is the simplicity of image and language in which such psychological insights are conveyed, making them easily comprehensible to a peasant audience. The DA by contrast, merely quotes the stanzas of the *Dhammapada* on the subject of vengeance.

14. . . . of the ten lakhs of monks gathered there, . . .

This extended imagery is very much in the sermon tradition. The repetitive elaboration (sometimes to the point of boredom) is perhaps in order to explain the Doctrinal point about the four stages of the Path to *nirvāṇa*.

15. The monk Tissa, though ripe in years and obstinacy was green in wisdom . . .

Again, there is no instant forgiveness. While so many thousands heard the Buddha's sermon and attained to various stages on the way to Enlightenment, the monk Tissa did not on that occasion attain even to the first stage of the Path *(sōvān)*. We are told that only much later (after he had rid himself of his stubborn traits), did he become eligible for the blessings of Spiritual Attainments.

The Demoness Kāḷī

As a bush fire burning out of control stops[1] only when it reaches a vast body of water, so the rage of one who vows vengeance cannot be quelled except by the waters of compassion that fill the ocean of Omniscience. We shall illustrate this with the story of the demoness Kāḷī.

How does it go?

There was once a young man, who on the death of his father, had no choice but to take on the responsibilities of the household himself. He ran the farm and the house and cared for his widowed mother. She saw what hardships he underwent and thought, "I cannot relieve him of the whole of his burden but, if I were to arrange a marriage for him, at least he could leave the household chores to his wife and so take a little rest himself. Besides, if I am to go on enjoying the benefit of his care and attention, I had better see to his welfare." So, one day she said, "Son, shall I arrange a marriage for you?"

"Mother, I don't want that. Let us not introduce any such complication. I will care for you myself as long as I live. Give me the opportunity to perform that act of merit,"[2] he answered.

"Son, don't say that. How can I be happy when I see you work so hard?"

The mother continued to bring the matter up again and again, so finally the young man fell silent. Sensing that he had agreed to her proposal,[3] the mother prepared to go to a certain household to make inquiries on behalf of her son. The son, seeing her get ready, asked, "Where do you mean to go?" When she told him it was to such and such a household, he stopped her, saying he preferred another, and directed her to the one of his choice.

The mother then entered into the necessary negotiations with that family, arranged an auspicious time for the marriage, and on the chosen day brought home the bride for her son. Unfortunately the young woman, his wife, was not blessed enough to have children, so like a tree that should bear fruit but does not, she was barren.

As they lived thus, childless, the mother said to her son, "Son, I arranged the marriage of your choice, but just as trees grown for their fruit yet fail to produce any, so where one needs a child to continue one's lineage, this wife of yours is barren. I live happily because I have you to care for me. When you are old and feeble, how will you manage without a child? Would you like me to arrange another marriage for you?"

The son said he did not want that. Perhaps because he felt it would be pointless to say more, he merely repeated that he disliked the suggestion, not just out of politeness, but sincerely.

The barren wife, hearing the discussion, thought, "A child may, twice or thrice, refuse a parent's request. However, since it is wrong to disobey, it is not unlikely that he will finally agree. Were he to marry someone of his choice and were they to have a child, then I will be relegated to a servant's status. But if I were to select someone myself, such a thing would not happen." With that in mind, she went to a certain household.

Deceit breeds in sin[4] just as good needs knowledge to flourish. Besides, since deceit is itself vile and needs to associate with vileness, it associates with vile women, because deceit often resides in women. Sometimes what one speaks, thinks, and acts is largely mixed with deceit, and what may seem done entirely in the interests of another is in fact done only for one's own welfare. Very often one is aware of the inadequacies of a certain action but does not reveal it to others. So (deceitfully) the wife selected a young woman of good family for the position. Since it was not a regular proposal, the young woman's parents did not agree.

To convince them, the wife said, "I am barren. If your daughter were to bear my husband a child, that child would become heir to great wealth and comfort. What use are riches to a barren woman like me?"

Thus, like a person in disguise, thinking one thing but saying quite another, she arranged a contract and brought the young woman to her husband.

Then again she thought, "If this woman were to have a child, she might end up as my mistress. Then the whole purpose of my plan is lost and what I told her parents when I asked for her, may in fact come true. Should that happen what use would my deceitful tricks have served? If by some means I can prevent her having children, I should employ those means." Then, with evil intent she went up to the bride one day and said, "Whenever you conceive be sure to tell me."

The young wife, thinking it a good idea, indeed told her as soon as she conceived. From that day on, all her food and drinks were prepared by the other. One day the barren wife found something that could be put into food to cause a miscarriage; she administered the medicine. Thus, she deprived her rival of a child, but in doing so extended her own journey through *saṃsāra*.

On the second occasion, too, when the young woman conceived, she gave her the medicine, that had by now been tested, and made her miscarry a second time.

At that point, the neighbor women said, "How is it that twice in succession you have miscarried? Is it because of something your 'elder sister,' a jealous rival, has done?" When questioned thus the young wife told them how she had mentioned the fact that she had conceived and how from that point on the barren wife had prepared special meals for her and how she had miscarried after eating that food.

They heard it all and said, "Fool, if the first time you ate what she prepared, you miscarried, why did you tell her when you conceived a second time? And even if you chose to tell her, why did you eat what she gave you without finding out what it was she cooked? Don't you know that for women there is no suffering greater than jealousy of a rival? From now on say nothing." So they admonished her.

The third time she conceived she said nothing. When the barren wife saw her rival's belly grow great with child, she was like a person who, because she cannot eat or drink, does not want others to do so either. Being barren herself, she was jealous of those who were fecund and inquired why she had not been told of the pregnancy earlier.

The young wife replied, "You brought me here and gave me to your husband.[5] When you disliked my staying on, instead of sending me back to my parents' home, you fed me medicine and caused me to miscarry. Tell me what kind of friendship is that?"

"Whatever has happened so far, now that she knows everything I am ruined," thought the barren wife. She decided to wait for an opportunity during childbirth. When she got the chance, she gave the young woman the medicine during labor. The pregnancy was now full-term. Thus, instead of being aborted, the child lodged horizontally in the womb. The young wife's labor became excruciatingly painful; her life hung in the balance.

As she was dying she said, "Alas, your deception was very great. Three children have died and now I, too, am about to die. You have killed four people. When I die, may I be reborn as a demoness powerful enough to devour you and the children you bear."

With that Fervent Rebirth-Wish, she died and was reborn as a cat in that very household.

The husband caught hold of the barren wife and shouted, "It is because of you that I have suffered this great loss." He kicked her and beat her with whatever came to hand,[6] and since there was no point in killing her, he finally let her go.

She died sometime after and was born as a hen in that household. The hen reached maturity and was ready to lay. Three times in succession, the cat ate the eggs she laid. The hen seeing that said, "As a man eats up all his seed grain and when that is over consumes even the discarded grain for lack of better, so she, who three times ate my eggs, will she not finally eat me, too? Therefore, when I die and am reborn, may I, too, be able to eat her and her young."

With that Fervent Rebirth-Wish, the hen died and was reborn as a tigress. The cat died and was reborn as a doe. Three times the tigress ate the young of the doe. Finally when she was about to eat the doe, the dying doe made a Fervent Rebirth-Wish.

"Three times this tigress has eaten the young I bore. Now she eats me, too. May I die and be born a demoness so that I can eat her and her children." So the doe was reborn as a demoness during the lifetime of the Buddha.

The tigress was born as the daughter in a certain nobleman's household in the city of Sävät. On coming of age, she was given in marriage and went to live in a village some distance from her hometown. She had a son from her marriage. The demoness, checking on households where children were born, heard of a birth from members of that household, and came there in the guise of a friend.

"Where is our dear friend?" she asked. When informed that she had given birth to a child, she said, "Did she have a son or a daughter? I would like to see her."

Thus, deceitfully worming herself into the inner chamber, she took the child in her arms as if to look at him, promptly ate him, got up, and left. The second time, too, when a child was born, she came and ate him. On the third occasion, when the young woman was pregnant, she said to her husband, "Twice in this place a demoness devoured the children I bore. Are not one's parents the best people to care for one's welfare? I will go to them to have my child." So saying, she went there and gave birth to a child of great Merit, who was destined to live long.

During this time, it was the demoness' turn to carry water[7] from the lake Anavatapta for King Vessamuni (overlord of Demons). She did this task for four months and again for another five months. Some demons even died of the hard labor. This demoness carried water for the prescribed time. Then, having completed her task, like a ravenously hungry person, who hurriedly deposits her waterpot on the pot stand in the inner room and rushes to the kitchen to grab some food, so she rushed immediately to the labor room, which had been her one goal all this time. Pretending to be a friend, she inquired where the woman was.

They said, "On two earlier occasions a demoness ate the children she bore in this place. She knew of no other way to protect them so she has gone to the home of her parents."

"Wherever she is, it cannot be as far away as the heavens amidst the stars. Besides, if the child is already born, it will make it all the easier to find him and eat him, like eating a plate of ready cooked rice," so thought the demoness. Calling on that other demon, her long-standing vow of vengeance, she set off immediately for the inner city.

The woman, who had twice given birth and twice been left childless, now completed the naming ceremony for her son; she decided that it was time to return to her own village. She was passing through the premises of the Devramvehera monastery, with her husband and child, when she decided to bathe in the pond not far from the temple; she gave the child to her husband to hold. She finished her bath, climbed back onto the bank, and was sitting suckling her child while her husband took his bath, when she saw the demoness approach. Having seen her twice before, she recognized her instantly. She shouted to her husband, "Quick, come ashore, the child-eating ogress is coming!" Without waiting for him, she ran to the temple and rushed in through the door.

At this time the Buddha, accompanied by a retinue of forty monks, was seated preaching in the temple. The terrified woman cut through the crowds, went right up to the Buddha and, as if placing a water jar on a pillow covered in a wondrously colored spread, laid the tiny infant by the Buddha and placed the young child's head on his feet, resplendent with the one hundred and eight auspicious marks.[8]

"Though I may never hope to be a Buddha, this child I give to you. I see him in great danger. Just as you once granted Prince Alavi the gift of life extending for one hundred and twenty years, and as you protected Alavi from demons, I beg you, protect this child from the demoness that seeks to hurt him." So she pleaded with the Buddha as with a friend or intimate, her fear being so great.

The entrance to the temple was guarded by the god Sumana,[9] who though his name meant "The Pleasing One" was displeased with the demoness; he did not allow her to enter.

As a beggar woman, dressed in rags, afraid to come too close, hovering around at a distance from the place where a meal is in progress, is invited in and offered a plate of rice, so in order to give this flesh-eating demoness the food of *nirvāṇa,* the Buddha called up the Senior Monk Ānaňda and said, "Ānaňda, go invite that demoness standing outside the door and escort her in."

Seeing the demoness enter, the mother of the little one, ignorant of the power of the Buddha and terrified that, even though the child was lying with his head on the feet of the Buddha, the demoness might still snatch and eat him, said, "Lord, there comes the demoness I spoke of."

As a mother hushes a hungry child with soothing words until the pot of rice is cooked, so the Buddha comforted her with words until he was ready to preach a sermon.

"She comes but you need not be afraid.[10] If you two had not met, then there would have been a reason for fear." Thus, he calmed her. He then said to the demoness, "Why do you do this? Just as truth and justice are forgotten if you never come in contact with those who know what is right and just, so if you two had not happened to come to me, your vengeance would have lasted over eons like the ageless enmity between a bear and a *Kōn* tree that we know from the *Phandana Jātaka,*[11] or the enmity between crows and owls as related in the *Ulūka Jātaka.*[12] It was a good thing I met you.

"Listen demoness,[13] when your body is filthy with spit, phlegm, and snot, you cannot clean it with that same spit, phlegm, and snot—in fact it will only get more filthy. So when you abuse those who abuse and revile you, or kill or beat up those murderers who beat you, or indulge in criminal acts against those who do criminal acts against you, it is like adding fuel to fire; enmity on both sides never ceases. Just as iron sharpened on steel cuts ever more keenly, so your rage increases. How then can that enmity be made to cease like a fire that is dampened?

As spit, snot, and such like are washed off with clean water, and that water, because it is pure, can cleanse a filthy body, so hatred that burns on the fuel of justifications must be quenched with the water of compassion, not fed with the firewood of reasons and causes. Compassion is fundamentally right, free of malice, and is the source for all good actions. Good, founded on compassion, destroys evil and puts out the fire of enmity. When that fire, which is most difficult to extinguish, is put out, then the ten other fires kindled by the various types of passions such as the desire for wealth, will also die. When there is no more wood, even fires that have been burning for long years die down. Once all eleven fires are extinguished, just as rice plants thrive in flooded fields, so in the rice field of the mind softened with the waters of Compassion, seeds of Moral Conduct and Contemplation will sprout, and a rich harvest of worldly blessings and of Spiritual Attainments can be had."

So he spoke and encouraged the demoness who, exhausted by her previous terrible crimes such as the taking of human life, had no strength left to enter the city of *nirvāṇa.* He set her on the first stage of the Path to Enlightenment, that of the Stream-Enterer, and until, at some future date, she was able to pound, husk, and prepare the rice meal of the Path and the Fruits, which would sustain her in her journey through the desert of *saṃsāra,* he gave her a handful of Stream-Enterer rice for the journey.

That demoness, who because she was a demoness had no fixed abode, now acquired a small room (since there were many others also there) in the nine-storied palace of the nine Supramundane States. Since she now had the heavenly body of a noble being, she was allowed to live there. Thus, she gave up eating human flesh, which was in every way despicable, and acquired a taste for *nirvāṇa.*

As if the weight of the child lying on his feet was too heavy for him, the Buddha now turned to the mother and said, "Give your child to the demoness to hold."

"Lord, I'm afraid to give the child to her," the mother replied.

"Do not fear. The Senior Monk Aṅgulimāla once said, 'I will cut a thousand fingers to perform my sacrificial rites' and killed many people and caused much trouble. I tamed him. Now he does not harm so much as an ant. The water with which they wash the seat where he recites the Protective Stanzas[14] is now used to ward off all dangers. Women in labor drink this sanctified water and give birth painlessly. In one of my former births, as the learned Mahauśadha, in this same manner, I stopped a demoness from devouring a young prince, and by the power of my wisdom enabled her, in that very life, to rid herself of the five sins. Did you think that I, now a Buddha, would ask you to carry your child to that demoness if she still ate human flesh? No harm will come to your child from her. No demon can harm one who has touched my feet."

As he spoke, the demoness was given the child to carry. She hugged and caressed the child as if to gather to herself some of that radiance the child had got from the blessed body of the Buddha, and handed him back to the mother. Then, as eyes struck by a powerful radiance gush forth tears, so she burst into weeping.

The Buddha, seeing her weep, said, "Those who come to me leave happy, having obtained the wealth of *nirvāṇa;* none leave weeping. You weep because you miss your worldly pleasures."

"Lord, formerly I ate living beings just to satisfy my stomach and yet I was never full. From now on, since I will no longer kill living things, the taste of *nirvāṇa,* though it will delight my mind, may not be sufficient to satisfy the hunger in my body. Therefore I weep, thinking, 'How will I live from now on?' "

The Buddha comforted the demoness and said to the mother, the lay devotee, "Take this person to your home and without fear keep her there. Give her the first serving of whatever you cook and look after her well."

She took the demoness home, and set her up under the rafters.[15] Whatever she cooked, she offered first to the demoness and ate only what was left. However, when the rice was being husked, by spreading it on the ground and pounding it with long pestles, the raised wooden pestles kept hitting against the demoness' body. Bothered by this, but being now set in the path of righteousness and so unable to act otherwise, the demoness called her friend, the woman lay devotee, and said, "This place is not convenient for me. Put me somewhere else."

She then took her and put her at the far end, in a room where the pestles were stacked away. Although the demoness now had no further occasion for evil actions that result in continued rebirths, the consequences of her past evil actions had to work themselves out.[16] Thus, each time the pestles were thrown into the room, they struck her on the head. She then said that that place, too, was unsatisfactory, so she was put at the end of the hall where they kept the water for washing. However, small boys while rinsing their hands and mouths splashed dirty water on her head. She complained that this was not satisfactory either, so she was put behind the hearth. Dogs shivering from the cold, having no other comfortable place, gathered there as if for her company, so that, too, was unsatisfactory. She was then taken and placed in a corner under the eaves. Little boys urinated and defecated there so that, too, was not satisfactory. She was then put out in the yard by the garbage heap. People would bring whole basketsful of garbage and throw it on her head so that, too, was troublesome. She was then placed at the entrance to the village. There, young boys, learning to shoot arrows, used her as their target so that, too, was unsatisfactory. She was finally taken outside the village to a place far from the public thoroughfare and there looked after and given rice gruel. She suffered no further discomfort and so remained there. Thereafter, she began to give advice to the household that brought her rice gruel.

"This year there will be heavy rains so your mudfields of rice will rot. Cultivate grains that grow on high land such as *Mineri,* and *Tana.*" Or she would say, "This year there will be little rain so your highland plantings will all die. You should farm your wet rice fields."

As a result of her good advice, their farming was always carried out with foreknowledge, and was successful. Others in the village had no such luck.

"How is it that whatever you plant does not die, while all our crops are destroyed?" they asked.

The householders answered, "Why, have you not noticed that we regularly take rice gruel to a place a little distance away from the village? We take it to a certain demoness. She tells us when there is going to be rain and when there is not. It is because of her that our farms are a success. If you do as we do, you will get the same advice and have nothing to worry about."

Thus, all the town folk began to render similar services to the demoness and, because of her association, they, too, lacked neither rice nor other grains. She in turn got much devotion, was given eight Ticketed Offerings,[18] and became famous as Kāḷī Barandhi. This practice continued until the writing of these commentaries.

Thus, vengeance is an extremely vile sin. Therefore, give it up. A mind full of compassion is good and paves the way to obtain the eleven powerful blessings.

As it is said:

> Mettārahita posena—natthi pāpaṃ akāriyaṃ
> Mettāsahita posena—natthi puññaṃ akāriyaṃ"*

---

*What is done without compassion, results in bad karma
A compassionate act can only result in good karma.

Therefore, set yourself on that path and purify your mind to go into the presence of the Buddha. Even though that Buddha is presently dead,[19] come into his presence by means of the stories of the *Jewel Garland of the True Doctrine*. Give up that most vile hatred such as you have heard and seen, fill your mind with compassion as he advised, and thus obtain blessings in this world and the blessings of Spiritual Attainments.

Endnotes

THE DEMONESS KĀḶĪ

Illustrates stanza 5 of the Yamaka Vagga.

> Na hi verena verāni . . . esa dhammo sanantano
>
> Hatred is never appeased by hatred in this world
> By love alone is it appeased. This is an ancient law.

1. As a bush fire burning out of control stops . . .

This image is yet another interpolation by Dharmasēna Thera. There is a play not only on the fire-water opposition but also on the word "Omniscience." The Buddha is often referred to as the Omniscient One. Thus, rage and vengeance can only be extinguished when confronted with compassion born of knowledge *or* when they encounter the Omniscient One.

2. ". . . Give me the opportunity to perform that act of merit, . . ."

An "Act of Merit" (s. *piṇkama*) refers to the Buddhist notion of actions that have good *karmic* results. Care for one's aged parents is considered a specially meritorious action. Note the shift here from the transcendental ethics of Doctrinal Buddhism contained in the opening image to the pragmatic ethics of daily life —merit-making.

3. Sensing that he had agreed to her proposal, . . .

This passage provides an insight into how marriages were traditionally arranged. The formal negotiations are done by the parents or "others" not the couple themselves, but the individual's preferences are taken into account. Thus, there is a tacit understanding on both sides as to who should be approached and how.

The negotiations for getting a "co-wife" are similar and there are codes to be followed. Both parties are aware that it will not be a "regular" marriage and that the second woman will not be mistress of the household. It is when the code is broken, as in the barren wife's deceitful aborting of the fetuses, that a wrong is committed.

4. Deceit breeds in sin . . .

This digression on deceit is introduced for the benefit of the monk Dharmasēna's thirteenth century listeners. Such interpolations or homilies occur at different points in all the stories, are easily recognizable, were introduced by the monk Dharmasēna into his version of the text, and are addressed to an "implied" audience.

The rather misogynist aside in which deceit is specifically associated with women is also characteristic of the writings of this period (most of it done by monks).

5. "You brought me here and gave me to your husband. . . . "

It was customary, in Sri Lanka, for a marriage to be considered dissolved if a woman returned to her parental home and chose not to go back to her husband. This traditional form of divorce was "legal" in Sri Lanka up to the early nineteenth century, when the British introduced a different legal system based on Roman-Dutch and English Common Law. The older custom, however, continued to function as a special law in the central parts of the country known as the Kandyan Provinces. In our text, the implication behind the statement is: "You could have sent me back to my parents and the marriage would have been dissolved. You did not have to commit these violent acts." The DA version does not suggest this. It merely says, "It was you who brought me here and twice caused me to suffer miscarriages." The custom of dissolving a marriage by returning to one's parents was possibly specific to Sri Lanka.

6. He kicked her and beat her with whatever came to hand, . . .

The statement is so casually made it suggests that wife beating was a common feature of peasant life and familiar to the culture.

7. . . . , it was the demoness' turn to carry water . . .

Note the shift of narrative focus to the demoness as she functions in the demon world. She is seen as a real person, a physical being not a spirit, engaging in the routine activities of her demon world. At the same time, the text clearly indicates that the demonic is also the embodiment of her vow of vengeance.

Lesser spirits like demons and ghosts are believed to be kept in bondage to Vessamuni, overlord of demons. They must perform certain tasks as penance for their sinful deeds. Hence the belief that magicians and sorcerers are able to enlist the services of Vessamuni and make him perform special tasks for them, too.

Note the image of the ravenously hungry demoness devouring the child like a ready cooked plate of rice. The very ordinariness of the simile heightens the macabre nature of the act. The effect is similar to Jonathan Swift's in *A Modest Proposal*.

8. . . . the one hundred and eight auspicious marks.

The Buddha as a *Mahā Puruśa* (Great Being) had thirty-two auspicious marks on his body. These marks are often iconographically represented on the palms of hands and soles of feet of statues and pictures. Here the number is given as one hundred and eight, perhaps because that, too, is an auspicious number.

9. The entrance to the temple was guarded by the god Sumana, . . .

The god Sumana was probably a reference to the god Saman, one of the guardian deities of Sri Lanka. In the Sinhala, there is a play on the word Sumana which means "pleasing" and *dummana* "unpleasing."

10. Once again we have an example of a contextualized sermon to a dramatized audience.

Paula Richman in her study of the Tamil Buddhist text *Maṇimēkalai* refers to similar use of: "The dramatized audience as a rhetorical device," which enabled "these small-scale preaching events to explore the practical implications of doctrines *in situ*." [Richman 1988, 46.] It was thus a rhetorical device common to both Sinhala and Tamil Buddhist literature of the medieval period. It is not a strategy found in the DA. There, the "teaching" is mainly in the form of a quotation of a stanza of doctrinal text followed by a brief comment. This tends to suggest that the use of a "dramatized audience" internal to the story was a relatively later stylistic device, at least as far as Sinhala writing was concerned.

11. *Phandana Jātaka* story,

The story of a lion who plotted to get a tree cut down and how he was outwitted by the deity of the tree.

12. *Ulūka Jātaka*

The story of a quarrel between owls and crows. At the period in question, crows used to eat owls by day and owls flew about nipping off the heads of crows by night.

13. "Listen demoness, . . ."

This interpolation of yet another sermon is addressed to the demoness but the style and formal tone suggests it is directed also at a rhetorical audience.

14. . . . where he recites the Protective Stanzas . . .

Stanzas referring to the Buddha's victory over specific evils are recited by monks in a ceremony known as *pirit* (p. *paritta*). This ceremony is performed to bring protection and blessings to laymen. Water that is "empowered" by the words chanted, is then given devotees to drink and a thread that is similarly empowered is tied around their arms. The conversion of the demon Aṅgulimāla is one of the stories in this recital. Those particular stanzas happen to be the ones that are recited specifically to ease the pain of women in labor. The practice is still common in Sri Lanka today.

15. She . . . , set her up under the rafters.

Household deities and images are often placed high up away from regular traffic in the household. In this case, the demoness, too, is treated as if she were a kind of idol or image and placed up under the rafters. The implication is that she has now reverted to her spirit form. But she continues to suffer physical pain, a consequence of her past bad actions. The women pounding grain lift the long pestles high up above their heads and in doing so hit the demoness who is up in the rafters.

16. . . . the consequences of her past evil actions had to work themselves out.

According to the Buddhist doctrine of *karma,* all actions have consequences. Thus, although the demoness, as a Stream-Enterer, may no longer commit demeritorious *karmic* acts, in accordance with *karmic* law, she must continue to suffer the consequences of her past bad actions. This is what is now being described in the story.

17. Cultivate grains that grow on high land . . .

Most Sri Lankan farmers even today, each cultivate a small extent of rice land or mudfields (s. *mada idaṃ*) and a slightly larger extent of high land or *chēna* (s. *goda idaṃ*). Rice, which requires standing water, can only be grown during the heavy monsoon. Grains such as Minēri and Tana need much less water and are sown on areas of cleared highland. But excessive rain can ruin the rice-fields just as a drought can quickly kill the highland cultivations.

18. She . . . was given eight Ticketed Offerings, . . .

The Sinhala, *lābat* (p. *salāka bhatta*) means literally "ticket rice" or food to be distributed by tickets or tokens. Rev. Sōrata in his dictionary [1952], refers to *salāka dāna,* as the offerings made by individuals or households whose names were written on pieces of paper that were then distributed among the monks. Buddhist monks, in their begging rounds, went to the specified households for their food. In the context of our story, the reference is probably to a similar practice, current even now in Sri Lanka, of allocating devotees a specific day to bring their offerings to the temple. I have translated it "ticketed offerings."

Thus, the Kāḷī story becomes an origin myth of Kāḷī, the goddess/demoness. Both the DA and the SR texts state that Kāḷī propitiation continued to be performed "until the writing of these commentaries," that is, they were in existence both when the fifth century DA was written and when Dharmasēna was translating in the thirteenth century. The fact that in both texts there is no mention of Kāḷī by name in the body of the text, suggests that the tale of the demoness was very likely an even older legend that was then incorporated to serve as an origin myth for the goddess/demoness Kāḷī.

Barāndha Kāḷī literally means "Kāḷī on the Balcony." One wonders whether it is not an attempt to link it to Badra Kāḷī (Kāḷī the Merciful), which is the name by which she is often propitiated. Such a connection would help legitimize the transformation of the flesh-eating demoness into a merciful deity, to be propitiated and placated as she no doubt was, during the time of the author.

19. Even though that Buddha is presently dead, . . .

To go into the presence of the Buddha means to achieve Enlightenment. It does not mean to enter a heaven where the Buddha is present as a living immortal god. The distinction is clarified and the Doctrinal position stressed by the monk Dharmasēna, perhaps for the very reason that it may have been a popular misconception among his peasant audience.

The Monks of Kosaṁbä

Moreover, to show what disasters follow from discord and quarreling and what great blessings come from amity, we shall relate the story of the monks of Kosaṁbä.

In the city of Kosaṁbä, in a temple built by the nobleman Ghosaka and named after him, there lived two monks. One was a great observer of the Disciplinary Rules of the Order and was skilled in their practice. The other, though not very meticulous in the observance of the Rules, was skilled in preaching the Doctrine. Each had a following of five hundred monks.

One morning, the Preacher monk went to the toilet to relieve himself and, after washing, left the remaining water in the vessel instead of emptying it or covering it as the rules required. A little later, the monk who was a strict follower of the Rules of Discipline went to the toilet and saw some water still in the vessel and the vessel not closed. When he had finished, he went to the Preacher monk and asked, "Was it you who didn't empty out the water after using the toilet?"

"Yes, it was me," the other replied.

"Didn't you know that it was a violation of the rules?" he asked.

"I did not" said the monk.

"Well, if you didn't know any better, I suppose you cannot be blamed for it" he said.

The Preacher monk thought, "My careless act might bring me rebirth in hell. Why should I let that happen? Since I can remedy it by admitting it to my fellows,[1] I shall confess and be absolved."

However, the monk who was expert in the Rules of Discipline said, "Since you did it unknowingly it was not a conscious act and so cannot be considered a sin." The Preacher monk, since he was expert only in Teaching, knew no better and believed that the words of the monk, who was expert in the Rules, had absolved him.

The latter, however, though he had earlier said it did not matter, now went around telling his followers, "This Preacher monk, just because he has studied a thing or two, goes around preaching to others. But as the shadows beneath a lamp are never dispelled, so he does not know his own shortcomings."

Then those monks went to the followers of the Preacher monk and said, "It seems your preceptor does wrong and doesn't even know it."

They in turn, then reported this back to their preceptor. The Preacher monk said, "This observer of the Rules told me at the time that I was not to blame for leaving the water in the pot, because I did it unknowingly. Now he says I was at fault. He lies. Does he claim to observe the Rules of the Discipline and yet lie like this? Do those rules, which he studies so well, condone lying? Doesn't he know that all manner of ills befall a liar? If he doesn't, how can he claim to know the Rules of Discipline?"

Those monks then went to the followers of the monk of the Discipline and said, "It seems your Preceptor lies." Thus, because of a handful of water, a conflict flared up and reached a point where even the Buddha could not quell it.

Then the monk, who was expert in the Rules of Discipline, since he already had a following, pronounced sentence of excommunication on the Preacher monk for not confessing his fault. The followers of each split into two groups.

The lay devotees who attended on the monks also began to take sides. The nuns receiving instruction did the same. Even the Protecting deities and their associates on the earth below, in the sky above, and extending all the way to the world of Brahma, all beings, even those who possessed no Attainments,[2] divided into two camps. There was a great conflict extending from the kingdom of the Four Kings to the Akanitā Brahma world. As the quarrel intensified, a monk went to the Buddha and said, "Lord, the followers of the monk, who pronounced sentence of excommunication, say he did right and have formed one group. The supporters of the monk, who was excommunicated, say it was wrongfully done and now have formed another group."

The Buddha, without commenting on whether it was right or wrong, merely said, "They should settle their differences." Twice he sent this message but they did not do so.

On the third occasion he said, "The *Saṅgha* is being divided," and he went in person to meet the two parties in the city of Kosaṁbä.

There he told the monk, who had pronounced sentence of excommunication, that he was wrong to have first said, "You are not at fault," and later pronounced excommunication. He pointed out to the excommunicated monk his fault in first deciding, "I will beg forgiveness" but then hesitating when told it was unnecessary, and persising in not doing so even after he was excommunicated. However, the two groups continued to hold onto their positions. The Buddha, therefore, instructed that they should perform their religious observances separately[3] and, that in the refectories and seating halls, they should sit down, leaving a space of one vacant seat in between.

When the quarrel did not stop even at that, he once more returned to the city of Kosaṁbä and said, "Monks this quarrel is very wrong. Nothing is gained from it. We are told in the *Laṭukika Jātaka*[4] how, simply as a result of a quarrel, even frail Käṭakirili birds were able to overcome elephants by the power of strategems.

Kākañca passa laṭukikaṃ—maṇḍukaṃ nīlamakkhikaṃ
Ete nāgaṃ aghātesuṃ—passa verassa verinaṃ*

He also related the *Vaṭṭaka Jātaka*[5] about the several thousand quails who, when snared in a net, each said to the other, "You lift up the net." "No you do it." And so they were unable to break free and all died. Even that advice was not heeded. Then one of the monks said to him, "Lord, don't bother to say anything more."

For as it is said:

Yāni karoti puriso—tāni attani passati
Kalyāṇakārī kalyāṇaṃ—pāpakārī ca pāpakaṃ
Yādisaṃ vapate bījaṃ—tādisaṃ harate phalaṃ"**

He who sows *Amu* seeds will reap *Amu* grain,[6] for we shall be known by our deeds. The Buddha then related the *Dīghiti Kōsala Jātaka*[7] about how an enemy captured the territory of King Dīgha Kōsala, drove him out penniless, and subsequently killed him. But his son, Prince Dīghāya[8] (Long-lived), heeded his dying father's advice who said, "Look to the future. Do not be shortsighted." And so he bore no ill will towards King Brahmadatta (the enemy) but lived in peace with him.

The Buddha said, "If even laymen, in a time when there was no Buddha, forgave each other, can not you who are monks, members of my compassionate Order designed for the forgiveness of faults, make peace with each other?"

Though he gave them the medicine of his advice, the disease of their discord was not cured. Unwilling to remain there and watch such conflict among monks of his Order, the Buddha took up his robe and bowl himself[9] and, having partaken of a meal begged from the city of Kosaṁbä, he left for the Bālalonakārāma hermitage, alone, without informing a single one of the monks. He preached to the monk Bhagu, who lived there, about the advantages of living alone. He then went to the Pācinavaṃsa Park and preached to Anuruddha and two other monks about the pleasures of living in harmony. From there he went to the Pāralīya forest, full of mangoes, *Jambu* fruits, and bananas. This forest was traversed by elephants, horses, bears, and such beasts, inhabited by parrots, peacocks, cuckoos, and other birds, and haunted by *sid-*

*Behold, the crow, the quail, the frog, and the blue-fly,
Together killed the elephant. How powerful is hatred.

**Whatever a man does, he sees his true self in his deeds
One who does good, sees good, the wrong-doer, sees wrong
What seeds a man sows—that harvest he will reap.

dha and *vidyādhara* deities. There were hundreds of ponds and lakes that were filled with water and constantly in motion, for they were stirred by the breasts of celestial nymphs bathing in them. There, wishing to be alone, the Buddha spent the entire Rainy Season, away from the company of crowds, accepting only the services of the elephant Pāralīya,[10] who had separated himself from the herd, wishing to be alone, too.

The lay devotees of the city of Kosaṁbä came to the monastery and, not seeing the Buddha, asked, "Where is the Buddha?" Hearing that he had left for the Pāralīya forest, they inquired, "Why did he go there? What was the reason for his departure?"

The monks answered, "Our conflict was intense, and we did not heed his advice or his attempts to make peace, so he went away." Thus, they spoke, unashamedly, because contentiousness knows neither fear nor shame.

The lay devotees then said, "You monks, who have all taken ordination in the Buddha's *sāsana,* did you reject the advice of the Buddha himself who is as compassionate as the earth that protects even those who trip and fall on it?"

When they admitted it was so, the lay devotees said, "By attending on these monks we can neither see the Buddha, who has gone away, nor have a chance to worship and serve him. Because of them we have now been deprived of a chance to attend on the Buddha. We shall no longer give these monks either rice or water.[11] We will not permit them to stay, and we will not worship them." So the lay devotees decided. From that time on they did none of that.

The monks lived by their begging bowls and had no other means of livelihood than the rice obtained as alms; so now they starved. After a few days, their bodies withered. However, the intelligence does not dry up as quickly as the body. They reconsidered their position, realized what was right, and their hearts were softened. They confessed their faults to each other and obtained forgiveness because they could not otherwise be at peace.

Then they went to the lay devotees and said, "Devotees, though we did not resolve our differences on the advice of the Buddha, your actions have brought us together again. We are now as we were before, so you, too, should revert to your former practices."

The devotees replied, "If you receive the Buddha's forgiveness then we, too, will resume our former practices."

Since the monks lived far away and it was not customary to go to the Buddha during the Rainy Season, they were unable to do so; they were forced to live under severe hardship for the duration of that Rainy Season. The Buddha, on the other hand, who had gone into the immense forest, suffered no hardships at all during that period.

That majestic elephant, Pāralīya, went up to the Buddha and greeted him. Noticing that he was not accompanied by any disciples, the elephant cleared the grass underneath the tree with his feet, then broke a branch off a tree, and swept the area with it. When the Buddha made his abode there, the elephant fetched drinking water for the Buddha[12] during the entire three-month Rainy Season. He carried the waterpot in his trunk.[13] He even provided the Buddha with water for bathing. When hot water was needed, he would break a twig, strike it against a stone, throw dry wood on it and make a big fire. He would then roll a stone into the fire, heat it, and with a stick roll it back into a small rock pool. When the water was sufficiently heated, he would test it with his trunk and then go to the Buddha and worship him. The Buddha would ask, "O Pāraleyya, is the water heated?" Then he would walk to the pool and take his morning bath. After that, the elephant would go into the forest and bring him offerings of various kinds of fruits. The Buddha would partake of them and afterwards preach to him.

If, on occasion, the Buddha went to a nearby village to beg, the elephant would take up the revered begging bowl, place it on his head and follow after. The Buddha would walk up to the boundary of the village and say, "O Pāraleyya, you cannot come any farther into the areas of human habitation," and, taking the bowl from him, he would walk into the village. The elephant would remain there until he returned. When he saw the Buddha approach after begging in the village, he would walk up to him, take the bowl and robes from him, place them on his head as if they were an unornamented crown for an elephant king, and walk back to the Buddha's resting place. Like one long experienced in performing services for a Buddha, he would place the robe and bowl in their correct place, provide water for washing his feet, and fan him with the branch of a tree to cool him and dispel his fatigue.

After the Buddha had eaten, the elephant would perform all the customary duties and services and stand guard over him day and night. Holding a huge stick in his trunk, he would walk the length and breadth of the forest throughout the three watches of the night until dawn broke. Thus, the forest became known as the "protected forest." In the morning, he would provide soft twigs for the Buddha to brush his teeth and water for washing. He would then sweep the area and perform all the customary services.

A monkey living in that same forest saw the services performed by the elephant and thought, "I, too, will render service." While roaming in the forest one day, he saw a honey comb in the hollow of a tree, broke it off, placed it on a banana leaf, which he tore off a tree, and presented it to the Buddha. The Buddha accepted it unhesitatingly, just as he accepted even cakes made of rice bran. The monkey looked on and saw that the Buddha continued to hold it without eating it. "Why does he not eat?" he thought to himself.

Though the monkey was ignorant of the laws of causation and had no knowledge of *karmic* consequences because of his animal condition, he yet had the wisdom born of the power of his good thoughts. He therefore realized, "It must be because there are still larvae in the comb." Then taking the honey comb in his hands, with his finely shaped little finger that seemed made for such dextrous work, carefully, without hurting them, he picked out the larvae and then offered the comb to the Buddha.

Even though the Dunduvelbä bees gather honey from many sources and so it does not have much flavor, on this occasion, the gods infused it with heavenly flavors. The Buddha ate it and preached to the monkey who, drunk with joy, danced. He was hanging, suspended, holding on to a branch with one hand and with his foot on another.

Unfortunately, Demerit is always in opposition to Merit, goes hand in hand with it, and waits for its opportunity. Thus, as if hostile to the good deed the monkey had just performed, the consequences of a sinful act from his past caught up with him, and both the branch he was hanging on and the one he was standing on broke. He fell on a stake and was pierced through by it. However, since he died with a serene mind because of the gift he had just given, he was reborn in the Tavtisā heaven, in a golden abode one hundred and twenty cubits tall. As when a gem, covered in a silk cloth, is thrown up onto a high shelf, and the force of the throw causes the cloth to fall away but the gemstone to alight up there, so he flung away his monkey form and was born as a god three leagues tall; he was accompanied by one thousand heavenly maidens. Just as the gods infused great sweetness into the Danduvelbä honey comb, so he enjoyed much heavenly bliss; he was destined also to enjoy a taste of *nirvāṇa*.

News that the Buddha was living in the forest attended by the elephant Pāralīya became known all over Jambudīpa.[14] The nobles of Sävät, such as Anēpiḍu, Viśākhā, and others, came to the Senior Monk Anaṅda and said, "We wish to see the Buddha." Indeed, about five hundred monks, coming from different directions, went to the monk Anaṅda and said, "Now that the Rainy Season is over. We have not heard a sermon from the Buddha in a long while. We would like to see him."

The monk Anaṅda led the monks to the forest. Reluctant to descend on the Buddha with so many, especially since the Buddha had spent the Rainy Season entirely by himself, he left the others on the outskirts of the forest and went alone to meet the Buddha. The elephant Pāralīya, seeing the monk Anañda approach thought, "This is an enemy." Snatching up a stick in his trunk, he rushed to beat him. The Buddha saw him and said, "O Pāraleyya, this man is my chief attendant. When the elephant Nāḷāgiri was sent by Devidat and came trumpeting to kill me, this man rushed out in front of me. Again in the *Swarṇa Karṭaka Jātaka*[15] this man, born as a golden crab, captured the crow who had come to pluck out my eyes and forced the snake, who had come to support the crow, to suck out, with his own mouth, the venom he had injected. He freed me of the poison and then killed the crow and snake so they would no longer harm me. He has been of great help to me in many former births. Do not stop him from coming here." The elephant then threw away the stick and offered to carry the monk's bowl and robes. The monk refused to give it, not because he was annoyed with the elephant for having rushed up with a stick to kill him, but because it was not correct that he should give it in the presence of the Buddha.

The elephant thought to himself, "He refuses to let me take the robes and bowl, I only hope he doesn't impolitely place them on a rock above the Buddha's head." The Senior monk Anañda, who knew much better than the elephant how to attend on a Buddha—since he had acquired that experience over eons of past lives — placed his own bowl and robes on the ground. Anyone who knew the rules and practices would not put his belongings on the chairs or the bed in which a teacher sleeps. Thus, the Senior monk Anañda put his robe and bowl away, greeted the Buddha, and stood respectfully to one side.

Though the Buddha knew he had not come alone, he asked him, "Are you alone?"

"Five hundred monks have accompanied me. Not knowing your intentions, I have left them on the outskirts of the forest," he replied.

"If so, bring them here," the Buddha said. At his command, the Senior Monk led them in. The Buddha talked to them.

The monks said, "Master, you are delicate, not used to such hardship. How did you live these past three months all alone? Not even the monk Anañda accompanied you, so who could have strained the water for you? You must have been seriously inconvenienced."

The Buddha answered, "Monks, do not think so. This elephant Pāraleyya attended to my needs, performing all the customary tasks without any shortcomings. It is blessed to live with one like him and to be the recipient of such attentions. If one finds such a companion, it is good to live with him. If not, one should live alone, like a king who abandons his kingdom, retires to the forest, and does not divulge the fact of his royalty." Thus, the Buddha advised them.

Just as men, who go without water for two or three months and are consumed by thirst, yet when they finally find water sip it very very slowly, so these five hundred monks, who for three months had longed to hear a sermon from the Buddha himself, now let the water of the Doctrine pour into the thousand containers of their ears and savored it with the mouths of their minds. They slaked the thirst of Defilements with the waters of the Teachings and attained *nirvāṇa.*

Since the messages sent by the nobleman Anāthapiṇḍika,[16] Viśākhā, and others had to do with hearing the Teachings, the Senior Monk Anaṅda said, "Master, the nobleman Anāthapiṇḍika and about five *crores* of other devotees, wait eagerly to see you. Since they are already firmly set on the Path of Attainments, they wish to attain *nirvāna."*

The Buddha knew that, like sticks that can be straightened only when they are heated by fire, the monks of Kosaṁbā were now united. He said, "If so, take up my bowl and robes." He got the Senior Monk Anaṅda to bring his bowl and robe. Just as in a past life, the Buddha, as the elephant Chaddanta, had himself attended on a *Pasē* Buddha, so in turn, he had enjoyed the attentions of the elephant Pāralīya. He now made ready to leave.

The elephant watched him as he prepared to go; and went and stood in front of him. The animal obstructed the path of the Buddha as if he were blocking his own path across the river of *nirvāṇa* in this very birth.

The five hundred monks said, "This majestic elephant obstructs the path of our majestic Lord, the Buddha. What is he doing?"

"Listen monks, he acts so for no other reason but that, having rendered services to me for the past three months, he now wants to render service to all of you, too. The merit he gains for the services he renders you are much greater[17] than what he gains from that which he has done for me. For you are the *Saṅgha,* the monastic Order. If we leave without staying here today, the delight that now suffuses his mind will be lessened. If the delight is less, its consequences are diminished. Whatever it is, we must not let that happen. He does not deserve to be shortchanged."

Even though the Buddha's compassionate thoughts toward[18] the elephant Nāḷāgiri, who had come charging to kill him, were the same as for this one, yet it was as if he had a special personal feeling for this elephant. In order that a creature so good could, at least in another life, attain to the blessings of Spiritual Attainments, the Buddha remained there with his monks. He did so not so much in consideration of the gift of alms he was about to receive, but out of respect for the elephant's goodness.

The next day, the elephant plunged into the forest and brought mangoes, *jambu* fruits, bananas, two kinds of ripe *jak* and other fruits, made a great heap of them, and offered them to the monks. The five hundred monks partook of them. Though they had successfully put an end to their Defilements, they were not as successful in consuming the supply of food that had been put before them. However, they finished their repast as best they could and led the Buddha out of the forest.

The elephant again threaded his way through the host of monks, up to the front, and stood blocking the road. Seeing him do what he had done before, the monks reported back to the Buddha.

The Buddha said, "He wants to send you all away and wishes to have me remain behind, alone."

Then he said to the elephant, "Listen O Pāraleyya. I must make this journey back. Even if I were to stay, you would not be able to achieve the Trance States of this world or the other-worldly benefits of the Path and the Fruits. You are not yet equipped for them. Thus, you must remain behind."

That majestic elephant heard him, rolled up his trunk in his mouth, and weeping and lamenting, followed him. Had the Buddha stayed, he would have served him to the end of his life. The Buddha walked with him to the outskirts of the village and then said to the elephant, "Beyond this point are the habitations of men, you must not follow me farther. Stay here." The elephant stood still, watching, and when the Buddha passed out of his sight, consumed by grief, he died. He was reborn in the Tavtisā heaven in a golden abode one hundred and twenty leagues high, attended by one thousand divine maidens, and was known as the god Pāraleyya. Just as he had offered heaps of fruits, more than could be consumed, so he enjoyed numberless kinds of heavenly pleasures.

The Buddha attended by his retinue of monks, arrived at the Devramvehera monastery. The monks of Kosaṁbä heard that the Buddha had come to Devramvehera and, inspired by a faith born of remorse, they went to beg his forgiveness.

The King of Kosol, hearing that the monks were arriving, went to the Buddha and said, "Lord, I will not permit those sinful monks to enter any region under my command."

The Buddha replied, "Oh King, their quarrel was serious.

For it is said:

> Kuddho atthaṃ na jānāti—kuddho dhammaṃ na passati
> Andhaṃ tamaṃ tadā hoti—yaṃ kodho sahate naraṃ.*

*An angry man knows not what is good, sees not what is right,
When anger is pervasive the result is blinding darkness.

They did not give due consideration to the facts of the case, or listen to my advice, but they are good men. They should not be abandoned on account of this one fault. They have now forgiven each other and have come to beg forgiveness from me, too. Do not stop them."

The nobleman Anēpiḍu said, "These are monks who, instead of walking the path of Discipline and righteousness, forced the Buddha to take to the forest, as if the forest paths they regularly walked were not enough. I will not allow such monks to enter the premises of my monastery." But he restrained himself because of the Buddha's appeals.

Since these monks had been divided in their opinions during their quarrel, the Buddha instructed that they be given separate sleeping areas. The other monks neither sat with them nor stood beside them. Visitors to the monastery would inquire of the Buddha, "Where are those monks from Kosaṁbä who quarreled?"

"They are those seated together in that corner," he would reply.

"Is it that fellow over there? Is it this fellow over here?" they inquired as if poking a finger in their eyes. The monks were even more ashamed. They went to the Buddha, worshipped him, and asked forgiveness.

The Buddha said, "Listen, monks. If a person is unaware of the ill effects of conflicts, it is because he thinks only of his own quarrel. Just as they abandon their observances and no longer practice meditation on the subject of death, so they tend to forget that we are all headed for death; that, however long we live, death is the end. A wise man on the other hand who knows what is good and bad, would say, 'This quarrel is painful while it lasts, but its consequences are equally painful.' In the city of Kiṁbulvatpura, about one hundred and sixty thousand kings fought over a dispute about water; they turned an entire river into blood. If they were made to think 'This is something one should never do, for any reason,' or if by some means the quarrel could be quelled, then such means should be used. If one acts in this manner, then all quarrels will end, just as this particular quarrel, which even I could not stop, has now ceased."

They heard the sermon, and those, who already had the proper requisites, climbed the ship of the Path and the Fruits and sailed across the sea of *saṃsāra* to the port of *nirvāṇa*.

Good men should know that quarrels are not the product of good thoughts and should be aware of their bad consequences. Instead of sensing the existence of a pit at night and then jumping into it in broad daylight, one should engage only in good deeds and purify the mind.

Endnotes

THE MONKS OF THE CITY OF KOSAMBÄ

Illustrates stanza 6 of the Yamaka Vagga

Pare ca na vijānanti . . . sammanti medhaga

Others do not know that we come to an end here
Those who know it have their quarrels calmed.

1. Since I can remedy it by admitting it to my fellows, . . .

According to the rules of the Order, monks could confess their faults to each other and be absolved. This is different from the Christian forgiveness of sin by God and had to do mainly with minor transgressions of the elaborate Rules of Conduct a monk had to observe.

2. That is, those who had not reached any one of the four stages of the Path to *nirvāṇa.*

3. The Buddha, therefore, instructed that they should perform . . .

Note the extremely practical measures suggested for preventing arguments, quarrels, and confrontations in the course of daily interaction.

4. *Laṭukika Jātaka* story,

It is the story of a quail and how she brought about the destruction of an elephant that had killed her young ones. The point of the stanza that follows seems to be that hatred, resulting from a quarrel, can generate enormous destructive power.

5. *Vaṭṭaka Jātaka* story,

The E. B. Cowell edition gives two versions of the *Vaṭṭaka Jātaka* but neither refer to this particular incident. *Vaṭṭaka Jātaka* referred to here is, however, well-known in the Sinhala tradition. It appears in the Jātaka Collection as the *Sammōdamāna Jātaka* and is about a flock of birds caught in a net who finally escape only when they are all united and fly away together with the net.

6. He who sows *Amu* seeds will reap *Amu* grain, . . .

The simple image with which he briefly sums up the content of the verse is in sharp contrast to the elaborate paraphrases of some of the other stanzas.

7. *Dīghiti Kōsala Jātaka* story,

A prince spares the life of the king who had slain his father and thereby wins him to repentance.

8. Prince Dīghāyu . . .

The text does not give the meaning of the name but I have included it because its meaning would be readily picked up by Sinhala readers. Dīghāyu is long-lived because he accepted good advice and did not go to war with his enemy.

9. . . . the Buddha took up his robe and bowl himself . . .

Under normal circumstances one of his disciples would carry his robes and bowl if he were leaving on a journey.

10. . . . , accepting only the services of the elephant Pāralīya, . . .

Sri Lankans traditionally took their names from the village or region from which they came. Here the elephant is given the name of the forest in which he lives. The SR text refers to both the forest and the elephant as Pāralīya. However, whenever the Buddha addresses the elephant he calls him, perhaps affectionately, 'O Pāraleyya.' I have kept the distinction.

11. We shall no longer give these monks either rice or water.

Withdrawal of lay support for monks or monasteries that did not keep the *vinaya* rules was one way of exercising control and enforcing the monastic rules of Discipline. Even today in Sri Lankan villages, laymen show their displeasure about the conduct of a monk who breaks one of the major *vinaya* rules by not giving alms and not worshipping at his temple. In the old days, since monks were dependent solely on the laity for their food, this was a serious restriction and therefore proved an effective check. It is not so now since monasteries and monks have become independently wealthy.

12. . . . Pāralīya, fetched drinking water for the Buddha . . .

It was the period of *vas,* so the Buddha was in effect, 'in residence' in the forest, but without lay support. Hence, the significance of the elephant's services.

13. He carried the waterpot in his trunk.

It is interesting that while all the actions performed by the elephant seem to be fancifully human, anyone familiar with elephants would find them perfectly plausible because they are all acts that an elephant could perform. The passage suggests a firsthand observation and knowledge of the ways of elephants. It occurs in both the DA and the SR texts, and very likely came from the original Sinhala source. Then as now, elephants, whether tamed or in the wild, were very much part of the Sri Lankan landscape. Thus, the description rings true and very different from the merely fanciful accounts found in western stories such as *Babar the Elephant*. So it is with the monkey.

All the services the elephant renders the Buddha are the formal courtesies that a disciple monk would perform for his teacher. Such formalities are still observed in the *Saṅgha*.

14. The traditional name for India used in the Buddhist texts.

15. *Swarṇa Karṭaka Jātaka* (The gold-clawed One)

The story is about the Bōdhisatva born as a farmer. He is attacked by a snake in league with a crow who wishes to pluck out the farmer's eyes. A crab with whom he had struck a friendship "Crushed both their heads like lotus buds with his claws and took the life from them" thereby saving the Bōdhisatva's life.

16. Since the messages sent by the nobleman Anāthapinḍika, . . .

Note that sometimes he is referred to in the text in the Sinhala form Anēpiḍu and at other times in the Pāli textual form as Anāthapinḍika. Perhaps when the monk Dharmasēna was translating closely from his text the Pāli form slipped in.

17. The merit he gains for the services he renders you are much greater . . .

The Buddha's statement seems to imply the characteristically modest claim that the *Saṇgha* as a collective group of monks is a more important and a more effective source for merit than the Buddha himself, who though their leader and the founder of the Order, is but a single individual.

18. Even though the Buddha's compassionate thoughts toward . . .

An interesting distinction is being made here. The Buddha's feelings of compassion, according to the Doctrine, are the same for all creatures whether it be the elephant Nāḷāgiri, who comes to hurt him, or the elephant Pāralīya, who renders him service. It is as if the author, however, while granting the Doctrinal position, cannot help making a special claim for the elephant Pāralīya and his deep affection for the Buddha.

The Monk Mahākāḷa (Great Kāla)

Moreover, when a person cultivates Liberation through practices such as the suppressing of a sinful thought with a corresponding positive one, he accumulates the wealth of Moral Conduct and Contemplation, just like earning a livelihood from agriculture and trade. If, however, he does not learn how to protect that wealth, or knowing it carelessly fails to protect it, then such a person will come to harm.

On the other hand, if a person knows how to protect such wealth but in spite of it keeps open the Sense-doors such as sight, then, while he wanders in the forest of Sense Objects, robbers of Defilements will enter and steal from the city of his mind the wealth he has acquired. One should therefore close the entranceway of the six faculties with the door of Mindfulness, and lock it with the bolt of Wisdom. A man stands to benefit from such action.

Besides, a person may deck himself in the ornaments of Moral Conduct and Concentration, but it would not be fitting unless he also wears the golden necklace of the True Doctrine. In case a person does wish to adorn himself in those Doctrinal ornaments, then for his benefit, we will string this jewel,[1] the story of the monk Mahākāḷa, on the golden thread of our story collection.

In Daṁbadiva, in the city of Setavya, there lived three wealthy men who were brothers. The eldest was Mahākāḷa (which means Kāḷa the Great), the second was Majjimakāḷa (which means Middle Kāḷa), and the youngest was Cullakāḷa (which means Little Kāḷa). The oldest brother often went on trading trips, taking the youngest with him, and leaving the middle brother behind in the city. What they bought was then traded by the middle brother.

On one occasion, the two brothers left on a trading trip with five hundred carts loaded with all manner of goods. They arrived at the city of Sävät. Since that city was heavily populated, the goods they brought sold quickly; they did not need to travel any further. They stopped their carts midway between Sävät and the Devramvehera monastery.

The older brother Mahākāḷa noticed many people going by at evening, all decked out and carrying perfumes and flowers.[2] Since he lived in the outer regions, he did not know what this was about and asked, "Where are all these people going?" He was told they were going to the monastery to hear sermons. Mahākāḷa had already performed ample merit and had good intentions, so he decided, "I will go, too." He called his younger brother and said, "Brother, see that the carts are well protected. I am going with these people to hear a sermon." He went, worshipped the Buddha, and because he was a newcomer, did not sit in front but at the rear of the crowd.

On that occasion, the Buddha recited the *Dukkha-Khanda* stanzas, preached of the evil consequences of worldly wealth,[3] the need to avoid attachment to gold, silver, pearls, gems, and other goods, and the importance of fixing one's desires on the goods of the Doctrine.

When a sick man goes to a good doctor for a cure and is told such and such things are bad for his ailment and that such and such things are good, he follows the advice however hard the regimen recommended may be, and learns to avoid wanting what is bad for him. Similarly, the devotee Mahākāḷa decided that only if he joined the Order and observed the monastic rules could he rid himself of the disease of Defilements and savor the honey of *nirvāṇa*. He thought, "I, too, will become a monk." Thus, when everyone had paid their respects and left, he went to the Buddha and asked to be ordained.

"Don't you have any kinsmen whom you should inform of your intention to join the Order?" the Buddha asked. "A younger brother," was the reply. Mahākāḷa was asked to inform him at least.

He then went to his brother and said, "Brother, all my wealth is yours. Enjoy it."

"What about you then?" asked the brother. Mahākāḷa said that he planned to join the Order of Monks. The brother raised several objections. But as a great river flows inevitably towards the sea, so Mahākāḷa's thoughts were bent on ordination. The brother therefore did not stop him but agreed saying, "Good! So be it."

The devotee Mahākāḷa obtained his brother's consent, went to the Buddha, and received ordination. Cullakāḷa thought to himself, "If I were to join the Order with my brother, be with him, and talk to him, I might persuade him to change his mind, which right now seems bent on ordination. Then, together we could revert to the lay life." In any case, irrespective of whether his brother remained a monk or not, Cullakāḷa resolved he would give up the robes after a time. Thus he, too, became a monk, thinking of it mainly as a means to preserve their wealth.

The novice Mahākāḷa soon obtained the higher ordination and went to the Buddha to find out what kinds of duties and practices a member of the Order had to perform. He was told they were of two kinds; the Practice of Scholarship and the Practice of Contemplation.

Mahākāḷa said, "Master, I took to the robes as an older man. It is hard for me to acquire learning and scholarship. That comes more easily to younger men. I shall undertake the Practice of Contemplation." So saying he undertook the sixteen practices of Cemetery Meditations.[4] He learned from the Buddha the observances, injunctions, divisions, and benefits of the practice of Contemplation leading to Enlightenment.

From then on, ten hours after the first watch, at midnight, when everyone was asleep, the monk, Mahākāḷa would go to the cemetery to look for an unpleasant object for contemplation. He would return at dawn before anyone was awake.

At this time, a female cemetery attendant named "Kāḷī" was in charge of the cremations. When she arrived at the cemetery where the monk came for his meditation, she noticed that the ground where the monk had sat meditating and the place where he had walked up and down was denuded of undergrowth. "Who comes here?" she wondered. "I will keep a close watch." However, though she meticulously observed everything, she could discover nothing, for the monk came only at midnight. One day, determind to find the cause, she lit a lamp inside the shelter built for occasional use and accompanied by her sons and daughters hid herself in the cemetery.

On that day, too, the monk arrived at the usual time. She saw him, greeted him and asked, "Your Reverence, is it you who live here?

"Yes, lay devotee," the monk Mahākāḷa answered.

"Master, a cemetery is in many ways a dangerous place. There are special observances one should know when one lives in such a place."

The monk did not say, "Who are you to teach me the observances?" He had himself not learned the Rules of Discipline or the Doctrinal Teaching, so what should he do? It is said:

Tadahu pabbajito santo—jātiyā sattavassiko
So pi maṃ anusāseyya—sampaticchāmi muddhanā*

He recited that stanza to her.

She heard him and replied, "Your Reverence, you are living now in a cemetery.[5] You must inform the cemetery keepers of it, and the chief of the group of monks, and the head of the village in which the cemetery is located."

Instead of saying, "Good I will do so" the monk asked, "Why is it necessary to report the matter to all these people?"

She replied, "Your Reverence, rogues who steal a treasure, when they are chased by the owner, often throw the stuff into a cemetery and run away, perhaps so as to blame it on those who work here. The owners, when they see their possessions lying about in the cemetery and see you moving about inside, may harass you. But if one has already informed the various officials concerned, they will say, 'This monk has been living here since such and such a day, even though you may not see any sign of his presence today. Therefore, there is no need to sus-

*If he be only seven years old, but is an ordained monk
Let him admonish me. I accept it with all my heart.

pect him.' That will put an end to any suspicions. You must, therefore, inform those three categories of persons. Besides it will in no way hinder the practice of your Meditation."

"Let me find out if there is more to this business of permission," thought the monk. He asked, "What else should I do?"

"Your Reverence, while you live in this cemetery you should not eat meats, fish, flour cakes, sesame sweets, and other such foods that attract demons. You should not sleep during the day and you should not be lazy. You should avoid deceit and trickery. Your thoughts should be pure. When you come to the cemetery, do so after everyone is asleep. When you go back to the monastery, do so before people awake.

"Your Reverence, a donkey, whether he sleeps on a garbage heap, at the edge of a street, at a crossing of three roads, at the entrance to a village, or on a heap of chaff, merely happens to sleep there. He does not live there for any length of time. So like him, you, too, whether you sleep on a mattress of grass, on leaves, on a pallet of sticks, or you spread out your animal skin, do not sleep too much, merely rest your body awhile. If you end this journey through *saṃsāra* and become Enlightened,[6] then when you die your body will be placed in a golden pavilion, covered with a carpet, and cremated in great splendor. But if you do not achieve Enlightenment, your body will be put on a heap of logs, covered over with wood, and burned without ceremony as they do for the poor. As it burns, the corpse will be poked with iron prods, taken off the pyre, cut up into pieces with an axe, and burned in bits and pieces." Thus, she advised him about matters that the Buddha had not instructed him in, even though he had taught him meditation.

As Tēmīya Bōsat, in the *Mugapakha Jātaka* story,[7] accepted the advice of the goddess, abandoned all desires for pleasure, and was strengthened in his desire to become a monk and attain *nirvāṇa,* so in order to overcome the enemy of Defilements and arrive at the land of *nirvāṇa,* the monk Mahākāḷa engaged even more intensely in the war of *Dhutāṅgas* or severe ascetic penances.

Then he told the cemetery keeper, "Let me know when you come across an object fit for contemplation, that arouses repugnance." He said this to the lay devotee, who though her name was Kāḷī, which means the Dark One, was by no means dark in her ideas.

From that point on, as chickens forage for food[8] all day and only curl up at dusk, at the end of the day, the monk Mahākāḷa swept the yard early, collected water, bathed, cleaned and cooled his body, worshiped at the Bo tree, paid his respects to the senior monks, sat, walked, and spent the night in meditation.

As chickens at daybreak step down from their roost, so in the morning, he dressed, completed his worship, and until it was time to set out to beg for food, went to a place free of crowds and again engaged in meditation. When it was time to go begging, he gathered enough food just to survive. Again, as chickens scratch the ground with their feet, examine everything, and only then eat what they find, he, too, in order to be free of any obligation to the giver, ate with the awareness that the food was not intended for pleasure but for sustenance. As chickens cannot see at night even though they have eyes, so he felt no attraction for objects that were attractive and suffered no sense of deprivation with regard to them. Though he had eyes he was as if blind. Similarly, pleasing sounds that fell on his ears did not attract him, nor did he feel displeasure at jarring noises. Though he had ears he was as if deaf. He did not feel the difference between sweet scents and stinking smells that affect the nose, or the bitter taste that registers on the tongue, or the comforts or discomforts that register on the body, or good and bad sensations of the mind. He was like a person without a nose, tongue, body, or mind.

As chickens, even if shooed away, invariably return to their former roosting place, so while sewing his robes, or engaging in new activities, or performing rituals or other obligating practices, he did not abandon his meditation, but lived continuously heedful and aware.

The monk Cullakāḷa, by contrast, constantly recalled the pleasures of his past life, his wife, and his children. "What is our brother doing without enjoying his vast wealth?" he asked himself. As if living in the same village but engaging in two very different kinds of business, though brothers, the younger lived in a state of great distraction.

Not long thereafter, a young noblewoman died after a brief illness. Her kinsmen brought her for cremation, instructed the cemetery keeper Kāḷī to attend to the matter, and left. When Kāḷī removed the cloth covering the face of the corpse and saw the golden form — the woman looked as if still alive — she thought, "It would be good to show this body to the monk."

She went to the monk, worshipped him, and said, "A corpse has been brought for cremation. Though it is ugly because it is dead,[9] your contemplation of it is not ugly, and though it will rot if not cremated, how you perceive it is not rotten. However, though this corpse is now mindless, it can evoke serenity of mind in you. Though it is devoid of thought, will soon reach a state of putrefaction, and is of the opposite sex to you — but the same sex as me — it would be good for you to contemplate this unpleasant object."

The monk went to the cemetery, removed the face covering, looked the body over from the soles of the feet to the head and said, "This corpse has still not reached the stage of swelling. There is no way to use it for Contemplation. Therefore, set fire to the corpse and inform me when it is burning. He then returned to the monastery.

The lay devotee did as instructed, set the corpse alight, then informed the monk. The monk arrived and sat contemplating it. The parts of the body that the flames licked, whitened like the white markings on cattle. The legs burned and began to hang down. The arms burned and curled up. The skin of the forehead was scorched. The monk sat contemplating it all.

"How beautiful was this form when I first saw it. Now, it is very different. Such is the nature of existence," he thought. He made this the object of his meditation and developed Insight. He thus made a dam of Contemplation across the river of Desire that swells and roars down into the sea of *saṃsāra*. He channeled the ocean of *saṃsāra* filled with the waters of Defilements into the giant mouth of the whirlpool of Knowledge,[10] which is the Path to Enlightenment. Thus, he emptied the ocean of *saṃsāra* and crossed over to the land of *nirvāṇa* and there enjoyed the tax wealth of the country of Enlightenment.[11]

Like a parent, who postpones a journey because of the pressing needs of a child, and when the matter is taken care of, then proceeds, taking the child along, so the Buddha remained until the monk Mahākāḷa achieved full Enlightenment, together with the fourfold powers of Analytical Knowledge. Then, attended by him and other monks he went to the city of Setavya and resided in the Hinsalu forest.

The former wives of Cullakāḷa heard that the Buddha had arrived and said, "The man who was formerly our husband must surely have come with the Buddha. Once he is here we will make him stay." In order to get him to come, they sent an invitation to the Buddha. As this was a household that the Buddha had not visited before, a monk had to go ahead to make the necessary arrangements.

A central seat had to be set up for the Buddha with one on the right for the Senior Monk Säriyut and on the left for the Senior Monk Mugalan. From that point, seating had to be arranged on both sides for all the other monks. The Senior Monk Mahākāḷa, while putting on his robes, said to his younger brother, "Go ahead and arrange the seating for us."

The moment the monk arrived there, the inmates of the house, perhaps knowing that his convictions were not all that strong, placed very low seats at the front and high seats at the rear.

"Don't do that. Place the high seats at the front and the low ones at the rear," said the monk Cullakāḷa. At that his former wives said, "What do you think you are doing? Are the seating arrangements that we set up not good enough? Who gave you permission to take on the robes? Why did you leave? And anyway, why have you now come back?" They snatched away his robes,[12] decked him in white clothes, placed a wreath of flowers on his head, and then said, "Since you came to make the seating arrangements, now take our message to the Buddha and conduct him here. We shall arrange the seating." He was the kind of person who went along with whatever requests were made and so he did as they bid him. He had not been in robes for very long so he was quite unashamed and went in that garb to the Buddha,[13] as if to indicate the change in his life. He invited the Buddha, and his retinue of monks, and arrived with them at the house.

They arrived and sat down to their meal. At the end of the meal, the former wives of Mahākāḷa thought, "These women made Cullakāḷa give up his robes and return home. We will make Mahākāḷa give up his robes and return home, too." They sent an invitation to the Buddha that food would be prepared at their home on the following day.

However another monk was sent to make the seating arrangements so they did not get a chance to accost the Senior Monk Mahākāḷa. Now Cullakāḷa had two wives. Majjimakāḷa had four wives, the same number as the number of hells. The monk Mahākāḷa had eight wives, the same number as that of the Eightfold Path to Enlightenment, which he had already attained.

When the Buddha arrived, they seated him and his retinue of monks and offered them food. Those who wished to eat outside, arose, and went outside. Those who wished to eat seated, sat inside and ate. The Buddha partook of his meal seated inside. At the end of the meal, the former wives of Mahākāḷa said, "Master, let the Senior Monk Mahākāḷa stay behind and preach the thanksgiving sermon to us. He can return later when the sermon is over. You should go on ahead." The Buddha knew there was nothing any of them could do, so he agreed and left.

When he reached the village gate the monks wondered, "Has the Buddha acted in this manner knowingly or unwittingly?[14] Yesterday Cullakāḷa went ahead to his house and his vows of celibacy were undermined. Today, because another monk had gone to make the arrangements, the monk Mahākāḷa had been saved from a similar fate. He is a holy man, disciplined, and restrained but what might they not do to him now?" So they wondered.

The Buddha heard their comments and asked, "What is it that you say?"

When they told him he replied, "O Monks, do you think that the Senior Monk Mahākāḷa is lacking in strength, like Cullakāḷa?"

"Yes, Master" they replied. "Cullakāḷa had just two wives, and they succeeded in keeping him back. This monk has eight former wives. How can he escape them? We are sure they will ensnare him and keep him back."

The Buddha replied to the monks who spoke thus, "O monks, don't say that ever again. Cullakāḷa, who had no understanding of the True

Doctrine, lived like a man who, when he sees a certain female form, is captivated and believes that feminine form the ultimate in beauty. He thinks the limbs beautiful, the feet beautiful, the fingers and nails, the slender waist, the hips, the belly, the eyes and ears, the mouth and face, all very beautiful. He allows no unpleasant thoughts to intrude. He did not close his mind-door. Instead he allowed the enemy Defilements free play. He knew no limits when begging and accepting food, was lazy in fulfilling his religious obligations, and made little sustained effort. He lived his life with a mind that constantly faltered in its allegiance to the *sāsana*. As a strong wind blows down a tree that stands at the end of an earth dam, men such as he fall from the *sāsana*.

"By contrast, the Senior Monk Mahākāḷa does not allow the enemy Defilements to get any opportunity to enter. He cultivates feelings of repugnance so as not to be attracted to the thirty-two Impurities, such as hair, which decay. He closes the entrance way of his mind with the door panes of the six senses and stops enemy Defilements from entering. He is moderate in food, cultivates devotion in the pursuit of the Path, develops his energies with effort, sets himself in the four pure disciplines and lives in this manner. Just as a strong wind can do nothing to shift an enormous rock, so no one can do anything to this monk."

Like the two wives who had made fun of Cullakāḷa the previous day, the eight former wives of Mahākāḷa surrounded him and thought that he, too, would succumb to them. As female jackals try to entice a lion king by making jackal noises, so they said many things. But because of the psychic powers Mahākāḷa had obtained at Enlightenment, the monk realized the true nature of these women and rose from his seat. He split apart the center of the roof, rose up through the air, and went to where the Buddha was, as if to prove the truth of what the Buddha had just said.

At the end of the sermon, the monks, who when returning from the meal had questioned, "Did the Buddha knowingly act this way?" and had been full of doubts, now were convinced. They rid themselves of the Defilement of Doubt and arrived at the various stages of Enlightenment, such as a Stream-Enterer.

Thus wise, good men, should not seek after Impurities like Cullakāḷa, but shed them like the Senior Monk Mahākāḷa. They should indulge in the threefold Virtuous Practices performed through body, word, and mind, and should each according to his disposition, reach one of the three states of Enlightenment.[15]

Endnotes

THE MONK MAHĀKĀḶA

Illustrates stanzas 7 and 8 of the *Yamaka Vagga.*

Subhānupassiṃ viharantaṃ . . . va dubbalaṃ
Asubhānupassiṃ viharantaṃ . . . va pabbataṃ

As the wind fells a weak tree so Māra overcomes
one who lives only for pleasure, with senses unrestrained,
immoderate in food, indolent and inert.
As the wind cannot move a rocky mountain, so Māra cannot overcome
one who lives meditating on Defilements, with senses restrained,
moderate in food, full of faith and resolute.

This story begins with a homily conveyed in an elaborately developed metaphor. Note that the images all have to do with trade, the acquisition of wealth, its protection, and possible loss. Thus, it is a fitting preamble to a story about merchants who earn their livelihood engaged in such activities. The images thus carry a considerable charge. The DA version by contrast has no such prefatory commentarial material.

1. . . . we will string this jewel, . . .

The writer is making an elaborate play on the title of the story collection, the *Saddharmaratnāvaliya* or Jewel Garland of the True Doctrine. Each story is a Jewel linked together by the golden string of the story collection, illustrating virtues that are the true wealth that one should accumulate in life and with which one should adorn oneself.

2. . . . , all decked out and carrying perfumes and flowers.

The scene is no different from what happens in Sri Lankan villages even today, where going to the temple to hear a sermon is as much a festive social occasion as it is a religious one.

3. . . . , preached on the evil consequences of worldly wealth, . . .

The Buddha's sermon, as always, is directed to the particular listener, in this case, the merchant Mahākāḷa. However, where the DA merely states: "The Teacher preached the Law in orderly sequence with reference to Mahākāḷa's disposition of mind," the SR spells it out using themes and images that deal with worldly wealth, goods, gold, and silver.

4. These are meditations on the impermanence of life undertaken in a cemetery while contemplating objects of death and decay.

5. . . . "Your Reverence, you are living now in a cemetery.

It is the cemetery keeper who, with due respect, admonishes the monk on what he should do when within "her" territory. She is not awed or put off by his quoting of the text. Instead she confidently instructs him on what he should eat and drink and how he should act, and even discourses on points of meditative practice and Moral Conduct. Her instructions are extremely practical both in terms of his functioning in the everyday world as well as in terms of his religious objectives. Although the monk quotes a stanza that establishes his superiority as a monk, there is an ironical reversal here. He refrains from saying "Who are you to teach me the observances?" because he realizes that he has not studied the Rules of the Vinaya. He finally accepts her advice "about matters that the Buddha had not instructed him."

This can be considered a commentary on the position of women in a Buddhist society. Here, a Senior Monk is admonished by a woman of the lower class, a cemetery keeper (in Brahmanical terms one of the most polluted), on matters of conduct and meditative practice. It is considered neither presumptious nor offensive. Interestingly the DA version is even less ambivalent in the readiness with which the advice is accepted. The DA text simply states: "The Elder did not say, 'Do you think I shall observe any rules of your telling?' Instead he said, 'What ought I to do lay sister?' " Shortly after he asks again, "Is there anything else I ought to do?" She gives him more instruction. There is no "qualifying" stanza about the status of a seven year old monk as in the SR text.

A comparison of the two texts make it tempting to speculate that sex differences were less important in early Buddhism. A senior monk can willingly accept the advice of a cemetery keeper, a professional in her own right. Society in Sri Lanka had clearly changed sufficiently by the thirteenth century, perhaps due to strong Hindu influences after the tenth century, to make the author of the SR qualify the story with the addition of the stanza about the higher status of monks. Hence, the subtle tension here between the world view of the author and the values implicit in the story.

Note also the subsequent comment that though her name was Kāḷī, which meant the Dark One, she was indeed enlightened (not dark) in her ideas.

6. If you end this journey through *saṃsāra* and become Enlightened, . . .

Being an expert on cemetery procedures, she tells the monk about the two possible kinds of last rites he would have. If he achieves his goal of Enlightenment, he will be cremated with great pomp and ceremony. If not, his body will be unceremoniously burned as they do for the poor.

E. W. Burlingame's translation of the DA is very confusing at this point. In it Kāḷī tells the monk, "In case, Reverend Sir, while you reside in the burning ground you succeed in achieving the goal of the Religious Life, *and they bring a dead body here and cast it away* (italics added), I will place it on the funeral pyre and rendering the usual honors . . . I will perform the funeral rites over the body. If you do not succeed, I will light the pyre, drag the body along with a stake, throw it outside, chop it to pieces with an axe, . . . and burn it." The SR version makes it quite clear that she is talking about what would happen to him, the monk Mahākāḷa, were he to die without achieving Enlightenment. The comment must thus be read as a continuation of her "sermon" to the monk on how to assiduously perform his meditative practices. Thus, the SR helps clarify possible scribal errors or distortions of meaning found in the earlier text or its English translation.

7. *Mugapakha Jātaka* story.

The Bōdhisatva born as a prince is alarmed at the prospect of becoming king and having to commit acts that could lead to hell. A goddess, who in a former birth had been his mother, advises him to behave as if he were deaf, mute, a cripple, and unintelligent in order to escape his fate. At last, as he is about to be buried, he opens his mouth and discourses on religion to his charioteer. He then becomes an ascetic and is followed by his father.

8. From that point on, as chickens forage for food . . .

The elaborately developed "chicken" imagery reveals both the author's excellent powers of observation of animal activities (seen also with the story of the elephant Pāralīya) as well as his ability to use these simple homely observations to describe religious practices and abstract Doctrinal teachings.

9. Though it is ugly because it is dead, . . .

Another indication that the cemetery attendant is herself well-versed in the Doctrine (perhaps by having been around meditating monks who seek out cemeteries) and knows what she is talking about.

10. . . . of the whirlpool of Knowledge, . . .

The reference here is to the *vadabha mukha*, a giant whirlpool in the middle of the ocean, which is able to suck all the waters of the ocean into it.

11. . . . there enjoyed the tax wealth of the country of Enlightenment.

Over and over again in this story the images are from the world of commerce and deal with trade, money, taxes, and so forth. They reveal the author's knowledge of subjects outside the bounds of doctrinal philosophy and tend to confirm that the author was a scholar-teacher monk, a *granthadhura*, who associated closely with laymen and was familiar with their affairs.

12. They snatched away his robes, . . .

These are not subservient long-suffering women as are generally pictured in Hindu literature. In fact both the female cemetery attendant and the wives show considerable independence of spirit and confidence in their interaction with men.

On the other hand, sensual pleasures, sexual or any other, are considered "Defilements" that undermine the ascetic life of monks. To the extent that Cullakāḷa's wives represent the sensual distractions of lay life, that finally "seduce" Cullakāḷa to give up robes, they are seen negatively. But this is not necessarily a negative comment on the sex. The case of the cemetery attendant in the same story is an example of the opposite.

By contrast, the authorial comments on women that are interpolated into this and other medieval Buddhist texts *are* negative remarks on the female sex. One is continuously struck by the considerable discrepancy or lack of fit between the Buddhist clerical view of women as being inherently evil and the positive image of many female characters in the stories themselves.

13. . . . went in that garb to the Buddha, . . .

When Cullakāḷa arrives unashamedly in his "lay outfit" to invite the Buddha, there is not the slightest criticism of his action. The Buddha simply accepts the invitation. Leaving the order was purely a personal matter; a monk was free to do so at any time.

14. . . . "Has the Buddha acted in this manner knowingly or unwittingly?"

The disciples' doubts are always aired, taken up by the Buddha and used as an occasion for teaching.

15. . . . reach one of the three states of Enlightenment.

One can reach Enlightenment as a Buddha, a *Pasē* (p. Paccēka) Buddha, or as a *arahat*.

Wearing the Ochre Robe

If a person whose mind is naturally untainted at conception and therefore pure, allows that pure mind to be tainted with impurities such as lust, then he is not worthy to wear the monk's ochre robe. A jackal cannot fit into a lion-skin. To illustrate this, we shall relate the story of "Wearing the Ochre robe."

Once upon a time, the two chief disciples, each with their respective retinues of five hundred monks, informed the Buddha that they were going to travel. They left the city of Sävät and, like two suns rising simultaneously, arrived at Rajagaha. Seeing the two revered visitors, a handful of rich citizens and large numbers of the poor, invited them in, offered them alms and the hospitality due to guests.

One day the Senior Monk Säriyut, the Captain of the Doctrine, preached a sermon on how to obtain the blessings of wealth and of followers. He said, "Listen devotees, there are those who give their wealth with some specific thought in mind but they do not include others in the act of giving. Since such people give only their own possessions, when they are reborn, they will obtain riches. However, because they have not allowed others to participate in this act of giving, they will not have the benefits of followers and companions in their next life.

"There is also another kind of person who, even if it takes a while, encourages others to make gifts. He expends energy and effort but does not give his own wealth. Such a person, since he gets things done by commanding others, will be blessed with a following wherever he is born. However, he will not have money even for his own survival.

"Then there are yet others who give no gifts themselves and because they give nothing cannot encourage others to give either. Wherever such men are born, they get neither the one nor the other.

"However, some people whose minds are filled with faith, believe in the working of *karma* and give alms. Compassionate, they engage others, too, in their activity. Such people, like Dhanañjaya, Meṇḍaka, and Jōtiya, wherever they are born, enjoy the pleasures of wealth as well as companions and followers." Thus, he preached.

A certain wise man hearing him thought, "I must try to obtain both these blessings." He invited both Senior Monks[1] to his home for the following day.

"For how many is the invitation?" the Senior Monks inquired.

"How many are there?" the man asked. He was told there were one thousand monks. The lay devotee invited them all and the Senior Monks accepted the invitation.

The lay devotee then went to the city and, intending to get everyone to participate, announced, "I wish to invite the two Senior Monks and their respective retinues to accept alms from us tomorrow. Everyone can join in and give in whatever way he can." So saying he got them all to participate.

The people made lists agreeing to give as much money as they could. Some said, "We will give to one or perhaps two monks." Some said, "We will give to four or five monks." Then some added, "To seven or eight"; some to "ten or twenty"; some to "thirty or forty"; some to "sixty or seventy"; some to "eighty or ninety"; and yet others said, "We will give to one hundred." Thus, they decided. Having agreed they thought, "If each of us were to prepare a meal in our individual homes, it would be too much trouble. We should cook everything in one place. Let us therefore gather together all that we need and prepare this almsgiving." They did so.

A certain nobleman brought a scented, golden robe worth one thousand gold coins and said, "If you are still short of items, sell this garment and buy whatever you need."

Because many people had jointly provided the requirements for the almsgiving, there was nothing lacking. The chief organizer then said, "The golden robe, which a certain nobleman gave is still left. To whom should we give it?"

As one who, when asked about rice fields, points out the most fertile field he knows, so someone suggested it be given to the Senior Monk Säriyut. He was a fertile field fed by the waters of Fervent Rebirth-Wishes, which he had made over a period of more than one incalculable and one hundred thousand eons, in order to become the Buddha's chief disciple.

Others, worthless themselves, as if pointing out a useless field, which has lain fallow for a long time and become an abandoned marsh, said, "This monk Säriyut is like a man who visits only when the pot of rice is cooked. He comes to stay for a week or a month and then leaves. The monk Devidat on the other hand is constantly with us. He is like a medicinal plant, of great use to us." Since usefulness is something that pleases everyone at all times, those, who considered usefulness a significant virtue, asked that the robe be given to him. In this debate, those in favor of giving it to the monk Devidat were in a majority.[2] Therefore, in spite of the fact that the monk Devidat did not belong to the order of the Āriyas, and so was lower in rank to the Senior Monk Säriyut, and was inferior in goodness, for he did not practice the virtues of Moral Conduct and Contemplation, and though he was lower in status, for he had not achieved the position of a disciple, and was full of wickedness, for he had nursed a grievance over a golden plate, that was unassuaged over a period of five eons, as related in the *Sērivānija Jātaka*,[3] they still gave the robe to him. He cut it up like a monk's robe and began wearing it.

People looked at him and said, "This robe is better suited to the Venerable Säriyut, Captain of the Doctrine, whose body is golden like a garland of *Kaṭukarańdu* flowers,[4] whose mind is golden because it is free of

Defilements. It is not suited to this monk on whom it sits like a decoration hung on a pole. Why does this monk wrap himself in it and walk about like a toothless man trying to sing?"

A monk, who traveled from Rajagaha to the city of Sävät went to the Buddha, saluted him, and when asked for news of the chief disciples, related the story of the ochre robe and all that had taken place.

The Buddha heard his story and thought, "If I were to tell a *Jātaka Story* with this as the central theme, it would be of great use to a great many people for a long time to come." So he said, "This is not the first time that this man put on the ochre robe for which he was not fit. He has done so in the past, too.

"Long ago when King Baṁbadat ruled in the city of Baranäs, there lived a certain hunter who went into forests, killed elephants, cut off their tusks, nails, and portions of meat from the fleshier parts of their bodies, and made a living from their sale. There was a certain forest in which thousands of elephants lived. As they roamed the jungles feeding on green leaves and grasses, they often traveled where a *Pasē* Buddha sat.[5] When they saw him they would kneel, salute him, and walk on.

"One day the hunter, who made his living killing elephants, saw this and thought, 'I can make a living by killing these creatures. These animals as they go back and forth, stop, kneel, and salute this *Pasē* Buddha. I wonder why they do that?'

"He realized that they were paying their respects to the Buddha's robe and thought, 'It would be a great help if I, too, could find a robe like that and so command their respect.' He stole one from a *Pasē* Buddha, who had left his robe on a river bank while bathing. (Because of this deed, he was to spend endless years in the underworld, naked.) The hunter then went to where the elephants passed and pulling the robe above his head to cover himself completely, sat, grasping a spear.

"The elephants seeing him did not realize that he was not a *Pasē* Buddha, for he was dressed in the robe of one. They thought, 'This must be the *Pasē* Buddha.' They saluted him, and went on their way. The hunter would wait till all the elephants had passed and then would hurl his spear at the one who came last. Thus, he would kill the animal that walked last, cut off his tusks, then dig a hole in the ground, and bury what was left in case the other elephants should see it.

"At that time, our Bōsat had been born as an elephant[6] because of a sinful act in a past birth. He happened to be the leader of that herd. The cruel hunter made his living by killing these elephants. The great Bōsat soon noticed that his herd was daily decreasing. As the powerful glow of a gemstone does not diminish even if it lies in a heap of garbage, so, though he was born an animal, he was not lacking in intelligence.

He, therefore, questioned his herd on what was happening. "Why are our elephants getting fewer and fewer? What is going on?" The others said they did not know.

"As a physician understands the root cause of a disease and so knows what medicines to administer in a given situation, so the Bōsat had the intelligence needed for the occasion. He thought, 'These elephants are disciplined. They will not go anywhere without telling me. There is certainly some grave danger lurking here.' He then thought of the possible sources of that danger and reasoned thus. 'There is no visible danger. But in that place a certain man sits, wrapped in an ochre robe. If any harm is being done, it must come from him.' In order to observe the situation, he sent all the other elephants ahead, and followed slowly at the rear.

"The hunter sat quietly until all the other elephants had saluted him and passed by. He saw the great Bōsat approach very slowly. Unaware that, though the animal was walking with a measured pace his intelligence was running in all directions, the hunter held his robe tight and hurled his spear.

"The Bōsat, who had merit enough to deflect the thousand weapons of the death-god Vasavat, stepped back, and avoided it. 'This indeed is the man who has caused the death of so many,' he thought and chased after him. The hunter flattened himself against a tree. He was covered by the tree but he was not protected from his sins. 'With my trunk I will grab both him and the tree, rip it out, smash him against the ground, and kill him,' thought the elephant. Then he saw the ochre robe the hunter was wearing and recoiled like a man fleeing who suddenly comes up against a high wall.

'I cannot think of harming this fellow while looking on this robe.[7] It would be a wrong done to the Buddhas and the *Pasē* Buddhas who rightfully wear this robe.' So he decided not to kill him and instead asked, 'Was it you, fellow, who killed so many of my relatives?

'Yes,' the hunter replied.

'Whatever harm men like you do, is done to yourself because your thoughts are wicked. Does one ask why soot blackens the outside of cooking pots? You, who are in every sense garbage,[8] have dared to put on this robe that only very pure beings wear. They are beings who, for over two incalculables and one hundred thousand eons, have striven to achieve the state of a *Pasē* Buddha. If you can do such a heinous act, what is there worse left for you to do? Or for that matter, what good act can you ever do? Understand the power of this robe by the fact that it has saved your life today.' Thus, he admonished him."

The Buddha related this story and added, "It was Devidat on that occasion who wore a robe that he was not worthy to wear. I was the elephant who advised him. If a man wraps himself in a monk's robe while his mind is stained with Defilements, it is as if he were to decorate the outside of a pot that contained feces. He has no right to such a garment. It is meant only for the virtuous. Who then is worthy to wear such a robe? A man who, living in an appropriate time, comprehends the Path and the Fruits and vomits out Defilements such as Lust through the mouth of Wisdom, and Knowledge of the Fourfold Path. Having done so, he does not then go back to eat up that same vomit. Instead, as a Kirala bird guards its egg, or a Yak protects its tail, or a person cares for his or her only son, or a one-eyed man looks after his one good eye, so he guards and keeps the Precepts he has undertaken to observe, without lapsing on any one of them. Then, just as the Wheel-Jewel[9] is not meant for anyone other than a universal monarch, so the robe is suited only for such a man."

The monk who had brought the news from Rajagaha heard this sermon and as a reward for bringing the message achieved the status of a Stream-Enterer. Many others, too, achieved that and other Spiritual Attainments. Thus, wise men interested in the good health of Realization of the Doctrine, should swallow the medicine of Insight[10] needed to cure the disease of Lustful Defilements that constantly arise in the mind. They should vomit them out through the mouth of Wisdom. Then, free of Impurities, they should avoid sinful acts, practice Moral Conduct and Contemplation, and purify the mind.

Endnotes

WEARING THE OCHRE ROBE

Illustrates stanzas 9 and 10 of the *Yamaka Vagga*.

> Annikkasāvō kāsāvaṃ . . . kāsāvamarahati
> Yo ca vanta kasāvassa . . . kāsāvamarahati
>
> He who wears the ochre robe but is not free of Defilements,
> uncontrolled, and untruthful, is unworthy of that robe.
> He who is free of Defilements, established in virtue,
> self-controlled and truthful, is worthy of the ochre robe.

1. He invited both Senior Monks . . .

In Sri Lanka, even today, when monks are invited to a home for a dāna, or ceremonial feast this question is asked. Laymen decide what number they wish to entertain. There is no obligation to invite an entire complement of monks resident in a temple. One may invite one or many. The kind of invitation described here is unusual and on a scale which requires large community participation. Note also the varying nature of the contributions. It is important that each man gives only what he can.

2. In this debate, those in favor . . . were in a majority.

The exercise of a vote and the acceptance of the decision of the majority was very much part of Buddhist monastic organizational practice. Here we see it percolating to the laity who use the same method to come to a decision. Note also that even though it is clearly the wrong decision, it is upheld.

The same procedure is referred to in the DA. "After a long discussion, it was decided by a majority of four to give the robe to Devadatta" [E. W. Burlingame 1979, 191], suggesting that the practice had come to Sri Lanka very early and existed even around the fifth century A.D.

3. *Sērivānija Jātaka*

Two hawkers are successively offered by its unwitting owners a golden bowl. The greedy hawker overreaches himself while the honest one is richly rewarded.

4. . . . golden like a garland of *Katukaran̆du* flowers, . . .

The sudden juxtaposition of formal, stylistically classical images such as this with homely images such as "like a toothless man trying to sing" is very characteristic of the author's style. It is a device he uses again and again very successfully.

5. . . . they often traveled where a *Pasē* Buddha sat.

This is the Sinhala term for a Paccēka Buddha.

6. . . . , our *Bōsat* had been born as an elephant . . .

Note that *karma* catches up even with Bōdhisatvas, as in this case. Only on becoming a Buddha or on achieving *nirvāṇa* is one free of it.

7. "I cannot think of harming this fellow while looking on this robe. . . . "

In the SR, the elephant stops in his tracks when he sees the robe and decides that to kill the hunter, while he is wearing it, would be an act of disrespect to all Buddhas and *Pasē* Buddhas.

The DA version is slightly different. "The Great Being thought to himself, 'If I offend against this man, the reverence, which thousands of Buddhas and Private Buddhas and Arahats feel *toward me,* will of necessity be lost." [Burlingame 1979, 193] [italics added] This is probably a mistranslation. The SR version makes much more sense.

There is an implicit contrast suggested here between the hunter who goes to the forest to kill and destroy and the *Paccēka Buddha* who sits in silent meditation, disturbing nothing.

8. You, who are in every sense garbage . . .

The language of the elephant's "sermon" to the hunter is strong, earthy, and carries a lot of punch. The same homely imagery and simple style is retained in the Buddha's sermon that follows immediately after.

9. Just as the Wheel Jewel . . .

The wheel or *cakra* is the symbol of a universal monarch, who is called a "*cakravartin*" or "wheel-turner."

10. . . . should swallow the medicine of Insight . . .

Once again the story ends with a medical metaphor based no doubt on current medical theory; medicines were given as emetics so that the "impurities" of disease could be vomited out.

There are hardly any such "medical" metaphors in the DA text.

The Chief Disciples

Those whose thoughts are good always associate with the like-minded. Just as light does not mix with darkness or fire with water, they do not associate with the wicked. To illustrate this truth, we shall relate the story of the chief disciples.

Not far from Rajagaha, at a time before the Buddha was born, there were two Brahmin villages called "Upatissa" and "Kōlita." One day, a Brahmin woman named Rupasāri, who lived in the village of Upatissa, conceived, and, on that very day, a woman named Moggali in the village of Kōlita also conceived. Both Brahmin families had maintained their family lines unbroken for seven generations. Both women performed the rituals for protecting the fetus on the same day, and because of that, exactly on the same day, without any mishap, both women gave birth to two sons of great merit.

At the naming ceremony, Rupasāri, who was so named because she was blessed with virtue and beauty, named her son Upatissa. His father was the chief of the village of Upatissa. The other child was named Kōlita because he was the son of the chief Brahmin of the village of Kōlita.

When they reached school age, both studied all the arts and acquired every skill. They learned a great deal and, because they could commit to memory all they had studied without having to go over anything twice, they completed their studies in a very short time.

The young Upatissa, whether he went to the river for sport, or to the pleasure gardens, was always escorted by five hundred chariots, drawn by horses sensitive to every command of their riders. Each of them had a retinue of five hundred young men.

Each year crowds gathered in the city of Rajagaha under the shadow of the rock, for a festival at which there was a lot to eat and drink as well as a performance known as the "*Giragga Samajja*" or Festival of the Rock. When the two young men went to see the performance, they were assigned seats together. Together they watched the performance, laughed when laughter was indicated,[1] and grieved where grief was called for. When it was necessary to give gifts, they gave generously. One day, while they were enjoying the performance in this manner, the *karmic* consequences of the Perfections, which they had cultivated in past lives in order to become the chief disciples of the Buddha, now reached the point of fruition.[2] As a result, on that particular day, the performance ceased to move them to laughter or tears nor did they participate in the feast that followed the performance. What was the reason for the change?

"What is there pleasing or worth seeing here? We who watch or they who perform will disappear within one hundred years, be erased like drawings on the seashore, and trampled on by the dance of death. There is nothing substantial here. Let us stop seeing these useless spectacles. Let us rather seek the Doctrine of *nirvāṇa* that frees us from birth and decay." That thought passed through Upatissa's mind at that instant because, for over a period of one incalculable and one hundred thousand eons of past lives, he had believed and acted on just such a conviction. The youth Kōlita, thinking the same thoughts, said to Upatissa, "Friend, today you are not as you were. When one is troubled by one's thoughts, it shows. What is the matter? Why are you troubled?"

"There is no point in seeing these performances, friend. They don't help us to acquire Merit. They only lengthen our stay in *saṃsāra*. Nothing is gained by extending our time here, we only prolong our suffering. Therefore, it is better to seek *nirvāṇa,* and shorten our stay in *saṃsāra*. If we experience *nirvāṇa,* the cycle of our births as human beings will gradually come to an end. It is to put an end to this cycle of rebirths, to cease to be, that I stopped myself from being moved by these performances. What were you thinking of, friend?" he asked Kōlita.

Kōlita admitted that he, too, had been thinking along the same lines. As the river Ganga merges with the river Yamuna, so young Upatissa realized that their ideas were one.

He said to Kōlita, "Friend, our thoughts are good thoughts. If we wish to seek *nirvāṇa,* then let us give up this lay life so full of complications and suffering and become monks. Now whose order should we join?"[3]

At that time, there was an ascetic named Sañjaya who lived at Rajagaha with a great following. He was so well-known that Kōlita and Upatissa decided to take ordination under him. They donated their five hundred chariots and five hundred palanquins to five hundred of their thousand followers and sent them back to their respective homes. With the remaining five hundred followers, they went to the ascetic Sañjaya and were ordained as wandering mendicants.

The ascetic Sañjaya received much honor and respect after these two young men took ordination under him; soon he became even more famous. Not very long after their ordination, Kōlita and Upatissa learned everything Sañjaya had to teach them.

"Master is this all you know? Is there no more?" they asked him.

"Listen, pupils, I have kept back nothing,[4] not even what is my teacher's right to withhold. I have taught you everything."

"If that is the case then there is no point in remaining mendicants under this teacher," said the young men to each other.

"We seek a certain kind of Enlightenment. Therefore, just as a person cannot obtain horns from a hare or flowers from a *dimbul* tree, so we cannot expect to get Enlightenment from this teacher. But this land of Daṁbadiva is vast. We who actively seek must surely find a teacher who has achieved Enlightenment and will teach it to us."

From that point on, whenever they heard of a learned Brahmin ascetic, they would go to him and enter into discussions. They found no one who could answer their questions, but they would answer any questions that were put to them. In that manner, they walked the length and breadth of Daṁbadiva in search of someone who could teach them the doctrine of *nirvāṇa*. Failing to find anyone who could, they returned to their native villages.

The ascetic Upatissa then said to the ascetic Kōlita, "We have searched long and so far we have not discovered *nirvāṇa*. But just because we have not found it,[5] that does not mean there is no such thing. If there is fire, there is also water to quench it. Therefore, if there is suffering, there must be the means to conquer that suffering. We seek to know what is not found in our present learning. Can we for that reason say that it doesn't exist? Let us look some more for someone who will teach us the path to *nirvāṇa*. Whoever first discovers it must come back and teach it to the other." Thus, they agreed.

At this time, the Buddha happened to stop at Rajagaha on his way to Ūravela to fulfill a promise he had made to King Bimsara. He took up residence at the Vēluvanārāma monastery.

> Aññākoṇdañña pamukhe—bhikkhu khīṇāsave jino
> Vidhātuṃ dhammadhūteyyaṃ vissajjēsi tahiṃ tahiṃ*

That is to say, he sent out sixty monks in different directions with the message that the Three Jewels had now appeared in this world.

The Senior Monk Assaji, who was one of those sixty and also one of the first five to become a monk, completed the task allotted to him and returned to the city of Rajagaha. The next day he went to the inner city to beg for alms.

It so happened that the ascetic Upatissa had eaten early and was on his way to the monastery of the wandering mendicants. He saw the Senior Monk Assaji and thought, "I have not seen an ascetic like this one before. Surely, if there are Enlightened Ones on this earth, or if there are any who perform the practices and disciplines to become Enlightened, this must be one of them. I can tell from his appearance. It would be useful to ask him about it. He is now begging for alms so he has no time for talk. The man who is thirsty is always in a greater hurry than

---

*To fulfill the task of spreading the Doctrine,
The conquering one sent in all directions
Monks, who had destroyed their Defilements
led by the Reverend Aññā Kondañña,

the one who dispenses the water. Since our thirst for *nirvāṇa* is great, I will not lose sight of this man. If he has obtained the water of *nirvāṇa* from the pond of an Enlightened One, I will ask for some myself, drink it, and assuage the thirst of my Defilements." Thinking thus he followed the monk.

The monk who had learned to be moderate in asking alms obtained only what he needed for survival and began to look for a suitable place to sit and eat. Upatissa the ascetic, as a preliminary to hearing the Buddha's teaching, prepared a place for him to sit and eat. At the end of the meal, he brought water in his own vessel for the monk to wash his hands and mouth and performed all the services due to a teacher. When he had rendered the service of disposing of the bowl after the meal, he began to engage in pleasant conversation with the monk.

"Your Reverence, even though you survive on the food obtained from begging, your physical appearance is beautiful, perhaps because your mind is pure. Where were you ordained? From whom did you obtain instruction?" he asked.

The Senior Monk Assaji thought, "These wandering ascetics are hostile to the Buddha's teachings. Thus, I will indicate to him that the lake of our Doctrine is deep and that it is not easy to step into it unless one knows the proper place or ford." So he said, "Listen, O monk, I am new and have not been in the order long. I have still not learned everything, therefore I cannot describe it fully."

The ascetic replied:

> Gaṅgāya vālukā khīye udakaṃ khīye mahaṇṇave,
> Mahiyā mattikā khīye lakkhena mama budhhiyā*

"I am the ascetic known as Upatissa. Do not worry about my capabilities. Whatever you know, whether it be much or little, speak. As one who chips off the outer soft wood and takes only the inner core of a timber tree, so even as you speak I will discard the various ornamentations of words and consonants and take only the core of the teachings of Enlightenment."

---

*There is not enough sand in the river[6]
or water in the deep ocean,
There are not enough clay particles in the earth
with which to reckon my powers of understanding.

Then the Senior Monk said:

> Ye dhammā hetuppabhavā tesaṃ hetuṃ tathāgato āha,
> Tesañca yo nirodho evaṃ vādī mahāsamaṇo."*

"That is to say, certain fruits or consequences, like the *saṃskāras,* stem from certain causes such as Ignorance. As coconut palms and talipot palms spring from coconuts or talipot-palm nuts respectively, or again, just as the nuts exist only because the palms exist, so because of causes there are results and because of results there are causes. Therefore, whether as cause or as result, the laws exist."

Thus, he preached the Law of Causation and the consequences that flow from Ignorance. Just as there are no coconuts or talipot-palm nuts where there are no coconut or talipot palms, so by eliminating the cause one can eliminate the consequence. Men like the ascetic Upatissa had the ability to make good use of the words of others. By hearing just the first two lines, he attained to the stage of a Stream-Enterer, a state endowed with one thousand modes of comprehension. The next two lines of that stanza,[7] he was to hear only long after.

"If I have sufficient intellectual powers to become a Stream-Enterer after hearing only the first two lines, then there must be some reason why I do not immediately attain to the other stages, too," thought Upatissa. He said, "Your Reverence, those two lines you recited are sufficient. I do not wish to trouble you to say more. If I wish to understand the Law of Causation, its Origins and its Resolution, and if Resolution can come only from a knowledge of the Doctrine of the Path and the Fruits, and the Doctrine of *nirvāṇa,* then tell me where is that Buddha, Teacher of the Three Worlds, who will teach me that all-inclusive Doctrine and not hold anything back. I who have seen the body of the Teachings must now also see the person of the Teacher."

The monk told him that the Buddha was in residence at the Vēluvanārāma monastery.

"If so your Reverence, will you go ahead. I have a friend with whom I long ago agreed that whoever first learned about *nirvāṇa* should inform the other. I must, therefore, tell him that I have found *nirvāṇa.* Since he, too, is looking for *nirvāṇa,* I will bring my friend to see the Buddha.

Thus, as if to free himself from the five Planes of Existence, he worshipped the monk, touching the ground with the five parts of his body.[8]

---

*The Buddha has made known Phenomena arising from a cause,
and the cause thereof.
The great ascetic has also taught how they cease.

Since he was now close to winding up the threefold Cycle of his Existence, he circumambulated the monk thrice. Upatissa then returned to the hermitage of the wandering mendicants.

The ascetic Kōlita saw his friend from afar and thought, "Today the color of my friend's face and body seem different. It is serenely beautiful. He is happy about something. It looks as if he has discovered the *nirvāṇa* he has been seeking for so long."

"What is it?" Kōlita asked his friend. "Have you found *nirvāṇa?* Are you now at peace?"

Like a man who finds something sweet,[9] eats half, and brings the other half back to a friend, Upatissa answered his friend's question by reciting the lines of the verse on the Chain of Causation that the Senior Monk Assaji had recited to him. On the day he attained Enlightenment, the Buddha had meditated on the Doctrine of Causation and had contemplated it from the beginning to the end, from the end to the beginning, from the middle to the beginning, from the middle to the end, from the end to the middle, and from the middle to the beginning. It consisted of twelve different constituents, twenty different ways, and three different parts, but it was not too deep for the Senior Monk Ańanda to comprehend,[10] just as water that is too deep for men may not be too deep for elephants.

As soon as the stanza ended, the ascetic Kōlita attained the Path of Enlightenment. Where the ascetic Upatissa had attained to the Path on hearing the first two lines, the ascetic Kōlita, like an unskilled merchant who buys with four gold coins what a skilled merchant buys with two, attained the Path of Enlightenment only after hearing all four lines of the stanza.

Having become a Stream-Enterer in this way, he asked, "Friend, is not the Doctrinal river the source of this sweet tasting water? Does it not come from the Himalayan Peak of the All-Knowing Buddha and issue forth from the lake of his mouth, from behind the rocky crags of his teeth, unheated by the sun of Defilements? I would like to see that Himalayan peak, the All-Knowing One. Where is he?"

The ascetic Upatissa answered, "That noble teacher is at the monastery at Vēluvanārāma. That was what the Senior Monk Assaji, my teacher, told me."

"If so, friend, let us go to him," Kōlita responded. At that moment, the ascetic Upatissa, who was always respectful of his teachers, remembered his former teacher Sañjaya and said, "Friend, let us tell the ascetic Sañjaya, too, of the *nirvāṇa* we have found. He is wise and it will be good if he, too, grasps it. If not, he can get just a description from us and go there himself. The Buddha preaches his sermons taking into consideration the needs of the person concerned, like prescribing a medicine after understanding the cause of a disease. Therefore, when the ascetic Sañjaya goes to him he will understand the Path, if he has sufficient good *karma* to do so. We are not Buddhas, so he may not get it from us, but he will surely get it from the Buddha, who, like a skilled archer, never fails to hit his mark. Let us go then." Together they went in search of the ascetic Sañjaya.

The ascetic Sañjaya saw them coming and asked, "What is it, pupils? Did you find someone to teach you how to obtain the heavenly nectar of *nirvāṇa?*"

"Yes, Reverend Teacher. Though neither you nor we had heard of it until now, the sun that is the All-Knowing One has arrived on earth and, with the rays of his Doctrine, he has destroyed the darkness of our Defilements. He has made disciplined men bloom like lotuses. You walk about exhausted, clinging to a useless activity, satisfied with lumps of dung while precious gems lie scattered around you. This is meaningless. Come with us to the Buddha."

Sañjaya answered, "You go to him. I will not come."

"Why will you not come?" they asked.

"Listen, all these years I have lived as a teacher to a great many pupils. How can I now serve another? Having once been a cooking pot, can I now become just a ladle? Given my reputation, it is not fitting that I should go to him now and become a disciple."

At that the two pupils said, "Reverend Teacher, the moment the seven Jewels of the Universal Monarch appear there is no one in all the universe of Sakvaḷa that does not become his subject. Similarly, once the Wheel of the Doctrine has been set in motion by that Universal Monarch, namely, the Enlightened One, his command extends to one hundred thousand million universes. Whatever you may decide, we cannot remain here. If you had heard the sermon of the All-Knowing One, you would have gone yourself without needing us to urge you. There is nothing to be gained by not going. We all know that. You must go to him."

As a sick man does not understand the potency of a medicine, and is reluctant to take it while those administering it know it will cure the disease and urge the patient to swallow it, so they strongly urged him. They strove to cure the disease of his Defilements by making him drink the medicine of the Doctrine.

The ascetic Sañjaya replied, "Are there more fools or wise men in this world?"

"Reverend Teacher, just as there is considerable chaff in a heap of grain, so there are a great many who lack wisdom. Like good grain, there are only a few wise men."

"If that be so, then those who are empty and stupid will be attracted to me and will seek me out. Men of great intellect will go in search of the monk Gōtama who has enough and more of it. Thus, I will have the greater number of followers. You, since you are wise and look for fertile minds, go to him. I will not come."

Though the two pleaded with him, he refused.

"May you then become famous by your action," they said and set off to see the Buddha. Since the two who left were the foremost of Sañjaya's disciples, many of his followers also left with them; the hermitage was deserted. Sañjaya, emptied of goodness just as his hermitage had been emptied of followers, looked on and was upset; the hot blood rushed to his head. Of the five hundred ascetics who were his followers, two hundred and fifty, strongly attached to Sañjaya, turned their backs on the city of *nirvāṇa*, their faces to the abyss of *saṃsāra*, and remained behind. Upatissa and Kōlita accompanied by two hundred and fifty followers went to the monastery at Vēluvanārāma.

The Buddha was seated surrounded by a retinue of one hundred monks to whom he was preaching. He saw the two visitors from afar; he had the vision to see things from four leagues away. He said to his monks, "Monks, do you see the two who are approaching? They will be my chief disciples."

The two young men came to the Buddha, worshipped him, and respectfully stood on a side. They asked that they be ordained and given the Higher Ordination.

Like a streak of lightning flashing from a red cloud, the Buddha raised his right hand and said, "Monks, come hither. In order to cross the desert of *saṃsāra* observe the practice of celibacy.

Thereupon these two ascetics and their followers put on the robes and took up the begging bowls that magically appeared. As if giving up their human forms for that of deities in the heaven of Brahma, they shed their lay garb, put on the ornaments of Moral Conduct and Contemplation, and were instantly transformed into Senior Monks seeming one hundred years old.

As when a great chieftain with his retinue visits a rich man[11] and, while they are discussing business matters their followers are given something to eat, so the Buddha kept the two who were to become his chief disciples, waiting, and preached to their followers. The followers for their part listened to the Buddha's sermon like those who eat a meal placed before them without wasting a thought on their chiefs. All two hundred and fifty of them achieved Enlightenment.

It is impossible to fill one's stomach by watching others eat. Similarly, though the two disciples had developed intellectual powers of a high order by cultivating the Perfections in order to become chief disciples to the Buddha, they did not achieve Enlightenment in spite of having heard the sermon preached to the multitude.

On the seventh day, after receiving ordination at the village of Kalavāla in the Magadha country, the monk Mugalan (formerly Kōlita) engaged in Contemplation. He used the Four Elements as the object of his meditation and did so in the following fourfold manner; that is, he first contemplated the elements in their totality,[12] in synthesized form, then he contemplated these elements in analytic form, then their characteristics in synthetic form, and finally their characteristics in analytic form. He cultivated Insight and fulfilled the three remaining stages in the twelvefold manner. Thus, he became the chief of those with supernormal powers, adept at such miraculous acts as transforming the earth into a clay oil-lamp, with the sea as oil, and the rock Mahāmēru as the central wick. Because he was able to perform such acts, he was appointed chief advisor of the Buddha's city of the Doctrine.

A fortnight after his ordination, the chief monk Säriyut (formerly Upatissa) was living with the Buddha near the city of Rajagaha in the rock cave known as the "Cave Dug by the Boar." While he was there, the Buddha preached to his nephew, the wandering ascetic Dikniya, the stanzas on the Cognition of Feeling. Like a man slipping his hand into another's rice bowl and eating from it, the monk Säriyut dipped the hand of his Insight into the meal of the sermon, assuaged the hunger pangs of his Defilements and thereafter achieved Enlightenment as an *arahat*.

As the Salkalaṇa tree hidden in the earth appears only at the time of a Buddha, similarly the city of *nirvāṇa* filled with noble *arahats*, though it exists as a concept, can be apprehended only in the time of a Buddha. Thus, wearing the insignia of the Perfections, which he had fulfilled in order to become a disciple, the monk Säriyut became Chief Commander of the city of *nirvāṇa*, which was filled with *arahats*. As Chief Commander, he had the power to teach the multi-faceted Doctrine to those scattered over limitless universes, to expel sinners from the city of the *sāsana* and, without showing favoritism, to bring the virtuous into the kingdom of *nirvāṇa*. He had the power to confer blessings of the world, and the blessings of Spiritual Attainments to the deserving; in addition, he was granted the power to preach the Wheel of the Doctrine after the Buddha's lifetime.

Of the two men, why was the Senior Monk Säriyut not the first but the last to achieve Enlightenment even though he had been ordained a monk? What was the reason for this? It is because in order to become a

Chief Disciple and sit on the right hand of the Buddha one must cultivate the Perfections to a heightened degree. For example, a poor man, if he decides to go on a journey, gets up, and leaves because there is nothing to delay him. But when a King travels, elephants must be caparisoned, and other elaborate preparations must be made. The delay must be understood in similar terms.

The very next morning, the Buddha assembled the monks. Of the two disciples, he appointed the Senior Monk Säriyut to the position of the foremost in wisdom, and the Senior Monk Mugalan the foremost in supernormal powers. They were selected from among all those near him. He pronounced them his chief disciples and preached the sermon on *Pratimokha* or the Rules of Discipline.

None of the other monks were happy about the appointment of these two as chief disciples. "Is the Buddha partial?" they all said. "Should he not have given the position to the five monks who initially accepted ordination under him? If not them, should he not have given it to the monk Yasa and his retinue of fifty-five monks? If not to them, he should have given it to the thirty monks of the Bhadhavaggiya group. If not to them, he should have given it to the three brother monks such as Ūruvela Kaśyapa. But to give the title of chief disciple to these two, who have joined the order at this late stage, seems to us an act of favoritism, whatever anyone else may think. Not just we, but anyone who hears of it will think that."

The Buddha, though he knew what they said because he heard it with his Divine Ear, asked them, "Of what do you speak?"

"Master, it is of nothing other than your acts of favoritism."

"You say that because of your ignorance. There is no favoritism here. Every one of these monks has performed certain special acts of merit and has made specific Fervent Rebirth-Wishes. For it is said:

Esa devamanussānaṃ sabbakāmadado nidhi
Yaṃ yaṃ devābhipatthenti sabbametena labbhati.*

"Hence what they get will be according to what they have wished and what they have striven to attain. Of these monks, the monk Aññā Kondañña, when he was journeying through the cycle of rebirths, made nine offerings of the first gifts of a single harvest. He did not, however, make a Fervent Rebirth-Wish to become a chief disciple. What was it he

*This (Rebirth-Wish) is a wish-conferring treasure for gods and men.
Whatever one aspires to and wishes for, all that will be realized.

wished for? He said, 'As this first gift of the harvest was given, so may I go to a Buddha and become the first to be enlightened.' "

"When did he make that Fervent Rebirth-Wish?"[13] asked the monks.

"Listen, O monks. In the ninety-first eon before this Buddha, a Buddha named Vipassi appeared on earth. During this time two brothers named Mahākāḷa and Cūḷakāḷa ploughed a large field of äl-rice. Then one day the younger brother, Cūḷakāḷa, went to the field, picked a young ear of äl-grain, crushed it, and ate it. It was very sweet. It tasted so good that he thought, 'If I were to make an offering of this very flavorful rice then, as a consequence, I might enjoy the even sweeter flavor of *nirvāṇa* one day.' He wished to make an offering of food prepared from the young grain to the Buddha and his retinue of monks. He went to his brother and said, 'Brother, let us husk these ears of äl-rice, prepare a meal of it, and offer it to the Buddha and his monks.' The brother replied, 'There is no tradition of giving food prepared from the young ears of äl-rice, nor will it be so in future. Do not waste the grain.' But since the younger brother was insistent on giving an offering of the young ears of äl-rice he added, 'In that case divide the field and do not harvest the section that belongs to me. Do what you wish with yours.'

'Good,' the other responded and he divided up the field, used numerous workers to crush the ears of grain, put the rice into pots, added no water, only milk, and when it was boiling added clarified butter, honey, and crystalized treacle; he prepared a dish of milk-rice. This he served to the Buddha and his retinue of one hundred and sixty-eight thousand monks. At the end of the meal he made a Fervent Rebirth-Wish, saying, 'Master, by this gift of the first fruits of the harvest that I have now made, may I be the first to enter the city of *nirvāṇa.*' The Buddha, knowing that it would come to pass, said, 'May it be so.'

"The younger brother went back to the field and, when he looked at the section where he had picked the grain, he saw fresh ears of grain appearing as if the sheaves were once more ready for harvesting. He thought, 'Whatever the fate of the other field, the field of my meritorious action is maturing well. Because I weeded out the grass and rubbish of miserly thoughts, not a grain was harmed and all of it has matured.' His joy at the sight of the uncut field was so great that he made another offering before the reaping. On the day on which the grain was reaped, he gave yet another offering. When it was bound into sheaves he made another offering. He made another, when the sheaves were heaped. When it was taken to the threshing floor, he gave another offering. When it was threshed and collected he gave another offering, and finally yet another offering when it was put in the granery. On nine occasions he gave nine offerings of food. Just as he had given unstintingly from everything he got, so the meritorious wishes he made each of the nine times, were fulfilled. Nor was his harvest diminished.

"Thus, he gave nine offerings of food and made the same Fervent Rebirth-Wish. One hundred thousand years earlier in the time of the Buddha Padumattara, too, he had given similar offerings for a whole week and had made the same Fervent Rebirth-Wish. Thus, in his present life on hearing a sermon, he became the first to achieve *nirvāṇa*. Others achieved *nirvāṇa* only after him. Now what do you say about that? If I had allowed others to achieve *nirvāṇa* before him, you could have found fault with me."

"What meritorious act was done by the monk Yasa and his fifty followers?"

"Listen, O monks. In the time of a certain Buddha, he and his followers performed many meritorious acts in order to become *arahats*. Then later, at a time when there was no Buddha, all of them were born on earth. They acquired merit by cremating the corpses of those who were too poor and needy and had no kinsmen to do it for them. One day they handled the corpse of a woman with child. Five persons were asked to perform the task of cremation. The others returned to the village. The young man Yasa was one of those kindling the fire where the body was burning. He made it the object of Contemplation and meditated on the repulsiveness of decay. He said to the others, 'Look, this person walked about not long ago. See what she is like now. Her hands burn and twist as in life they bent, refusing to perform an act of merit. The foot bends as when an older child is about to kick someone in play. The teeth that she brushed, standing in front of a mirror, now splutter like melon seeds. Eyes that were decorated with unguents now mix with ash and soot. Look at the filth that was inside that belly, once massaged with oil and saffron.' Thus, he evoked thoughts of revulsion in all of them.

"The four of them returned to the village and told the others about it. The young man Yasa went to his home and told his parents and his wife, too, of this. All of them listened to what he said and thereafter spent a lifetime engaged in the meditative exercise of the Contemplation of Decay. However, they made no Fervent Rebirth-Wish to become chief disciples. Therefore, I did not give them that position."

"Be that as it may, what meritorious act did the monks of the Baddhavagga group perform?"

"Listen, O monks, they, too, performed meritorious acts necessary to become Enlightened Ones. Just as in this eon the thirty of them wished to achieve Enlightenment, so at that time they desired to drink palm beer. The Doctrine I now preach will last five thousand years but the doctrine preached by a pig at that time lasted sixty thousand years.

For the duration of that entire period, the thirty of them decided to desist from the five acts of Demerit and observe the Precepts and make Fervent Rebirth-Wishes to become *arahats*. They did not wish for any other position, so I did not make them chief disciples."

"Be that as it may. But what acts of merit did Ūruvela Kaśyapa and others perform?" they asked again.

"Listen, O monks, he, too, performed meritorious acts wishing only to become Enlightened. In the ninety-second eon prior to ours, there were two Buddhas born on earth named Tissa and Phussa. The father of the Buddha Tissa was named Mīdu. That Buddha enjoyed the pleasures of the lay life. Then he made the great act of renunciation, became a monk, performed the major acts of striving to acquire Spiritual Attainments and became a Buddha. The son of the king by another queen became his chief disciple, who sat on his right. The chief minister's son became the disciple, who sat on his left. Then the King went to the Buddha and said, 'You, my oldest son, have now become a Buddha. My younger son is your chief disciple. The son of my chief minister is now your other disciple. You, the Buddha, since you are born of my seed, are part of me. Thus, the Doctrine you preach is also mine. The monks who carry forth that Doctrine are mine.'

"He spoke, thus, with a strong sense of egotistical pride. Then he bent low, worshipped the Buddha and added, 'Master, consider the period just passed as if it were merely a time spent in sleep at the end of ninety thousand years. Whatever you may have done in the past from now on, do not go begging to the houses of others.[14] Accept my hospitality and preach to me as long as you live.' Thus, he invited him and began to attend on him.

"The king had three other sons. Of the brothers, the eldest had five hundred followers, the second had three hundred followers, and the youngest two hundred. They saw their father attending on their elder brother and thought, 'We, too, would like to perform some service for our brother.' They asked their father's permission but they did not get it.

"At the time, there was some trouble in the countryside, and they were sent there by their father to restore order. They did so and returned. The king was pleased with their success and showed his affection by granting them a boon. They postponed asking for it in order to strengthen his affection. At a later date, they reminded the king of his promise and he in turn asked them to make their request. They replied, 'Your Honor, we need no other boon but that from now on we, too, be allowed to attend continuously on our brother. Give us that opportunity.' The king refused.

'Then, let us do it at least for seven years,' they said.

"The king did not agree to that either. They then asked for a period from six to one year, but they could not get even a year. They asked for a period from eleven to three months. That, too, they did not get.

"They said, 'O King, ignoring even the fact that we are your children, you are reluctant to grant us permission. Give us at least, each one month, for a period of three months.'

'I agree, my children, for what will you think if you don't get any turn at all. Each of you may take one month and thus you may give gifts of food for a three month period.' Thus, he granted them permission.

"The three brothers appointed one person to be in charge of the treasury and one man to record income and expenditures in case those handling expenditures might tend to chicanery. Under them were one hundred and twenty thousand others. The three princes summoned all these people and said, 'For the next three months we are going to observe the Ten Precepts, wear ochre robes, and live with the Buddha in his monastery. Take the rice and grain that you normally pay as tax and for the ninety days of the next three months, prepare meals for the ninety thousand monks, for the Buddha, for us, and for our one thousand soldiers, and bring it to the monastery. This is our only command. We shall not tire ourselves with any others. While we strive, however, you, too, should not be lazy. Follow our commands to the letter.' They then took their retinue of one thousand men and went to the monastery, observed the Ten Precepts, put on ochre robes, and remained in the temples.

"The treasurer and the scribe would take provisions each day from the store of one of the three brothers in turn. The family of one of them would prepare the meal and offer it. The children of the cooks, seeing the rice gruel, cried, wanting some. The cooks would feed the crying children with some of the rice gruel while waiting for the monks to arrive. This was like giving them molten metal to drink[15] or lead pellets to swallow. Thus, there was nothing left over when the monks had finished eating.

"Time passed and the adults preparing the food could not control their greedy thoughts either. Blaming it on the children, they, too, began to eat. During the ninety day period four hundred and eighty thousand people stole the food and consumed the alms intended for the monks. But, in order to digest the food so pilfered, they were born as *pretas*[16] and thus suffered as much pain as they had experienced pleasure eating the stolen food.

"The three brothers and their one thousand soldiers died and were born in heaven. Their merit was great so they remained in heaven for ninety-two eons. These three did many acts of merit and made Fervent Rebirth-Wishes to achieve Enlightenment. Just as you reap rice if you sow rice seed, so they got what they wished for.

"King Bimsara was the accountant in those days. The lay devotee Visākha was then the Treasurer. The four hundred and eighty thousand who stole food were born in the world of *pretas* and suffered much during that time. What could they do? They spent the ninety-two eons in pleasant and unpleasant states. In the Bhadra eon, though the eon itself was a blessed period graced by five Buddhas, since they had done nothing good, they spent the entirety of four Buddha periods in the world of the *pretas*. This should teach those who fear sinful acts not to take what belongs to the *Saṅgha*.

"Those *pretas*, while spending time in this manner, went to the Buddha Kakusaňda, the first Buddha to be born in this eon; his dispensation was destined to last forty thousand years. They asked when they could get some rice to eat. Just as there had been no limit to the food consumed, that had been prepared for the *Saṅgha*, so he, too, prescribed no time limit and said, 'You will not get to eat rice in my time. When I am dead and my teachings, too, have disappeared and when the world, which grows one inch every one thousand years has grown to a height of four leagues, the Buddha Koṇāgamana will be born. Ask him.'

"They spent that time in the *preta* world, since they had stolen sufficient to keep them there for that length of time. When the Buddha Koṇāgamana, whose dispensation lasted thirty thousand years, was born, they went to him. He, too, said, 'You will not obtain rice in my time. When I die and my Teachings disappear, and the earth grows four leagues, as was said before, the Buddha Kasub will be the next Buddha. Ask him.'

"They lived that period, too, in the *preta* world and when the Buddha Kasub was born, whose dispensation lasted twenty thousand years, they asked him, too. Just as they were not slow to eat the alms intended for monks, so they were not slow to question him. He, too, said, 'You will not obtain rice in my time. After me, when the earth, as was said of old, grows four leagues, the Buddha Gōtama will be the next Buddha. In his time, there will be a king named Bimsara. He will give offerings of food to the Buddha and his Order of Monks and gain merit thereby and transfer it to you.[17] At that time, you will be given food.' He then repeated what the previous two Buddhas had said.

"The *pretas* heard him. Just as the stars seen from the world of men are only six minutes from the heavens of the gods, and fifty years on earth are equal to just one day in heaven, so the time span between two

Buddhas was as one day to these *pretas*. The food they had eaten, which had rightly belonged to the *Saṅgha,* had been consumed over a period of ninety days. It had tasted so sweet that it had seemed, at the time, insufficient.

"The *pretas* had been told by the Buddha Kasub that in the time of our Buddha,[18] King Bimsara would offer alms and transfer the merit so gained to them. Therefore, they did not bother to question our Buddha. Instead, they appeared that night before King Bimsara, who on the previous day had made offerings of food to the monks, but had not transferred the merit to them.

"The king went to Vēluvanārāma the next day and told the Buddha of their appearance. The Buddha said to him, 'Great King, those *pretas* were your kinsmen two eons ago, in the time of the Buddha Phussa. They were asked to prepare food as alms for monks but they stole the food. Thus, unable to destroy the Threefold Cycle of Existence, they were born in the *preta* world. After an interminable period, they left that world and spent ninety-two eons more in other good and bad existences. In this eon, too, as retribution for eating alms, they were born again as *pretas* and forced to wander around suffering. They asked the Buddhas Kakusaṅda and Koṇāgamana, who had preceded me, when they would get some rice to eat; they were given no specific time. On the third occasion, they asked the Buddha Kasub and were told that in the time of my dispensation, you, who are kinsmen to them all, would intervene and obtain rice for them. The period between the two Buddhas has seemed to them no more than two days, and wishing for this one thing, they have been wandering around. Yesterday you offered alms but did not transfer merit to them, so they have now appeared before you.'

" 'If I offer it now will they receive it, Master?' the king asked.

" 'Yes, they will and it will amount to the same thing."

"On the second day the king gave a gift of alms and transferred the merit, wishing that the *pretas* might obtain food and drink. They then got heavenly food and drink. But the next day they appeared again before the king, naked. Again the king reported the incident to the Buddha.

" 'Listen, O King. It is because you have not given gifts of garments and transferred the merit to them."

"The king then offered garments and transferred the merit to them. It is not unusual to get celestial food once one participates in an act of transferred merit. Just as food, though swallowed in lumps, when digested releases nutrients that are transformed to produce a beautiful bodily form, so they received the merit transferred by the king and obtained heavenly food and garments. In keeping with that, they were instantly released from their *preta* existence and by the power of former good deeds they were transformed into heavenly beings."

The Buddha wished to give those,[19] who now had received the benefits of heaven, the additional blessing of *nirvāṇa*. Therefore, he preached a sermon from the *Thirokuḍḍa sutta* of the *Khuḍḍaka Nikāya*, beginning with the words, 'Thirokuḍḍesu tiṭṭhanti.'[20] On hearing this sermon, eighty-four thousand beings realized *nirvāṇa*.

Thus, in relating the story of the three brothers, he also told the story of the *pretas* that arose from it. He then continued, "The brothers got what they had made a Fervent Rebirth-Wish to obtain. Where then is my favoritism?"

"Be that as it may," they replied, "But what acts of merit did these two chief disciples specifically perform to reach that position?"

"Listen then if you wish to hear what merit they have done. Less than one incalculable and one hundred thousand years ago, the senior monk Säriyut was born in a family of Brahmins of great wealth, as if to make his beginning appropriate to his end whatever may have happened in between. (Such families had a treasury of eighty million and an expenditure of two bushels of gold coins a day.) His name was Sarada. The Senior Monk Mugalan was born into a farmer family also of great wealth. He was named 'Sirivadu.' As his name indicates, he cultivated friendships, and both groups lived in great friendship.[21] On the death of his parents, the Brahmin youth Sarada inherited great wealth. One day he thought to himself, 'I know only about this world and know nothing of the other world. Since birth is inevitable and marks the beginning of all our race, so death is inevitable to all who are born. Therefore it would be better to become an ascetic and search for release from birth, decay, and death.'

"He went to the householder Sirivaḍu and said, 'Friend, Sirivaḍu, I want to become an ascetic and realize *nirvāṇa*. Will you join me and also become an ascetic?'

"I cannot do that. But you can become a monk," Sirivaḍu replied.

"When one dies, one does not take relatives and friends along. All one takes is one's Merit and Demerit. Why then do we need all this that we cannot take along?' " So thought Sarada and opening the doors of his store houses of gems, he gave gifts to the poor and destitute and went to the Himalayan regions and became an ascetic.

"When the people heard he had become an ascetic they thought, 'If he gives up such wealth to become an ascetic then it must be something worth doing for us all.' First one became an ascetic, then two, then three, and so on until about seventy-four thousand became ascetics with matted hair.

"The ascetic Sarada attained the Fivefold Superior Knowledge and the eight Trance States and taught the seventy-four thousand matted hair ascetics the practices of meditation. Under his instruction, all of them attained the state of Superior Knowledge and the Trance States.

"At that time, the Buddha Anōmadassi had appeared in the world. The name of the city where that Buddha was born was called 'Candrāvati.' His royal father's name was Yasavat. His mother was Yasōdhara. His tree of Enlightenment was the Kumbuk tree, and his chief disciples were the two monks Nisabha and Anōma. The monk who attended him was called 'Varuna.' The nuns Sundarā and Sumanā were his two chief female disciples.[22] That Buddha had a life-span of one hundred thousand years. His height was fifty-eight cubits by a carpenter's measuring stick. His body's radiance spread to a distance of forty leagues. He had one hundred thousand monks permanently in his retinue.

"One day at dawn, that Buddha, who daily initiated twelve million lakhs of people to the Trance States of the Path, and twelve million lakhs to Trance States of Compassion, making a total of twenty-four million lakhs, arose from his Trance, looked over all the world, saw the ascetic Sarada and said, 'Today, if I go to that ascetic Sarada, I will cause a great Doctrinal rain to fall on the Himalayas. The ascetic Sarada will then make a Fervent Rebirth-Wish to become a chief disciple. Later his friend the ascetic Sirvadu, without hesitation, will also make a Fervent Rebirth-Wish to become the other disciple. By the time the Doctrinal rain ceases, the seventy-four thousand ascetic followers of Sarada will quench the great heat of their Defilements and become Enlightened; their achievements will be an ornament to my *sāsana*. Thus, if I go, much benefit will come of it.' So taking up his bowl and robe himself, without even calling up the monk who attended on him, he descended from the sky like a lion-king and appeared in full view of the ascetic Sarada, whose followers had gone to the forest for fruits and greens.

"Since the god Mahā Brahma has incorporated an account of the identifying marks of a Great Being into the *Vēda mantras,* he will recognize that I am a Buddha if only by his study of the *vēdas,*" thought the Buddha. "He then descended from the sky before the very eyes of the ascetic Sarada and it seemed as if all the beauty of the world were concentrated in his person. The ascetic saw the power of the Buddha and his beautiful form, which was like a painting by an artist trained in the art of abstract contemplation. It was the painting of one who, for a period of four incalculables and one hundred thousand eons, does nothing but take up the pigments of the Threefold Virtues and with the brush of his mind draw a portrait of a Buddha, endowed with the thirty-two marks of a Great Being together with the eighty minor marks and the halo a fathom wide that envelops a Buddha's body. Thus, he recognized the blessed marks of the Buddha, consulted his traditional sources regarding the marks, realized they were the same mirror images of each other, and knew that anyone with those marks would, if he were a layman, become a world conqueror. He would be famed throughout the universes with jewels equal in number but not in quality to the Sevenfold Noble Possessions of a Buddha. But if such a person were to join the Order and if there was no other Buddha in that eon he would be a Buddha, an All-Knowing One.

"Thus, he concluded that this Great Being was without a doubt indeed a Buddha. Realizing that it was not courteous to just stand there staring, he went on ahead and set up a seat for him. Just as he had achieved Superior Knowledge by merely practicing the Five Precepts, so because he wished to obtain the highest position, he arranged seating for the Buddha in such a way that he could worship him.

"The Buddha arrived like the dawn sun shining with one thousand rays from behind the Yugañdara mountain. He sat there glowing and shining with the Sixfold Buddha rays. Sarada, the ascetic, then set up a seat for himself[23] that was appropriate in relation to the Buddha and sat there.

"The seventy-four thousand ascetics, bearing fruits and greens, returned to their teacher. They saw where the Buddha was seated and where their own teacher was, and said to him, 'We thought there was no one better or even equal to you. But the place where you are now seated leads us to question that. Are there ascetics greater than you?'

"The ascetic Sarada replied, 'Pupils, what should I say? It is as if one tried to compare the Mahāmēru mountain with a mustard seed. If one considers it simply from the point of view of goodness, why, he is far superior. If one were to put all the Mahāmēru mountains that exist in all the infinite and immeasurable universes and place them one on top of each other, the goodness of the Buddha would exceed even that. Do not compare me to the Buddha, for I have not even as much as a mustard seed of goodness in comparison.' The ascetics heard him and thought, 'If this person were his inferior, our teacher would not describe him in such glowing metaphors. Just as his seat is higher, so he must be greater in goodness.' They paid obeisance to the Buddha.

"The ascetic Sarada addressed the worshipping pupils thus: 'Attend on the Buddha to the best of your ability. What you have now gathered was collected without much care or discrimination. It is therefore not good enough for him. Go find fruits that are as sweet as his teachings.' So he asked them to bring fruits and greens. Just as his thoughts were pure, so he washed and cleansed his hands and put it all into the Buddha's begging bowl. When the Buddha accepted the fruits and greens, the gods, as if to sweeten them with a further addition, introduced divine flavors into them, making them fit to be consumed by him and none other. The ascetic Sarada himself brought water for the Buddha, water that he had first strained. After the Buddha finished his meal, the ascetic, together with all his pupils, stood before the Buddha talking.

"At that moment the Buddha thought, 'My two chief disciples attended by their permanent followers of about one hundred thousand should enter now.' They in turn had been anxiously waiting, thinking, 'How can we enter without being sent for by the Buddha?' Now they sensed the Buddha's wishes and flew through the air putting to shame the swans of the swan kịng Dhratarāṣtra. They entered, worshipped the Buddha, and stood respectfully on one side.

"The ascetic Sarada then called up his pupils and said, 'Pupils, the chair on which the Buddha sits is too short for one so great in goodness. Nor are there seats for the one hundred thousand monks. You should render services to the Buddha and his followers who have visited us here. Go fetch flowers of all colors and perfumes from the Himalayan forests.' Thus, he ordered them.

"It is difficult to imagine the magical powers of ascetics who have achieved the powers of Trance States but, almost immediately after the monk Sarada spoke, they returned bearing flowers and constructed a flowered seat four leagues high for the Buddha. They prepared a seat three leagues high for the two chief disciples, since the Fervent Rebirth-Wishes and the austerities performed to become a chief disciple are much less than those needed to become a Buddha. For the others they constructed seats two leagues high. There were no seats smaller than that.

"How did they construct such seats in a temple where only seventy-four thousand mendicạnt ascetics had lived? It was because the magical powers gained from the Trance States enabled them to make the seats large if they so wished. When they had completed the task of setting up the seats, the ascetic Sarada worshipped the Buddha and said.

Nā nā pupphañca gandhañca sannipātetva ekato
Pupphāsanaṃ paññapetvā idaṃ vacanamabruvi.

Idante āsanaṃ vīra paññattaṃ tavanucchaviṃ
Mama cittaṃ pasādento nisīda pupphamāsane.

Sattarattiṃ divaṃ buddho nisīdi puppahmāsane
Mama cittaṃ pasādetvā hāsayitvā sadevake.*

---

*Having gathered various blooms and perfumes
And prepared a seat of flowers, he said,
"This is your seat; Lord, one that befits you
Give me pleasure and occupy it."
For seven nights and seven days, the Buddha on that flower-seat sat
Gave much pleasure as he preached to all the heavenly beings and me.

"Please occupy these flower seats and together with your retinue remain here in *saṃsāra* for a long time for my benefit."

On this invitation the Buddha, his two chief disciples, and their followers, sat on the flower seats prepared for each of them. The ascetic Sarada held seven large blossoms over the Buddha's head. The Buddha thought, 'May this offering of flowers made by this ascetic bring him great merit.' and put himself into the Trance State of Cessation. The chief disciples saw the Buddha attain the Trance State of Cessation and they and their followers also proceeded to attain that same Trance State. They remained thus for one week. While they were in that Trance State, the seventy-four thousand pupils of the ascetic Sarada ate fruit and greens at their appointed mealtimes. Not satisfied to survive just on that, however, at other times, they fed on the joys of being in the presence of a Buddha.

"During that week the ascetic Sarada quelled all desire for fruit or greens and spent the entire week holding the seven flowers over the Buddha's head, feeding on the sweet fruit of joy. When the week was over, the Buddha rose from his trance and in order to stimulate in the mind of the ascetic the desire to become a chief disciple, he called the Senior Monk Nisabha, the chief disciple who sat at his right hand, a monk of great wisdom, and said to him, 'Tell this ascetic, who has offered flowers, of the great merit that he has acquired from this offering.'

"Like a giant soldier who has been granted a special favor by a universal monarch and is extremely pleased that he has been chosen from among all others for this special honor, so the chief disciple was pleased and preached a sermon on the merits gained by offering flowers. He did so in accordance with his capacity for wisdom as a chief disciple. When he had finished the Buddha called on his second chief disciple and said, 'You, too, preach a sermon.'

"The Senior Monk Anoma, the Buddha's second chief disciple then preached a sermon. He did so as if churning the great ocean of the Doctrine confined in the Three *Piṭakas* with the churning stick of his intellect, and as if pouring the clarified butter of his teachings to cure the earache of Defilements.[24]

"Though the earache was cured by the sermons preached by the two disciples, they were not completely cured of the sickness of their Defilements, so they did not reach the shore of *nirvāṇa*. Thereafter the Buddha began to preach. Only he could read the minds of his listeners and preach accordingly. It was as if he were lifting, single-handed, a weight that several people could not carry. The seventy-four thousand matted hair ascetics listened to the sermon and all of them, except the ascetic Sarada, discarded their headgear of Defilements,[25] which was in the form of their matted locks, and put on the crown of Enlightenment.

"With merely the words, 'Monks, come here,' the Buddha obtained for them the three necessities of a monk, that is, the two robes and bowl. They rid themselves of their matted hair, and put on instead the robes of monks and received the higher ordination.

"How was it that the ascetic Sarada did not achieve Enlightenment when those who were his pupils achieved the Trance States of Superior Wisdom and became *arahats*. Was he lacking in wisdom? No, it was not for lack of wisdom. It was because he lacked concentration. Was he unable to concentrate because he had not eaten for a week? No, it was not that. The moment the chief disciple sitting on the Buddha's right began to preach, the ascetic Sarada had thought, 'How good it would be if I, too, could one day become a chief disciple and sit at the right hand of a Buddha. Thus distracted, he was unable to direct his thoughts along the path of the Doctrine that was being preached and so could not attain *nirvāṇa*.

"Though he did not achieve *nirvāṇa*, he was not disheartened but worshipped the Buddha and asked, 'Who was the monk who sat beside you when you asked him to preach? He did so without the slightest hesitation. What position does he hold in your *sāsana?*'

'That monk is no ordinary person. He will perpetuate the Wheel of the Doctrine that I set in motion. He has fulfilled the discipline necessary to achieve the status of a chief disciple who sits on my right.'

'Master, if that is so, even though I have not done any very great act of merit, yet because I held an umbrella of flowers over your head for a whole week without going forth even to gather fruits or food, by the power of that service, rendered with such effort, I do not ask for the wealth of a Sakra or a Brahma. Just as I did not go to look for fruits, so after one incalculable and one hundred thousand eons are completed, not before, may I end my *saṃsāric* journey and may I, too, become a chief disciple of a future Buddha and be seated on his right like this monk Nisabha,' the ascetic Sarada made a Fervent Rebirth-Wish.

"The Buddha thought, 'This man's wish is great. Will it come to pass?' With his powers of prescience, half of which extend into the future, he looked into the future and knew that the day would come after one incalculable and one hundred thousand eons when it would happen.

"So he told the ascetic Sarada, 'Ascetic, the Fervent Rebirth-Wish you made is destined to come to fruition just as a pebble thrown in the air is destined to fall down. In time to come, when one incalculable and one hundred thousand eons are over, there will be born in the world a prince who in his lay life will be called 'Siduhat.' When he becomes a Buddha, he will be called 'Gōtama,' according to his clan name. His mother will be queen Mahāmāya. His father will be king Suddhōvan.

He will have a son called 'Rāhula.' His attendant monk will be Anañda. The second chief disciple will be the monk Mugalan. You will be Säriyut, that Buddha's chief disciple on his right and will be called 'Captain of the Doctrine.'

"Thus he spoke and then together with his retinue of monks, the golden Buddha rose up into the sky like golden streaks drawn across a green meadow.

"The ascetic Sarada went to the monks in his retinue and said, 'Your Reverences, when you return home please tell the householder Sirivaḍu, my friend, that I have made a Fervent Rebirth-Wish to be a disciple sitting at the right hand of the future Buddha. Tell him he, too, should make a Fervent Rebirth-Wish to be the disciple on the Buddha's left.'

"Since the ascetic Sarada was himself endowed with psychic powers, he went ahead of the monks to Sirivaḍu's palace. His friend was glad to see him after such a long time. He set up a seat for him and he himself sat down in a lower position and said, 'Master, where is your retinue?'

'Friend, the Buddha Anomadassi visited us. We rendered every service that we could. The Buddha preached to those who provided him with fruit, and the seventy-four thousand ascetics became *arahats*. I saw the power and glory of the disciple sitting on his right, the monk Nisabha, and made a Fervent Rebirth-Wish to attain a similar status. You, too, should make a wish to be the second chief disciple."

'At that the householder Sirivaḍu said, 'I am not acquainted with the Buddha so how can I do that?'

'You can because from a long time back in the past you and I have been associating with Buddhas. You should now prepare an offering of alms.'

"The householder thereupon cleared an area close to his mansion big enough to sow one *yala* and two *amunas* of seed. He scattered white sand over it and strewed five kinds of decorative material and created a pavilion similar to a hall of the gods. He thatched it with blue lotus petals, the color he himself would be in his final existence, and prepared a seat for the Buddha. He arranged seats for the other monks, too, and prepared to render whatever other services were necessary. He then asked the ascetic Sarada to invite the Buddha.

"The ascetic, accompanied by the Buddha and his retinue came to the mansion. The householder walked up to the front, invited the Buddha, took up his revered bowl, and carried it to the special pavillion. He led the Buddha and his retinue in and seated them all. With his own hands he served a meal. At the end of the meal, he presented gifts of robes and said, 'Since this is not something I do for a minor Fervent Rebirth-Wish, please do me the favor of accepting my invitation and spend a week here.' Thus, he invited him.

"During that one week, the Buddha and his retinue of monks sowed the seed of Merit in that rice field, completed the work, and hoped to gather the harvest from it after one incalculable and one hundred thousand eons had passed. Sirivaḍu worshipped the Buddha and said, 'Master, if my friend the ascetic Sarada has made a Fervent Rebirth-Wish to become the chief disciple on the right hand of a Buddha, then I, too, would wish to be disciple on that Buddha's left.'

"The Buddha looked into the future and learned that this wish would be fulfilled and said, 'One incalculable and one hundred thousand eons from now you will be the second chief disciple to the Buddha Gōtama.' He made him happy about being given the opportunity to aspire to that position and then left, accompanied by his retinue of monks."

Our Buddha related all this and addressed his monks thus. "Listen, O monks, that is how these two made their Fervent Rebirth-Wishes. It is not that I gave them a position through any favoritism."

At that the two chief disciples worshipped the Buddha and said, "Master, when we were laymen, we went one day to see a performance." And so they narrated the story up to the point of listening to the sermon of the monk Assaji and becoming Stream-Enterers. "Lord, we then went to the ascetic Sañjaya and wished to bring him to you. We told him his philosophy was useless and that yours was far superior. Even at that the ascetic Sañjaya refused to come." They then repeated to the Buddha what the ascetic had said.

The Buddha replied, "O monks, it is like the act of the man Sunakkhatta, who while walking along with me, saw Korakkhatta practicing dog asceticism.[26] He thought it something worthwhile, and left me to go to him. A man who values teachings, which are preached solely in order to obtain the four requisites of food and robes, and the sixty-two false doctrines, with their attendant prestige and profit, is like Sunakkhatta who dismissed the Buddha's virtues such as Moral Conduct and Concentration as worthless and rejected the sermon on Right Understanding and Primary Causes as trivial. Such men do no acts of Merit and so do not obtain the blessings of wealth. They do not accept the Teachings of the Triple Gem or observe the rules of Moral Conduct and so do not achieve Spiritual Attainments.

"But if a man discards False Beliefs and Defilements as valueless, then, like the wise Mahauśada in the story of the *Ummaga Jātaka*,[27] who intelligently figured out the top and bottom ends of the Kihiri sticks, even though the sticks were finely planed and each a span and four fingers long, he would realize that Moral Conduct and Concentration are indeed valuable. Just as Mahauśadha, in that same story, dismissed the empty boasts of the chameleon, who, because he received four rice grains weight of gold, imagined himself equal to King Vēdeha who possessed millions, similarly, such a man should engage in generous acts and thereby gain both material wealth such as grain and riches, and finally realize the wealth of *nirvāṇa*."

Many attained Enlightenment as a result of this sermon. Good men should discard sinful acts that are no use, perform acts of merit that are worthwhile and useful, purify their minds, and enjoy material blessings as well as Spiritual Attainments.

Endnotes

THE CHIEF DISCIPLES

Illustrates stanzas 11 and 12 of the *Yamaka Vagga*.

> Asāre sāramatino . . . micchāsaṅkappagōcarā
> Sāraṃ ca sāratō ñatvā . . . sammāsaṅkappagōcarā
>
> Those who imagine the unreal in the real and the real in the unreal, [and] who dally in the pastures of wrong thoughts, do not comprehend the real.
> They who know the real as the real and the unreal as the unreal live in the pastures of right thought and comprehend the real.

In the DA, this story begins with a section on the life of the Buddha, from the time of his past existence as the Brahmin Sumeda to his birth as Prince Sidhārta, his renunciation, achievement of enlightenment, and his life as a teacher resident at the Vēluvanārāma monastery. It is at this point that the two disciples come to him. The story of Upatissa and Kōlita is thus the second section of the story.

The SR by contrast omits this preliminary section and focuses only on the story of the two disciples. Thus, it begins at section two of the DA story. The monk Dharmasēna has suitably included the story of the Buddha in the very beginning of the SR as part of an extended prologue. [Refer *Sūvisi vivaraṇa katā*.]

However, in spite of this cut, the story of the chief disciples is still, long and full of digressions or "branch stories." But the overall structure is very carefully plotted out. It begins with the childhood and youth of Upatissa and Kōlita, and their appointment as chief disciples. Then the controversy over the appointment is taken up and several branch stories are introduced as explanations of why they and not others were given that title. The branch stories are related by the Buddha and cover the past lives of several specific monks. The two disciples then tie up the story by briefly referring to their recent efforts to find Enlightenment, bringing the story up-to-date. Finally, the Buddha preaches a concluding sermon that enables many to achieve Enlightenment.

1. Together they watched . . . , laughed when laughter was indicated, . . .

Upatissa and Kōlita are clearly connoisseurs or in terms of Indian aesthetic theory *"sahṛdaya."* The term literally means "men with heart or taste." E. C. Dimock in the introduction to *The Literatures of India* defines the Indian aesthetic concept of a *"sahṛdaya"* as one whose mind has become "lucidly receptive like a mirror, through effort and constant practice of poetry." The text implies that the two young men were such connoisseurs.

The practice of giving gifts of money to individual performers, often immediately after a performance, is still followed in traditional areas of Sri Lanka. It is so even in a ritual performance context like the *Kohoṁba Kankāriya* where gifts of money are given by members of the audience, to indicate their appreciation of an individual performer or a particular dance sequence. The action is perhaps the equivalent of the western show of applause by clapping.

2. . . . the *karmic* consequences . . . now reached the point of fruition.

The consequences of past *karmic* actions can lie dormant for a long or short time and come to fruition often after several existences.

3. ". . . Now whose order should we join?"

Clearly there were many to choose from. Historically, the time of the Buddha was a period of great intellectual ferment, debate, and controversy among different groups of monks and wandering ascetics. This is suggested in several of the stories.

4. "Listen, pupils, I have kept back nothing, . . .

Teachers were not expected to teach everything they knew. There was one special item of knowledge that was traditionally withheld and passed on only to a chosen pupil, and that often at the point of death. Many medical practices and magical formulas were handed down from master to pupil or father to son in this manner.

5. . . . , But just because we have not found it, . . .

The statement is typical of Buddhist sceptism. Not only must one question what one sees, hears, or has been told about, but one must also not assume that what one does not see or hear of, therefore, does not exist.

6. There is not enough sand in the river . . .

Note that the image Dharmasēna uses to paraphrase the verse is not the same as that in the verse itself. Dharmasēna perhaps assumed that as this particular stanza was well-known and often quoted, he did not have to render the exact meaning. Alternatively he may have thought that his image conveyed the idea better.

Similarly with the next verse. The stanza gives a two-line summary of the Doctrine of Causation. The author in his explanation of the verse adds homely images and simple examples to illustrate the text.

7. The next two lines of that stanza, . . .

In the DA the text clearly states: "After he had attained the Fruit of Conversion, the Higher excellence failed to appear." [Burlingame 1979, 201] The SR statement is less definite, it merely implies that it would take a while before Sāriputta would gain full Enlightenment. The legend that Sāriputta had wished first to be a chief disciple to a Buddha and only thereafter attain *nirvāṇa* was probably well-known to his audience, so the meaning of the statement would have been clear.

8. It is a form of paying special respect. One worships in such a manner that one's head, hands, elbows, knees, and toes touch the ground.

9. Like a man who finds something sweet, . . .

It is interesting to contrast this entire section with the corresponding section in the DA. "The wandering ascetic Kōlita saw him approaching from afar and said to himself, 'Today my friend's face has a hue not as of other days; it must be that he has attained the Deathless.' Therefore he asked him at once whether he had attained the Deathless. Upatissa said in reply, 'Yes, brother, I have attained the Deathless.' So saying he pronounced the same stanza Assaji had pronounced. At the conclusion of the stanza Kōlita was established in the fruit of conversion." [Burlingame 1979, 201]. The SR version gives life and color to the relationship between the two friends and the differences in their characters and capabilities.

10. . . . it was not too deep for the Senior Monk Anaňda to contemplate, . . .

The Buddha's disciple Anaňda had a reputation for profound learning and familiarity with the Doctrine. In that area he was superior to all other disciples.

11. As when a great chieftain with his retinue visits a rich man . . .

This is still a custom in traditional Sri Lankan homes. The servant or retainer of a guest is often fed and cared for first, even before the guest himself. In this instance the followers achieve Enlightenment before their masters, thus underlining the kind of reversal which was an implicit critique of the Brahmanic position.

12. . . . he first contemplated the elements in their totality . . .

This passage gives some indication of the detailed manner of categorization and analysis according to which the Doctrine was taught.

13. When did he make that Fervent Rebirth-Wish?

Note how the branch stories are introduced—not just by extending into the past births of the main characters but also into the past births of secondary characters. The author consciously uses this narrative device, and even draws the reader's attention to it with the line, "Thus, in relating the story of the three brothers he also told the story of the pretas." Sometimes, as with many Jātaka Tales, these branch stories tend to break off and take on a life of their own.

14. . . . from now on, do not go begging to the houses of others.

The Buddha's father would have his son forget his period of life as a mendicant monk. Henceforth, he would wish him to accept his royal hospitality and stay and preach to him alone so he could acquire Merit. His selfishness is further seen in his refusal to give his other sons a chance to participate in the meritorious activities.

15. This was like giving them molten metal to drink . . .

Buddhists consider it wrong to eat food that is prepared for the *Saṅgha* before it is served to the monks. The food prepared for monks is first put aside and whatever is left after the monks have eaten (or symbolically accepted) is then distributed among the laymen.

16. A *preta* is a spirit or ghost, often of a dead ancestor or member of the immediate family, who restlessly haunts the place where he formerly lived. A *preta* must be propitiated with ritually polluted food offerings.

17. He will . . . gain Merit thereby and transfer it to you.

The transference of Merit by the doer of a good deed to one's dead relatives, who may have been born in less fortunate states and so be unable to perform meritorious acts themselves, is a special part of all merit-making ceremonies. Offerings of food to monks are a common form of merit-making; the merit is then transferred to others, especially dead kinsmen.

18. . . . in the time of our Buddha . . .

Note the voice here is that of the author even though presently the story was being told by the Buddha. The two voices blend and the lines between author/narrator and the narrator within the story become blurred.

19. "The Buddha wished to give those, . . . "

The Buddha's story seems to end here and the narrator's voice officially takes over. However, as noted earlier, the distinction is not always carefully maintained and in the paragraph immediately preceding, the voices again overlap.

20. An incomplete stanza. "They stand against the wall . . . "

21. In one of the birth stories of the chief disciples, they are born as Sarada, the son of a wealthy Brahmin, and Sirivaḍu the son of a wealthy farmer. Note the friendship between the two boys that cuts across caste lines. Note also that both, irrespective of caste, are equally wealthy. However, it is easier for the Brahmin to take to the ascetic life than it is for his friend the farmer, for he is weighed down with worldly responsibilities.

22. The nuns Sundarā and Sumanā were his two chief female disciples.

The reference indicates that women were not only allowed in the Order but were also given high rank. The Doctrinal position is thus quite different from that reflected in the author Dharmasēna's comments and asides about women, which punctuate his text.

23. Sarada, the ascetic, then set up a seat for himself . . .

Seating arrangements within the organization of the *Saṅgha* were carefully regulated according to seniority. In Sri Lanka, even today, formal seating arrangements are made whenever monks are invited to any gathering or ceremony. Seating is arranged in consultation with one of the monks who is specially assigned for this task.

24. . . . as if pouring the clarified butter . . . to cure the earache of Defilements.

According to indigenous medical practice, the medicine for an earache is slightly warmed oil poured into the ear. Here the elaborate (mixed) metaphor ties together the mythical reference to Vishnu churning the ocean, with the image of butter-making. This again is tied to the idea of clarified butter as a medicinal oil. The point of the image is to emphasize the soothing effect of the sermon on the ears of the listeners.

25. . . . , discarded their headgear of Defilements, . . .

Buddhist monks shaved their heads in contrast to Hindu ascetics who allowed their hair to grow long and matted as a sign of their holiness and asceticism. To discard the headgear of matted locks was thus to symbolically give up Impurities and Defilements and literally to shave their heads and join the order of Buddhist monks.

26. . . . , he saw Korakkhatta practicing dog asceticism, . . .

At the time of the Buddha, there were a group of ascetics who wandered around imitating dogs, hunting for food, and drinking in the manner of dogs. The term *balu tapas* (dog asceticism) has since also come to connote fraudulent asceticism.

27. *Ummaga Jātaka*

See reference to this Jātaka in notes to the Nāgasēna story. This is yet another of the exploits of the wise sage Mahauśadha, who is the hero of this *Jātaka* tale.

The Senior Monk Nanda

Enthusiasm for the Teachings decreases without instruction. To inspire those who are slow to practice Discipline and therefore are unable to realize *nirvāṇa,* we shall relate the story of the Senior Monk Nanda.

How does it go?

The Buddha, after he attained Enlightenment, visited the city of Rajagaha on the invitation of King Bimsara, and stayed at the Vēluvanarāma monastery. During that time, he also visited Kiṁbulvat, on the invitation of his father, and rested at the Nigrodha monastery.

The day after his arrival, he walked into the inner city of Kiṁbulvat and begged for alms. Then, as if making a gift of what he had acquired, the Buddha recited a single stanza of the Doctrine for his father, whom he had not seen in a long while, and made him a Stream-Enterer. His father would not be born again in the human world more than seven or eight times thereafter, possibly only two or three more times.

He recited a second stanza for the great Prajāpati Gotamī, his stepmother; he enabled her also to become a Stream-Enterer. She would be born a human only one more time. By this act, he seemed to be repaying her for the milk he had suckled at her breast. Then, as if to confer an even higher title on his father, he made him a Once-Returner.

That very day, after his meal, he related the *Canda Kiṇara Jātaka* story[1] to illustrate the good qualities of Queen Bimbā (his former wife), qualities, which he had already assessed in a former life as the wise sage Mahauśadha[2] when too, she had been his wife.

The next day happened to be a day of celebration. It was Prince Nanda's coronation, the day of his inaugural entry into his palace, and his wedding day, all in one. The Buddha, however, thought, "Greater than all three is the celebration of *nirvāṇa.* I will, therefore, introduce him to it." Thus, he went into the city to beg and at the end of his begging round, as if making a gift of *nirvāṇa,* he placed his begging bowl in Prince Nanda's hands. Since the begging bowl was given to mark the fruition of Rebirth-Wishes Prince Nanda had made in past lives, the Buddha did not ask for it back.

Prince Nanda had no desire to follow [the Buddha to the monastery]; he wished to remain behind. Yet out of respect for the Buddha,[3] he could not bring himself to say, "Please take back your bowl." Instead he followed after him thinking, "Perhaps he will ask for it back at the top of the stairs." When the Buddha did not do so, he thought, "Perhaps he will take it now at the foot of the stairs." The Buddha did not take it there, either. Although Prince Nanda was anxious to remain behind, he could not ask the Buddha to take back his bowl lest it be disrespectful, so he kept following him unwillingly, hoping all the while, "He will take it here. He will surely take it there." Thus, the Prince was reluctantly directed along the road that was later destined to lead him to end his *saṃsāric* journey.

Then the people went to the Princess Danav Kalana (Most Beautiful One in the Region), who was not only Prince Nanda's cousin but also his betrothed. They said to her, "The Buddha, on his visit to his father's palace, has taken away your betrothed, Prince Nanda, and led him away." She happened to be bathing when she heard the news. Without stopping to even tie up her wet hair, she ran after him and said, "If you must go, my betrothed, do return quickly." Those words remained fixed in his mind[4] like wood-apple gum that makes paints adhere to a surface.

Without taking back his bowl, the Buddha led Prince Nanda to the monastery and said, "Prince Nanda, will you become a monk?" Just as a ritually planted post[5] once placed cannot be dislodged, so the Buddha's words could not be disregarded.

Therefore, instead of saying, "I do not wish to be ordained," Prince Nanda responded, "Yes, I will become a monk." And so he pledged himself.

"Ordain him," the Buddha then instructed his monks. Thus, on the third day after he arrived at Kiṁbulvat, Prince Nanda was ordained.

On the seventh day, Queen Bimba saw the Buddha with his retinue of twenty thousand *arahats,* begging in the city. She pointed him out to her son, and said, "Look, my son, do you see that person? Though he walks around begging, he has four huge jars filled with treasure. Each of them have a mouth that is two to four leagues wide; they are as tall as the thickness of the earth. I have not seen him since he left to become a monk. Thirty-two men who have studied such things as the thirty-two marks[6] of a Great Being have predicted that you will become a universal monarch. Will you not need wealth? Go and ask him to bequeath to you his treasure." She dressed him up and sent him to his father. The prince followed after the Buddha, asking for his patrimony.

The Buddha did not stop the prince. Nor did his followers stop him. Since the child was accompanying the Buddha (his father), they did not think it right to stop him. Like a star following the moon, Prince Rahal followed after the Buddha all the way to the monastery.

The Buddha thought, "He asks for my wealth to which he is the legitimate heir. Great are the sufferings that are rooted in material wealth. I exchanged the one treasure of my Omniscient Knowledge for seven other treasures. I will give him those seven treasures." He called the Senior Monk Säriyut and said, "Listen, O Sāriputta,[7] this Prince Rahal asks me for my wealth. On my journey to become a monk, I left behind no guards to protect it and therefore do not have the kind of wealth he asks. But is not the treasure I now possess equally valuable? Therefore, in order to give him the seven treasures, ordain him a monk." Thus, he commanded and had Prince Rahal ordained. Once he was ordained Prince Rahal became just like the Buddha, even in the way he wore his robes.

King Sudōvan was greatly grieved that Prince Rahal, too, had been ordained a monk. The King, who could no longer bear his grief, went to the Buddha and said, "The grief I felt when you left to become a monk was assuaged by looking on the faces of Prince Nanda and Prince Rahal. When Prince Nanda became a monk, I consoled myself somewhat by looking on the face of Prince Rahal. Who is left to me now that he, too, has become a monk? Does affection for a son and grandson well up only in me? No, it is so for all men. Now that this has happened to me, let it pass. But henceforth, lay it down as a rule, that no child shall be ordained without the permission of his parents."

"It shall be so," the Buddha promised.

One day, the Teacher of the Three Worlds, the Buddha, entered the palace of King Sudōvan. When he was seated and ready to eat, the King said, "Lord, when you were performing penance, suffering in order to attain Enlightenment, a minor deity came to me and said that you were dead. When I heard that, I told him 'Like flowers that do not fade until they have bloomed at the right season, so my son will not die before he becomes a Buddha.' I did not believe what the deities told me."

"Great King, you who have seen the thirty-two marks that appear only on one destined to be a Buddha, and you who have seen the miracle of the thirty-two signs at my birth, how could you accept such a statement? In a past life, when you were born as Prince Dharmapāla, even though they brought you goat bones to convince you that I, your son, was dead, you said, 'In our clan, one who is born does not die until he has completed his total life-span.' " At that point the Buddha related the *Mahā Dharmapāla Jātaka* story,[8] and when the king heard it he attained the status of a Non-Returner or *anāgāmin*. However, he was destined to achieve full Enlightenment only on his death bed, not before.

The Buddha's work was not over, so to complete his work as a Buddha he left for the city of Rajagaha accompanied by his monks. Then he requested the great nobleman Anēpiḍu to build him a monastery at Devramvehera, and when it was complete and he was invited to reside there, he went with his monks to the city of Sävät and took up residence at the Devramvehera monastery.

While the Buddha was living there, the Senior Monk Nanda kept remembering the words of his betrothed, the princess. It was as if the colors of her words mixed with the gum of love were painted on the walls of his mind. Gazing on that painting, he became dissatisfied with the monastic order and said to a fellow monk who was a close friend, "I have no love for the *sāsana*. I intend to give up my robes."

The Buddha heard about this, called him up, and asked, "Is it true Nanda, that you said such a thing to this monk?"

When he replied, "Yes, it is true, Master," the Buddha asked, "Nanda, why do you wish to give up the robes?"

Nanda replied, "Master, while I was on my way here, I was of two minds whether or not to be ordained. The Princess Danav Kalana followed after me without even stopping to tie up her wet hair and said, 'Please return soon.' I think often of her words and so have decided to go back."

At that point, as if administering medicine for a serious and chronic disease, the Buddha used his own powers to take Nanda by the hand and lead him to Tavtisā heaven; the monk did not have the strength to do so himself. Along the way, he created a vision of a burnt out plot of abandoned farmland with a shriveled, old, she-monkey seated on a charred log. He then led him on to the Tavtisā heaven and there showed him Sakra's five hundred or more celestial maidens.

"What do you think, Nanda? Who is more beautiful, these celestial maidens or the Princess Danav Kalana?"

"Master, what are you talking about? Having set eyes on these celestial beauties, the Princess Danav Kalana now seems no better than that twisted and withered she-monkey that we saw by the newly burnt jungle clearing."

"If that is so, Nanda, practice the Precepts with enthusiasm for the *Sāsana* and, even though you may not rid yourself of all Defilements, I will guarantee that you will be born in heaven and obtain those celestial maidens."

Thereupon the monk Nanda replied, "If I have such a good guarantee for obtaining those celestial maidens, then I will certainly practice celibacy here on earth."

In this way the Buddha fostered in him an attachment to the *sāsana*. As one leads an undisciplined man to a public place and there forces him to act as he should, so in order to make the monk Nanda practice the Precepts, he took him to heaven. Then, as if not to hide from him the fact of his guarantee, he said:

Bodhaneyyaṃ janaṃ disvā[9] satasahassepi yojane
Khaṇena upagantvāna bodheti taṃ mahāmunī*

He vanished from heaven and in a second descended to the Devramvehera monastery.

*When he sees those who can comprehend the Doctrine, the Great Sage travels a hundred or a thousand leagues to make them understand.

The monks heard of this and said, "The monk Nanda is after all the Buddha's mother's sister's son.[10] He practices monastic Discipline just as if he were doing routine household chores. Only for the sake of celestial maidens! Moreover he has asked for guarantees from the Buddha. It is not fitting that he should do so." They went to the monk Nanda and wore him down with their remarks.

The monk Nanda felt very ashamed of the monks' criticisms. He gave up his desire for the celestial maidens and, as if firmly securing something about to fall off, he turned his mind again to monastic practices. Having given up the kingly life, he now lived diligently, seeking only the bliss of *nirvāṇa.*

A squirrel, when he meets an enemy his own size, puffs his tail, strikes him with it, and drives him away. Similarly, when enemy defilements drew near, the monk Nanda struck them down with the weapon of the Four Meditations; he drove them away.

A leopardess, who has only one litter and does not give birth a second time, is barren. Likewise, he decided to do nothing that would extend his cycle of rebirths beyond this one life. And just as the leopardess hides in tall grasslands to leap on her prey, so he went to huge trees and to the foot of rocks, to mountain ranges, caves, and cemeteries in search of the prey of Enlightenment. A leopardess, when she kills a prey, will not eat it if it has fallen on its left side. Similarly, the monk Nanda did not eat anything[11] that was obtained by any one of the twenty-one improper ways, such as making a verbal request. He avoided such foods as if they were poisonous concoctions. Instead, he cultivated Insight and, wearing the crown of Enlightenment, he received a coronation to substitute for the one he had abandoned. In place of the inauguration ceremony, which he had missed, he enjoyed the ceremony of entering the house of *nirvāṇa*. In lieu of the marriage feast he had rejected, he received the Path and the Fruits of Spiritual Attainments and gained a share in the kingdom of *nirvāṇa* belonging to the Buddha.

That very night a certain deity went to the Buddha, who was living at the Devramvehera monastery, worshipped him, and said, "Master, your younger brother Nanda has become an *arahat.*" Just as the Buddha knew when he took the journey to heaven that Nanda would end his journey in *saṃsāra* and had been watching for it, so now he knew of it even before the words were spoken.

At dawn the Senior Monk Nanda went to the Buddha, worshipped him and said, "Master, when you went to heaven you promised me five hundred celestial maidens. I now have no desire for anything, let alone celestial maidens. You no longer have to keep your promise."

The Buddha said, "Nanda, we already knew you had attained Enlightenment. A deity announced it to us. Therefore, whether you said it or not, we had already been released from our promise." Nanda's face, which glowed with the attainment of Enlightenment, then became even more beautiful.

Not knowing that Nanda had become an *arahat*, the monks went to him and said, "What has happened? Formerly you wanted to give up the robes. Now do you think differently about it?

"I have no desire to be a layman," Nanda replied.

"In the past, he had no love for the *sāsana*. Now he says he has no love for the lay life. The man is lying," they said and reported this to the Buddha.

The Buddha answered, "Monks, a house that is not well-thatched[12] may weather the dry season, but it will leak during the rains. Similarly, if you do not have the thatch of Tranquil Meditation and Insight Meditation your mind-house will not be protected from the rain of Defilements. A mind protected by the strong roof of the twofold Meditations will not get wet even with the great downpours of Defilements that fill the Ocean of *saṃsāra*."

On hearing him the monks, who had come to complain about Nanda, also reached the state of the Stream-Enterer and received the blessings of Spiritual Attainments. These monks, who now realized what was true and what was false, comprehended the Four Noble Truths.

A story went the rounds of the Council of Monks.[13] It went thus:

> The Buddha is most wondrous! He enabled his brother, who was about to lose his chance of achieving *nirvāṇa* on account of the Princess Dannav Kalani, to receive an even better gift. Just as one distracts a child clamoring for some object by showing him a better one, so by showing him the celestial maidens he distracted him from the Princess Danav Kalani. Could anyone else do such a thing?

The Buddha heard with his Divine Ear the stories that were circulating among the monks. He thought, "These monks talk about the manner in which Nanda was drawn to the *sāsana*. I will go there and say to them, "Listen, O monks, this is not something that happened just this once. In the past, too, I have distracted him in a similar manner. I will then tell them a story of the past to illustrate this. For five thousand years to come this *Jātaka Story* will benefit many."

He then went to the Council of Monks, saw that modest and restrained assembly and thought, "This assembly of monks is most beautiful. It is like a forest of lotuses blooming and swaying around a golden boat. If I do not begin the proceedings, no one will speak before I do. I will therefore begin the discussion."

So he said, "Monks, what were you talking about before I arrived?"

When they told him, he continued, "O monks, it is not only in the present that the Buddha, Lord of the Three Worlds, was invited by his monks and related the story of former times, which lies hidden like fire under ashes.

"Long ago, O monks, when a king named Bam̆badat was ruling in the city of Baranäs, there lived in that city a merchant called 'Kappaṭa.' He had a mule who could carry the weight of ten *amunas*.[14] He could walk twenty-eight leagues carrying such a load.

"During a certain season, the merchant carried his goods by pack mule to the city of Taxila. While he traded his goods, he let the mule out to graze. The mule, grazing along the edge of the city moat, saw a she-mule and went up to her. She engaged him in pleasant conversation.

'Where are you from?' she asked.

'From Baranäs' he replied.

'Why have you come on this long and difficult journey?'

'I have come to trade.'

'How much weight do you carry?'

'About ten *amunas* weight of goods.'

'With such a heavy load, how far do you walk each day?'

'About twenty-eight leagues,' he answered.

'You walk such a distance and with such a heavy load! Is there no one to massage your limbs once you get to your destination?' Thus, she spoke, hiding her true intent.

'No one.' he replied.

"Though she was an animal, being female, she was not lacking in feminine wiles.[15] Thus, even though animals do not massage each other's limbs, she made out that he was suffering some kind of deprivation in order to draw him to her. She indicated that if she were to live with him he would lack nothing. The mule believed what she said and was ensnared.

"Meanwhile the merchant sold the goods that he had brought with him and said to the mule, 'Let us go now.'

'You can go back. I intend to stay on here.' the mule answered.

"Though urged again and again he remained stubborn for no other reason than that he had become ensnared by the she-mule's words. When he refused to come the merchant said,

> Patodante karissāmi soḷasaṃgulakaṇṭakaṃ
> Sañchindissāmi te kāyaṃ evaṃ jānāhi gadrabha.*

---

*I will make a thornstick goad sixteen inches
And I'll break your back, know that, you mule.

"I will make a stick with thorns, sixteen inches long. I will get a stick and beat you."

"If you do that, I will plant my forelegs firmly on the ground, kick you with my hind legs, and smash your teeth," replied the mule.'[16]

"The merchant thought, 'Until now this animal has never said anything like this. What can be the matter with him?' He looked about him and saw the she-mule. 'It is surely because of her that he has become so stubborn,' he thought. Since he was a wise man with the kind of intelligence that could determine at what point to thread an eight-faceted gem stone, he said:

> Catuppadiṃ saṃkhamukhiṃ nāriṃ sabbhaṃgasobhiniṃ,
> Bhariyaṃ te anayissāmi evam jānāhi gadrabha.**

'If you return with me, I will give you a she-mule that is the most beautiful of your kind, with a face like a conch shell.'

"The mule was greatly pleased at the prospect. He felt no more affection for the she-mule he had seen, but instead felt a strong attraction to the she-mule he had just heard about. So he said, 'In that case, I will take up the load and go, not just twenty-eight leagues but even an additional twenty-eight leagues if need be—fifty-six leagues!'

'Good!' said the merchant and he led the mule home.

"After a few days, the mule reminded him about the she-mule. The merchant said, 'I will not forget my earlier promise. I will surely bequeath a she-mule to you as a mate. But there is one thing you should consider. I will pay only for the cost of your keep. She renders me no service. What you earn may perhaps be enough to feed the two of you, but then again it may not. I don't know about that. Later, she may bear you many young ones. Whether they be wife or children, and whether they be few or many, I cannot increase your wages because there are already many others who depend on me. Therefore, like the king in the *Suppāraka Jātaka* story,[17] who was descended from a barber and who gave only eight gold pieces to everyone irrespective of whatever skills were displayed, so, whether it be enough or not enough for you, and however many you be, I will give you only the wages of one.' At which point the mule transferred his attachment from the she-mule to his wages." Thus, ended the Buddha's discourse on the Jātaka.

Therefore, wise men should keep away from sinful deeds, establish themselves in good actions such as Contemplation, and suppressing Defilements, purify their thoughts and minds.

**I will bring you a wife with a face like a conch,
A four-legged wife, lovely of limb, know that, O mule.

Endnotes

THE SENIOR MONK NANDA

Illustrates stanzas 13 and 14 of the Yamaka vagga.

> Yathāgāraṃducchānaṃ . . . samativijjhati
> Yathāgāram succhānaṃ . . . na samativijjhati

> As rain penetrates an ill-thatched house, so lust penetrates an undeveloped mind.
> As rain does not penetrate a well-thatched house, so lust does not penetrate a well-developed mind.

The story of Nanda the Elder is divided into sections in the DA. Section (a) is said to be almost word for word from the *Nidānakathā, Jātaka* i, 85–92 and section (b) is said to be almost word for word from the *Udāna*. [Burlingame 1979, 217] The SR version omits the first paragraph (of section [a] of the DA), which tells of King Suddhōdhana's repeated requests to the Buddha to visit him. It progresses to an account of the Buddha's first visit to the city of his birth after Enlightenment and the events that occurred, that is, the ordinations of Prince Nanda and of Prince Rahal. Thus, the structure is much tighter. As always, the story is framed with a brief opening paragraph stating the didactic intention, and concludes with a brief exhortation.

The city of Kiṁbulvat (p. Kapilavāstu) was the Buddha's home. The story concerns his immediate family, his father, King Sudōvan (Suddhōdhana), his stepmother Prajāpati Gōtamī, who nursed him when his mother died, Queen Bimbā, his former wife, his son Rāhal (Rāhula) and his half-brother Nanda. This was the occasion of the Buddha's first visit to his home since he attained Enlightenment.

1. *Canda Kiṇara Jātaka*

This is a story of two fairies who dwelt on a beautiful hill and how, when the husband was wounded, the wife made lament until Sakra came to the rescue.

2. . . . her former life as his wife when he was the wise sage Mahauśada.

Another reference to the *Ummaga Jātaka*. Here, the sage tests Amarā Devi's intelligence and character by a series of questions. She answers him with equal skill and he then marries her.

3. Yet out of respect for the Buddha, . . .

It was considered impolite and rude to question the actions of one's teachers or elders. Prince Nanda could not bring himself to refuse the Buddha's implicit gift. In accepting the bowl and following the Buddha, he was symbolically accepting the life of a monk. His dilemma was that while he could not bring himself to return the bowl, he did not also wish to take on the celibate life of a monk. All he could do was to follow after, hoping that the Buddha would himself ask for his bowl, and so relieve him from this impossible bind.

4. Those words remained fixed in his mind . . .

Various types of gums and resins were traditionally mixed with vegetable dyes to make the paint adhere to the surfaces on which it was used.

5. Just as a ritually planted post . . .

Many ritual performances are inaugurated by the planting of a ritual post or *kap*. The kap symbolizes the *kalpa vrukṣa* or wish-fulfilling tree. A *kap* once planted cannot be dislodged until the ritual is completed.

6. Thirty-two men who have studied such things as the thirty-two marks . . .

The thirty-two auspicious marks of a Great Being are associated with one who will become either a Universal Monarch or a Buddha. They are most commonly used to identify a Buddha. Here the author suggests that Prince Rahal (Rāhula) also had the thirty-two marks. Therefore, he was expected to become a Universal Monarch. This connection neither appears in the DA nor is it part of the popular tradition. The Buddha's words in the following paragraph, "You who have seen the thirty-two marks that appear only on one destined to be a Buddha" seem to contradict this.

7. "Listen, O Sāriputra, . . .

Note the use of the Sanskritic form of the name on this occasion. It adds a note of formality to the request.

8. *Dharmapāla Jātaka* story.

This is the story of how a father refused to believe that his son was dead even when shown what were supposedly his bones, because, he claimed, it was not the custom in his family to die young. This was the result of good living throughout several generations.

9. Bodhaneyyaṃ janaṃ disvā . . .

This verse does not appear in the *Dhammapada Commentary.* Nor does the monk Dharmasēna give his usual explanation of the Pāli stanza in the body of the text. It could be a later interpolation.

10. "The monk Nanda is after all the Buddha's mother's sister's son."

Implicit in the monks' remarks is the charge of favoritism and a criticism of the Buddha's method of conversion in this particular case. As always the Buddha takes up the questions and criticisms raised by the monks, answers them, and by that further expounds on some aspects of the Teachings not hitherto clarified.

11. Similarly, the monk Nanda did not eat anything . . .

The proper and improper ways to beg for alms were all carefully laid down in the Rules of the Vinaya. The animal images introduced by the author Dharmasēna, which do not appear in the DA, make vivid the hardships of the ascetic life practiced by the monk Nanda.

12. "Monks, a house that is not well-thatched . . .

In the DA, stanzas 13 and 14 from the *Dhammapada* are introduced at this point. The author Dharmasēna has instead only a prose summary of the Dhammapada text in the SR.

13. A story went the rounds of the Council of Monks.

There is a double-edged quality to the comments. They could be read as an ironic criticism of the Buddha's methods or of wonder and appreciation of his skill. In the image of the child being distracted the author, Dharmasēna seems to attempt to explain the Buddha's actions. The subsequent passages mark a subtle shift to this latter position.

14. He had a mule who could carry the weight of ten *amunas*.

An *amuna* is a grain measure of five or six bushels. It is also used for a measure of land, i.e. that extent of land which requires an *amuna* of grain for sowing.

15. . . . , Being female, she was not lacking in feminine wiles.

Another gratuitous comment about women, characteristic of this and other writers of the medieval period.

16. In the DA, the mule's reply is also in verse. The author of the SR however, gives it in prose, and in so doing, makes the confrontation more dramatic, also perhaps more readily understood and enjoyed by his Sinhala listeners and readers.

17. *Suppāraka Jātaka* story.

This is the story of the Bōdhisatva, born as the son of a master mariner. Blinded by the salt water, he ceases to be a mariner and becomes chief assessor and valuer to the king. Though blind, he was wise and very skilled at his task and served the king well. The king, however, always paid him eight gold pieces for whatever services he rendered. Disgusted by the king's cheap ways, the mariner remarks, "This is a barber's gift; this king must be a barber's brat. Why should I serve such a king?" He returns to his own seaport hometown.

The Pig-Killer Cunda

Moreover, to show those who avoid doing good the ill effects of sinful acts, we shall relate the tale of the Pig-killer Cunda. How does it go?

For nearly fifty-five years the pig-killer, with his nets and water, lived by killing, eating, and selling pigs. In times of famine, knowing that the value of pigs would drop, he would take grain to the interior areas and trade one or two measures of it in exchange for piglets. The carts in which he carried the grain he then filled with piglets and on returning set up a sty behind his house. The food for the pigs was placed in the sty itself. The pigs ate and grew fat and he, too, fattened on such sinful acts.

When he decided to kill a pig, he would take the animal, tie it tightly to a firmly fixed post, and beat him with a four-sided club in order to tenderize the meat. He did not realize that, while the meat softened, his own sins swelled. He hadn't a clean thought himself but, as if to clean out some part of the animal's past bad *karma,* he would force open the pig's mouth (just as his own mouth was to be forced open in hell) thrust a stick to stop it from closing, and with a metal spoon he would pour intensely boiling water down the animal's throat. In like manner, molten metal would be poured down his throat in hell.

The boiling water in the stomach would churn up all the excrement inside the animal and pass out through the digestive tract. If there was the least bit of impurity left in the stomach, the water would come out turbid. But when all the impurities were flushed out, the water expelled would be clean. When the insides were clean, he would pour the remaining water on the pig's back. The black skin would burn and peel off. He would singe the hairs with a flare made of grasses and would cut off the animal's head with a sharp iron blade. He would then collect the blood flowing from the severed neck into a pot and dip the pieces of meat in a paste made from the blood. Then he would sit with his wife and children and eat. Whatever was left over, he sold.

He lived thus for fifty-five years. This man, committing such sinful acts, lived in close proximity to the monastery of Devramvehera, that Field of Merit so attractive to most other people. But though he had every opportunity for performing acts of Merit, he offered neither flowers, incense, nor lights; neither did he give gifts of alms nor do any good deed.

After fifty-five years, he became very sick. Long before he died, he began seeing the fires of the Avīci-hell, a portent of where he was to go in his next birth. These hell flames were such that, if one were to look at them even from a distance of four hundred leagues, one's eyes would burst out of their sockets. If one were to throw a rock as big as a house into those flames, it would melt instantly. How was it then that if a rock melted in it, a being born there was not instantly consumed? For this reason: a creature conceived in a mother's womb is not destroyed by the heat of that womb, similarly the power of bad *karma* can stop one from being immediately destroyed.

From the moment the pig-killer began to see those hellfires, what he had done to the pigs began now to happen to him.

For it is said:

> Yena yena pakārena yaṃ yaṃ pāpaṃ kataṃ purā
> Tassa tassānurūpaṃ ca phalaṃ hoti asāhiyaṃ*

He fell on his knees, squealed like a pig and crawled yelling and screaming from the front door to the back. The people in his house held him down and forcibly closed his mouth when he tried to scream. Just as he had formerly forced open the pig's mouth by thrusting a stick, so now he could not close his own mouth and screamed continuously. Neighbors, for seven houses on each side of him, a total of fourteen homes, could not get a night's sleep. Just as the pig had suffered greatly at his hands, so now the people around him also suffered great inconvenience. He ran back and forth like a mad dog; so they bolted the doors of his house and stood guard outside. Inside, Cunda the pig-killer, crawled back and forth crying loudly. For seven days he got no chance to eat any pork. For seven days he squealed and screamed in this way. On the seventh day he died and was reborn in Avīci-hell.

This hell was enclosed with four gleaming walls of flame[1] four hundred leagues long, broad, and high and about thirty-six leagues thick. It had an iron floor and a metal covering. Just as he had lived a life-span of fifty-five years on earth, so he was forced now to live in Avīci-hell for a part of an eon.

During the seven days that he spent yelling and screaming, monks passed by his house on their begging rounds. They heard his screams and thought it was the sound of pigs being butchered. They went to the Buddha and said, "Master, Cunda has closed his doors and is killing all his pigs. They are yelling and squealing. It is now over a week. It must be for some special feast of his. In all this time we have not seen even a glimmer of a compassionate thought in him or any sign that he would stop his killing. We have never encountered anyone so callous."

The Buddha replied, "Listen, monks, he has not spent these past seven days killing pigs. It is he who screams. Fearing death, he is des-

*Certain kinds of sinful acts committed in past lives
have similar consequences, unbearable though they be.

perate to show other sinners the magnitude of the hellfires that he now sees, so that they may not, like him, commit such sinful acts. Today he has died and been born in Avīci-hell. Therefore, whether you be monks or laymen know this. If a man immerses himself in sinful acts like this man did, at the point of death he will say, 'I have done nothing good in my past life.' He will grieve over what he has not done. In the other world, he will undergo great suffering and will grieve even as he suffers. Sinners suffer remorse in both worlds. Whichever way they look, they see nothing good that they have done. They grieve and suffer seeing only their base acts."

Many who heard this sermon became afraid to sin, avoided acts of Demerit and set themselves on the path of goodness. Thus, they ended their sufferings in *saṃsāra* and attained the Path and the Fruits. This sermon will benefit many for over five thousand years. Thus, good men should avoid sinful acts, do only acts of Merit and purify their thoughts.

Endnotes

THE PIG-KILLER CUNDA

Illustrates stanza 15 of the Yamaka Vagga.

> Idha sōcati pecca sōcati . . . kammakiliṭṭha mattanō
>
> The wrongdoer grieves here, he grieves hereafter,
> He grieves in both places,
> He grieves; he is afflicted, seeing his own impure deeds.

The story of Cunda is very close to its original in the DA. Perhaps for this very reason, it is one of the shorter pieces in the SR. It stands therefore in sharp contrast to many of the other stories, which are full of elaborate interpolations, of extended metaphors, digressions, and authorial comments. Here the comments are often confined to a brief aside or interjection as "The pigs ate and grew fat, *and he, too, fattened on such sinful acts.*" Or again, "He did not realize that, while the meat softened, *his own sins, too, swelled. He hadn't a clean thought himself* but, as if to clean out some part of the animal, . . . " The details of the procedure adopted in killing and cleaning the pig does remain the same in both works.

While making brief analogies that stress the moral implications of such actions, it is as if the author does not want to distract from the horror of the actual procedure. The detailed and extremely graphic account of the butchering of pigs occurs in both the DA and SR texts. It suggests that raising pigs for meat was probably a fairly common practice in the fifth century Sri Lankan world even though it violated a basic Buddhist precept. Perhaps for that very reason, it was used here to illustrate the bad karmic consequences of such acts.

Sri Lanka, though Buddhist, has not had a tradition of vegetarianism, unlike Hindu India that does. But it is interesting that today pig rearing is practiced mainly in the South West region of Sri Lanka by a largely Catholic population. Interesting too is the fact that the same technique for tenderizing the meat, as described in this text, is still in use.

1. This hell was enclosed with four gleaming walls of flame . . .

Note the precise detailed description in the SR as if the author were describing a familiar earthly structure. The DA passage is an interesting contrast, for the description is given within parentheses and in the words of others. "The fire of Avīci is a consuming torment able to destroy the eyes of one who stands a hundred leagues away and looks at it. Indeed, it has been described in this wise saying, 'Forever and ever it shoots forth its flames continually one hundred leagues in all directions.' Moreover, the Elder Nāgasēna employed the following simile to show how much more intense is its heat than that of ordinary fire, 'Great king, reflect that a rock even as big as a pagoda goes to destruction in the fire of Hell in but an instant. However, living beings who are reborn there, through the effect of their past deeds, suffer not destruction, but are as though they reposed in their mother's wombs.' " [Burlingame 1979, 226]

In the monk Dharmasēna's brief description, the sense of overwhelming terror comes from the very precision of the measured details and the feeling of being inescapably shut in. The image of the womb has very different connotations even though the sense of entrapment is similar. Depictions of hell in the frescoes painted on temple walls in Sri Lanka have a similar kind of precision; the heightened degree of realism seeks to intensify the horror for the beholder.

The Lay Devotee, Dhammika

Just as we give water to quench the thirst of those who have walked a long way in the hot sun so we have preached sermons such as the Dēvadūta Sutta to show good men the benefits of virtue. And to calm those who may be terrified[1] by the sufferings just briefly described, we shall now relate the story of the lay devotee Dhammika, and set you on the path of righteousness.

How does the story go?

Five hundred lay devotees lived in the city of Sävät and spent their time in peace and righteousness. Each of them had a retinue of five hundred persons. Thus, there were in all about twenty-five thousand lay devotees there. Their chief was the lay devotee Dhammika, who initiated all their acts of merit.

Dhammika had seven sons and seven daughters. Just as the aerial roots that hang down from a sandalwood tree are all equally fragrant, so the children were all equally good. They held the same ideas and beliefs as their parents. The two devotees and their children, a total of sixteen people, had a regular roster for the giving of alms. They gave gifts of rice every fortnight. Since in India[2] the people offer alms even when they see the new moon, so they made sixteen such additional offerings, too. They also each made an offering at the end of the rainy season to those monks who had completed the duties of that *vas* period. Like plants that bear sweet fruit because they grow in fertile soil, so these sixteen were greatly blessed.

However, just as a tree hitherto unscarred, may later develop a callous, so the lay devotee Dhammika developed a disease. The oil of his life burned low and the wick sputtered and approached the extinction of death. He wished to hear a sermon and, since the chanting of the Protective Stanzas are a kind of sermon, he requested the Buddha to send about eight or sixteen monks.[3] The Buddha sent them to him. They stood around the lay devotee's bed. The dying man saw the monks who were surrounding him like clusters of red lotuses so that his mind might be made tranquil at the moment of death.

Dhammika said to them, "Your reverences, soon I shall not be able to see you. While I still can, will you preach a single sermon for me to hear?"

"What text would you like?" they asked.

"Master, as the *Sihivaṭan Sutta*[4] is one that all the Buddhas have preached, it would be good if you could recite that for me." The monks did as he wished and started to chant the *Mahā Sihivaṭan Sutta.*

At that very moment, six chariots, each about six hundred leagues long, drawn by one thousand white horses, like white-lotus petals,[5] arrived from the six heavens of the gods and appeared in the sky.

The gods sitting in each of these chariots said, "O you, who are free of suffering, climb into the chariots we have brought with us, and, as you would break a clay cooking pot in order to replace it with a golden one, be reborn where you can have the blessings of heavenly worlds." Each god in turn, said this to him.

The lay devotee, concerned that the new arrivals would interrupt the recital of the sermon, said to the gods, "Please, stop a moment."

The monks thought he had addressed them and stopped their chanting. The lay devotee's children thought, "Our father is usually even more fond of sermons than he is of us. And yet he, who invited the monks to come here, and requested them to start the chanting, now asks them to stop. Alas! there is no one who is unafraid of death." Thus, they wept.

The monks throught, "He does not want us to chant *Protective Stanzas,*" and they returned to the monastery.

After some time, the lay devotee regained consciousness and asked, "Why do you weep?"

"Father, you invited the monks, asked them to chant the *Protective Stanzas* and while they were doing so, you stopped them, as if stopping someone in the very act of drinking nectar. We realized then that even you were afraid to die. If that is so then none of us can remain unafraid."

"Where are the monks?" asked the lay devotee.

"They have returned to their monasteries," the children replied.

"I did not ask them to leave. Why did they go?" he asked.

"You told them to stop. We heard it, too. To whom then did you speak?"

"Gods from the six heavens, as if to bring heaven close to me, brought six decorated chariots and placed them in the sky. They invited me to come to heaven. It was to them I said, 'Stop a moment,' so that I could finish listening to the chanting," he answered.

"If they brought their chariots, how is it that only you have seen them and we have not?"

Since it was impossible to make visible to others the chariots that had appeared to him, as a portent of his next life, he thought of a way to make them understand.

"Are there any flower garlands that have been prepared for me to give as offerings?" he asked.

"Yes," they answered.

"Of the seven heavens, which would you consider most attractive?"

"Father, the Tusī heaven[6] is where all the Bōsats and their parents live. That heaven is most blessed. There one can listen to the sermons of the Maitreya Bōsat," they answered.

"If so, take a garland and throw it and wish that it might hang on the chariot that has come from that particular heaven." They did as they were told.

The garland stuck fast to the head of the chariot and hung there as if all its beauty were spilling over. Many people saw the garland hanging up there, even though they could not see the chariot.

The devotee asked, "Do you see that garland hanging there?"

When they replied, "Yes," he added, "That garland hangs from the chariot that came from Tusī heaven. It means that I will go there when I leave here. You should weep only if the place to which I go were full of dangers. Therefore, be not sad. Instead, make Rebirth-Wishes to go there yourselves, and do good as I have done." So saying he died and was reborn in that chariot.

The instant he was reborn, he was endowed with a heavenly form,[7] three leagues tall, and adorned with sixty carts of ornaments. One thousand heavenly maidens accompanied him. An abode made of gems about one hundred leagues high also appeared. The god Dhammika, looking like Sakra, entered the jeweled abode adorned by that carpenter —his virtuous actions.

The Buddha asked the priests who returned to the monastery, "Is the chanting over?"

"Yes, Master. We started to chant the *Mahā Sihivaṭan Sutta* but before we could complete it, the devotee, Dhammika stopped us. Everybody started to weep. We said to ourselves, 'What is the point of chanting while everyone is weeping? There is no need to be doing both.' So we left hurriedly."

"Monks, he did not mean to stop you. Gods from the six heavens brought six chariots and asked him to climb in. He did not wish to interrupt the recital he was listening to, so he said to the gods, 'Stop a moment.'

When the monks heard that, they asked, "Master, where has he been reborn now?"

"In the Tusī heaven," the Buddha said. Then he added, "O Monks, a man who is not slow to do good is happy. Because he is of a happy mind he takes pleasure in doing good. In his next life, too, he is happy, seeing the blessings that have accrued from his past good deeds. Therefore, the virtuous man thinks only of the good he has done, whether in this life or another. He contemplates the blessings he has thereby obtained and is happy, like the god Dhammika."

Thus, he provided a drink of the Doctrine to these monks who were tired out[8] by chanting the Protective Stanzas. He eased them of the weariness of their Defilements and gave them a taste of nirvāṇa.

This sermon, like the wish-fulfilling tree,[9] the vine, and the pot, was of use to a great many people. Just as those who enjoy rice, when given a mixture of rice and *amu* grain, can pick out the rice from *amu*, so those who involve themselves in doing acts of Merit should learn to discard Demerit and choose only what is good. Then, with the seed of Virtue they should sow the field of the Three Refuges and gather a harvest of the blessings of the world and the blessings of Spiritual Attainments.

Endnotes

THE LAY DEVOTEE DHAMMIKA

Illustrates stanza 16 of the Yamaka Vagga.

> Idha mōdati pecca mōdati . . . kammavisuddhi mattanō
>
> Here he rejoices, hereafter he rejoices,
> He who has done good rejoices in both places,
> He rejoices exceedingly, seeing his good deeds.

Like the story of Cunda this story too follows the original fairly closely with only the occasional interpolated metaphor or comment.

1. . . . and to calm those who were terrified . . .

Here again the author consciously links the story with the one gone before by using it as a counterpoint. The DA makes no such connections.

2. Since in India, . . .

This is another aside typical of Dharmasēna, drawing attention to the fact that the story is after all located in India where the Buddha lived and preached, even though his present audience is Sri Lankan and have different customs and practices.

3. *Pirit* (p. paritta) is generally chanted by monks, alternating in groups of four, hence the number eight or sixteen.

4. The *Sihivaṭan Sutta* is another name for the *Satipaṭṭāna Sutta,* which is often recited at the moment of death, for it focuses on the Teachings of Impermanence and Decay.

5. . . . one thousand white horses, like white-lotus petals, . . .

Interestingly the DA version refers to one thousand Sindh horses. Identifying the horses as a particular breed of a specific region of India suggests possibly the DA author's Indian background. Horses, unlike elephants, are not a familiar part of the Sri Lankan landscape. Hence, the description is almost of an imaginary creature made real by means of imagery and simile.

6. The Tusī heaven is another name for Tusita heaven

7. . . . , he was endowed with a heavenly form, . . .

The descriptions of heaven and of the gods resemble closely their depictions in paintings to be seen even today on the walls of temples in Sri Lanka. Similarly with the depictions of hell found in the Cunda story.

8. Thus, he provided a drink of the Doctrine to these monks who were tired out . . .

This is a typical touch that makes Dharmasēna's characters come alive. They would appeal to readers familiar with attending on monks, who, when they come to chant *pirit* in their homes, have to be plied with warm drinks so they do not become hoarse.

9. . . . the wish-fulfilling tree, the vine, and the pot, . . .

The three items referred to, the *kapruk* (wish-fulfilling tree), the *kalpa lata* (wish-fulfilling vine), and the *badra ghata* (wish-fulfilling pot) are supposed to exist in heaven.

Devadatta

Let us illustrate with the story of Devadatta the enormity of the suffering that results from heinous sins so that those with sinful thoughts will be drawn out of such ways and set on the path of righteousness.

How does it go?

When our Buddha, teacher of the Three Worlds, was living in the mango grove named Anupiya belonging to the Malla kings of Kusināra, most of the eighty thousand young men who were assigned to him took to the robes saying, "Be he a king or be he a Buddha may he walk escorted by followers." However, the young princes Bhuddiya, Anuruddha, Bhagu, Kimbila, Ānanda, and Devadatta, did not join the Order.

The parents of the young men who had become monks[1] spread distasteful rumors about the others saying, "Our children have become monks. Perhaps the parents of those six don't happen to be kinsmen of the Buddha. That's why they don't have them ordained." As the talk spread, a brother of the young Anuruddha, named Mahānāma, also of the Ṣākyan clan, came to his younger brother and said, "Brother, no one from our family has yet joined the Order; that is a serious shortcoming on our part. As a result we do not get to share in the honors and respect paid to the Order of our distinguished kinsman. That is indeed a great loss. Therefore, why don't you, at least, become a monk? If you are unwilling, then I will join this Order to make good the lapse.

Now the young Prince Anuruddha was extremely delicate, having been brought up in the lap of luxury. Not only did he have no idea of the austerities of the life of a mendicant monk but he also had never lacked anything or even heard the word 'no.'

How was he so ignorant? I shall illustrate.

One day Bhaddiya and his six young friends were playing a game with balls of thread. Anuruddha lost and sent a message home for some rice cakes, for they were what he had staked. His mother sent him the cakes. The six of them sat down, ate the cakes, and played again. Anuruddha lost again. Once more he sent for cake. They ate the cakes and played for a third time. Anuruddha lost a third time. The stakes each time were rice cakes. They played a fourth round and once more Anuruddha lost and sent a message home for cakes.

Since his mother had already sent three rounds of cakes, there were no more left in the house. She sent a message saying, "There are no cakes." Since "no" was not a word that he had ever heard before, he assumed they were a special kind of cake and so told the messenger, "If there are only 'no-cakes' then bring me some of those."

The mother heard his message and thought, "My son does not understand the meaning of the word 'no.' I will teach him what it means with a simple illustration." She took an empty golden bowl, covered it with another bowl and sent it to her son. However, though it happened to be empty of cake, it was certainly not empty of Merit.

How so? Because the guardian deities of that city had said to each other, "This Prince Anuruddha, when he was born as the destitute Annāhara in a previous life, gave a gift of alms to the *Pasē* Buddha Uparitta. The food, which he had prepared for himself, was not too tasty but, instead of saying he had nothing, he gave what he had with a full heart. While doing so he made the following Fervent Rebirth-Wish. 'May I never again know what it is to do without, or ever hear the word "no." May I never have to even know where the rice comes from.'

"Now, if this empty bowl reaches Anuruddha, the gods will blame us for negligence. They might refuse us entrance into the Assembly of the Gods or our heads could split in seven pieces." Therefore, they filled the empty bowl with heavenly cakes. Just as rice even when prepared from unpolished grain, leaves no residual taste of its origin once it is cooked, so were these cakes transformed.

The bearer placed the dish before the young players, and as if to illustrate the meaning of the word 'no' he opened the lid of the dish. Whatever the meaning of the word may have been, the moment he did so, the scent of the cakes within suffused the entire city. It seemed rather an illustration of the power of goodness. The instant one ate even a small piece of these cakes seven thousand tastebuds were gratified.

Prince Anuruddha ate the cakes and thought, "My mother has not loved me till now. She has never prepared such cakes for me before. From now on I will eat only this kind of cake." He could think in this way because he had not yet tasted of *nirvāṇa*.

Anuruddha went home and asked his mother, "Mother, do you love me or do you not?"

His mother replied, "Son, what are you saying? As a one-eyed man loves his one eye so I love you."

"If so why have you never before given me the kind of cakes you sent today?"

At that the mother called the bearer and asked him, "Boy, what ever was in that dish that you took to my son?"

"My lady, the dish was filled with cakes. I knew it by the weight of the dish on my head."

The mother thought to herself, "My son must indeed be greatly blessed. The gods have filled the dish with heavenly cakes because of his great goodness."

Anuruddha then said, "Mother, from now on when you send me cakes, send me only this particular kind."

From then on, the mother, without wasting either oil or flour, sent her son an empty dish with a cover on it. The gods continued to fill the dish with heavenly cakes for as long as he remained a layman, for this man was of great merit.

Therefore, now when his brother asked if he would become a monk, this young man, who did not know even the meaning of the word "no," had no idea what it meant to become a monk. He asked what one had to do.

"Brother, one must cut one's hair, wear robes, sleep on a pallet of sticks or a hardbed, carry a clay bowl and beg. That is what one must do to be a monk."

"But brother, I am very delicate. I can't bear the weight of robes that are heavy with dye. It is impossible for me to sleep on a pallet bed, and I cannot beg. Therefore I just cannot do what you suggest. I will not become a monk."

"In that case, dear brother, remain a layman and work for a living. One of us two must join the Order, so I will," replied the brother.

This Prince Anuruddha, who was of such great merit that he had no idea where the rice he ate came from, had even less of an idea what it was to work for a living. Let us first illustrate his ignorance of where rice came from.

One day, the young Kimbila, the young Bhaddiya, and the young Anuruddha sat talking about this and that and someone asked where rice came from.

"It comes from a barn" said young Kimbila.

"You know nothing," said Bhaddiya. "I know where it comes from. Rice comes from a cooking pot."

At that the young Anuruddha cut in saying, "Neither of you know anything about it. Rice comes from a golden dish that has an eighteen inch border of flowerbuds and one hundred fine lines around its rim."

How was it that these three young men could make such statements? Were they imagining these things[2] or were they speaking from experience?

Young Kimbila had once seen unhusked rice being taken out of a barn and so assumed that rice came from a barn. Clearly he had not been anywhere near a rice-field. Young Bhaddiya had once seen rice being dished out of a cooking pot and so thought rice was produced in a pot. Not only had he not been near a rice field, but he had also obviously not even been near a barn. The young Anuruddha had neither seen rice unloaded out of a barn, nor had he seen it being dished out of a pot. He had only seen the rice as it was served before him in a golden dish, and so believed that rice came from a dish.

Thus, completely ignorant of how rice was grown, he now asked what it meant to work for a living. He was told, "First the field must be cleared.[3] Then the soil must be turned. After that it should be ploughed twice. Then the earth bunds should be built up and the land must be ploughed a third time. Then the clumps of earth must be broken and the earth smoothened. Afterwards the field must be muddied, sown, and then fenced. What was sown must be kept moist, the field irrigated, and certain remedial magical charms performed to prevent disease. When the grain ripens, it must be cut and stored. Then once more the stubble must be removed, the field weeded, burned, cleared, and sowed. In the next six months, when the rice grain ripens, the same process must be repeated." Thus, he spoke as if there was no end to the work that continued all year round.

Prince Anuruddha thought, "This endless round of work is like the continuous cycle of rebirths. If the work is never over, when does one get to enjoy its benefits? That being the case, then you, brother, can continue to live the lay life and engage in this endless work. I will shorten mine by becoming a monk, which does have an end in sight." Thus, he developed a taste for the monkhood and went to his mother to inform her of his decision. Three times she tried to stop him. However, his taste for *nirvāṇa* was now even greater than his taste for 'no-cakes.'

Thinking to stop him by one other means, she said, "If your friend Bhaddiya decides to join the Order, then you can do so, too."

Anuruddha went to his friend, talked with him at great length, and said, "My becoming a monk now depends entirely on you." He extracted a promise from him that they would be ordained together seven days later. Thus, he became even more strongly fixed in his decision to become a monk.

Thereafter, the six young princes, Bhaddiya, Anuruddha, Ānanda, Bhagu, Kimbili, and Devadatta, together with their personal attendant Upāli, like heavenly deities, spent one week enjoying all the royal pleasures. Then, as if going to sport in the pleasure gardens, they left accompanied by their fourfold escort.[4] When they reached the border and crossed over into foreign territory, the six princes ordered their troops to halt. They then took off all their jewels and ornaments, tied them up in a bundle, and saying, "Upāli, take this. It should be enough to provide for you for as long as you live," they gave it all to him. Unable to oppose the princes' command, Upāli stayed behind, weeping and lamenting.

When Upāli and the princes separated, it seemed as if the very forest cried out deafeningly around them. The great earth seemed to tremble. The attendant, Upāli, followed after them for some distance thinking "These princes may be kinsmen of that most compassionate Buddha, but the Ṣākyans are a very inflexible people. When I go back alone, having left the young men here, their kinsmen will say, "The princes have not returned because this man has killed them," and, not bothering to inquire about what actually transpired, they will kill me no matter what. These six royal princes have abandoned princely comforts, given me all their valuable ornaments, and have left to become monks. Becoming a monk cannot be bad for me, either. I, too, will join the Order." So he untied the bundle of ornaments, and hung them upon a tree like the decorations on a wish-fulfilling tree. Then saying, "Let anyone who wants them, help himself," he left to join the princes. They asked why he had followed them; he told them what he thought.

The princes took him with them to the Buddha and said, "Master, because we were princes of the royal Ṣākya clan, we were stiff with pride[5] like pythons who had swallowed plough heads. This man is our attendant. Is he not therefore of lower status? If you will ordain him first, we will then have to pay him obeisance and offer him our love and service. In doing so our pride will shrink, for pride is not something that we need in the Order of the Buddha." So they allowed the servant to be ordained first and the six of them took on their robes only after him.

Of the group, the Senior Monk Baddhiya, in the early hours of the evening, acquired the knowledge of all past births, which the Great Teacher had achieved on the night of his Enlightenment. He also achieved the Divine Eye of Wisdom that the Teacher acquired during the middle hours. And though he did not achieve the complete Wisdom of a Buddha, which the Teacher had attained in the dawn hours, he did attain the Knowledge of the Path as an *arahat*. The monk Bhaddiya thus acquired the three kinds of Wisdom and also all the other benefits of the Order such as worldly blessings and Spiritual Attainments.

As a tortoise[6] though he comes on land, does not give up his home in the pond, which is his refuge, so Bhaddiya did not give up his thoughts of compassion to all humans. Like that same tortoise, who swims with his head out of the water but dives down to the depths the moment he sees someone, so, on the great pond of the Buddha's teachings, Bhaddiya raised his head observing the Precepts of Moral Conduct. But the moment he saw the enemy of lustful Defilements, he withdrew into the waters of Contemplation. As the tortoise comes out of the water to warm his shell, so he dried out the damp of his impure desires with the warm sun of Right Effort and Striving. As the tortoise mines his way beneath the earth and, afraid of danger lives isolated, so he gave up riches and comforts and, for fear of continued rebirth in *saṃsāra*, took to the forest and lived amidst trees, mountains, and caves.

Again, as a tortoise, when out walking hides his four legs and head under his shell the moment he sees someone or senses danger, so when unwanted forms or objects hit his six sensory organs, since enemy Defilements such as lust lurk in the lonely forests of sense objects, he cultivated constant Awareness and vigilance over his thoughts.

As it is said:

> Te kilesamahācorā ālambaṇavanāsayā
> Na dhaṃsenti manogehaṃ satārakkhe upaṭṭhite*

He closed the six sense doors such as the eyes and stopped the enemy thieves from stealing the gold of goodness stored within. In three months he studied the three *Vēdas* of Threefold Knowledge, with the various sections, the Precepts of Moral Conduct, as well as the injunctions in the Doctrinal texts. Thus, having begged for alms in the countryside of the *arahat,* he arrived finally at the city of the Teachings of the King of the Universe, the Enlightened Buddha.

That city had a long wall made of Morality,[7] a moat made of the restraints, Fear and Shame, a city gate of Wisdom, with lintels of Effort, a protective column of Faith, and watchmen of Mindfulness. It had a nine-storied palace of the Nine Spiritual Attainments, four roads of the Fourfold Path going in four directions and the Three Signs, Impermanence, Sorrow, and Soullessness, pointing in three directions. It had also the Hall of Justice named the "Rules of the Monastic Order" and a royal thoroughfare called "The Path of Mindfulness." There were market stalls selling the flowers of Higher Knowledge, stalls selling perfumes of Moral Conduct, and fruit stalls selling the Fruits of the Path. There were also stalls selling medicinal preparations of The Teachings of the Thirty-Seven Buddhas for curing the disease of Defilements, and even a stall that sold the nectar of Awareness of Bodily Components, which could destroy Decay and Death. In addition there were stalls full of the gems of Moral Conduct and Contemplation, which could bring Enlightenment. There was a stall that was filled with the blessings of high status, wealth, long life, good health, good looks, and intelligence; and also the blessings of the human world, the heavenly worlds, the Brahma worlds, and of *nirvāṇa.* These goods were all available to the deserving, each according to his merits.

Just as one concentrates on the *Saṃskāras* and cultivates Insight so the Senior Monk Anuruddha, as a consequence of an offering of lights that he had made acquired the Divine eye and later became an *arahat.*

The Senior Monk Ānanda, like a bamboo that bends with the wind and not against it, was turned by the winds of the study of Texts and bent only in the direction of Right Conduct and became a Stream-Enterer. He postponed the stage of full Enlightenment[8] until after the death of the Buddha. Thus, he obtained a small portion of nirvāṇa.

---

*Defilements, those great robbers that live in the forests of sensory objects,
Do not attack the house of the mind if protected by the guard, Mindfulness.

The two monks Bhagu and Kimbili were flexible like bows which when bent, curve from tip to tip. They were malleable in their youth, in their middle years, and at maturity. Like crows, who live in constant fear, they lived in fear of sin, and just as crows share what they find with their fellows, so whatever they got as alms they shared, thereby practicing the discipline of sharing. Monkeys, when they settle in a certain area, live in the topmost branches of large trees where they are most comfortable. Similarly, these two lived restrained, disciplined, and blessed lives. Since there was much they wished to hear and say, they always had the benefit of good companions who loved and respected the Doctrine and instructed them when they were at fault. A gourd vine, as it grows, supports itself with its tendrils and climbs on the back of whatever it can, be it grass or sticks, and spreads itself around. Similarly, by virtue of the vine of the Path of Enlightenment, supported on the back of Meditative Insight necessary for achieving Contemplative Knowledge, they grew, matured, and bore the Fruits of Enlightenment.

The Senior Monk Upāli, accompanied by one thousand monks, heard the Buddha's Rules of Discipline, was appointed chief of Discipline and finally became an *arahat*.

The monk, Devidat,[9] although he had joined the Order together with the young noblemen Bhaddiya and others, was like the man who goes to where gold is being distributed but gets none. He did not achieve *nirvāṇa*. He cultivated the Eight Meditative Attainments[10] and developed Special Knowledge.

Just as the tributaries of many great rivers all flow together at its mouth, so streams of devotees began to render all manner of services and offerings to the Buddha while he was in residence in the city of Kosam̆bä. And just as he had had no respite, when he was cultivating the Perfections in order to become a Buddha, so now he had no respite from their attentions. People came to the monastery, carrying robes and other offerings and asked, "Where is that Buddha, the most virtuous of beings? Where is that Captain of the Doctrine, his chief disciple on his right? Where is that monk Mugalan who sits on his left? Where is the monk Mahasup,[11] the chief of the desireless? Where is Bhaddiya, the chief of the three kinds of Wisdom? Where is the colorful orator the monk Kumāra Kasub? Where is the monk Anuruddha, the foremost in Divine Vision? Where is the monk Rāhula, the most amenable to advice? Where is the monk Sīvali, who receives the most gifts of alms? Where is the monk Ānanda, the foremost in attending on the Buddha? They walked around asking after the eighty great disciples.

No one asked after the monk Devidat, since he was not famous for anything. At that, Devidat said to himself one day, "I came here together with Bhaddiya and others and became a monk. All of them came from royal families, which they left to become ordained. I did so, too." Forgetting the fact that though of royal birth he was far behind them in virtue, he continued, "All the people who bring gifts and offerings ask only after them. No one asks for me or even notices me. What ruse can I use to entice people to follow me and how can I get some profit from it?

"King Bimsara[12] became a Stream-Enterer on the very first day that he saw the Buddha, he and ten thousand others. A man who has taken a firm oath cannot easily be weaned away from it, so this man cannot be enticed into our way of thinking. Just as royal swans head for lotus ponds not the piles of garbage, so those who have once tasted the divine food of the Path, will not turn away from the Buddha.

"The King of Kosol has not himself attained *nirvāṇa* but is drawn to the Buddha's teachings because of his association with Queen Mallikā. He, too, cannot be influenced to do what we want. Those who are not royal princes are of no use to us. But King Bimsara's son the prince Ajāsat, because of his hostility to his father the king, which was there even before he was born, is ready to be enemies with anyone. He has no sense of a person's good or bad qualities. I will join forces with him."

Thereafter, Devidat left the city of Kosaṁba for Rajagaha. Since Prince Ajāsat was still young, he took on the guise of a dwarf[13] with two cobras wrapped around each arm, two around the legs, one around his neck, one hanging down from his shoulder, and one coiled up and tied like a turban around his head.

He entered the palace, alighting out of the sky onto Prince Ajāsat's shoulder and made him recoil in fear.

"Who are you?" the prince asked.

"I am Devidat," he replied. In order to calm the prince's fears, he took on the guise of a monk and stood before him. He soothed him, won his confidence, and obtained much gain in the form of a supply of five hundred containers filled with rice. Carried away by material gain, he now developed the sinful thought, "I will usurp the kingdom of the Buddha and live surrounded by monks." Consequently, he immediately lost even the little merit he had acquired to help him through *saṃsāra*.

Devidat went to the Vēluvaṇarāma monastery where the Buddha was, worshipped him with his hands high above his head, and said, "Master, you are old. You should now retire without straining yourself any further. I know how to handle this organization, so let me control the monks. Give over your Order of Monks to me." When the Buddha refused, Devidat was displeased. It was now the fifth eon since he had first vowed enmity to the Buddha on a matter of rivalry over a golden plate, as related in the *Sērivānija Jātaka*.[14] Now, as if to add to that enmity, he left the Order, which he had just joined, just as a man very near death is as good as dead. The Buddha, too, dismissed him from the Order.

Devidat, knowing he had been expelled, said, "This Gōtama-monk has thrown me out.[15] Because he has done so I, too, will do him harm." Just as in the past the Bōdhisatva had made a Fervent Rebirth-Wish to become a Buddha so he, too, had made a Fervent Rebirth-Wish to kill the Buddha. The incidents had occurred five eons ago.

Now he went to King Ajāsat. When milk is contaminated it curdles. Similarly, in order to contaminate the king's milklike good thoughts with his own wicked ones he said, "O Prince, men who were born in the old days enjoy a long life-span. Men of today do not. If you wait for your kingdom until King Bimsara dies, there's no telling what might not happen in the time between. Kill your father and take over your kingdom and I, on my part, will kill that Gōtama-monk and take over the Buddha-kingdom."

Like a person who imagines he can get to the world of Brahma without meditating or attaining to the Trance States, or as an unfortunate one not destined to achieve *nirvāṇa* imagines he can do so in this very birth, so Devidat imagined he could take over the kingdom of the Buddha, that kingdom that can only be obtained after four incalculables and one hundred thousand eons spent in Fervent Rebirth-Wishes.

Thus, Devidat incited Ajāsat to kill his father and become king. Then he asked King Ajāsat for archers and sent them to shoot the Buddha. The archers were unable to shoot the Buddha, but they did shoot down their own enemy Defilements. Thereafter, they became Stream-Enterers, stopped all killings, and refrained from committing any of the five sins. When Devidat heard this, he said, "Only a man like me, no one else, can look on the face of that Gōtama-monk and perform the heinous act. Therefore, I myself will do it."

He climbed the rock mountain Gijukula (Vulture Peak), and rolled down a boulder onto the Buddha. As the rock rolled down, the earth split apart and threw out another boulder to stop its progress. As the rocks clashed, a splinter struck the upper part of the Buddha's foot and drew blood. Hurting a Buddha is one of the five heinous crimes, so by that act alone Devidat confirmed his journey to the Avīci-hell.

Unsuccessful in his attempt to kill the Buddha by this means, he next forced the elephant Nālāgiri, who usually consumed only eight pots of palm beer[16] to drink sixteen pots, and sent him forth, intoxicated, to attack the Buddha. Seeing the elephant advance, roaring and thundering, the Senior Monk Anaňda stepped forward and stood in his path saying, "Kill me but spare the Buddha." In this act of self-sacrifice he showed his feelings for the Buddha. However, the Buddha overtook him and, with the medicine of soft words, he calmed the maddened animal, controlled him, spoke to him, and made this creature, who was as black as a pot of collirium, became as white as an elephant from the clan of Caddanta.[17]

The Buddha then left the city and returned to the monastery. There he partook of the large feast of alms that the thousands of devotees had prepared on a vast scale, preached a sermon to the one hundred and eighty million people living in that inner city and let eighty-four thousand of them into the city of *nirvāṇa.*

The monks began to say, "Behold, what a man this Senior Monk Anaňda is! When Nālāgiri, thundering, came to kill the Buddha, he stepped out in front."

The Buddha then spoke to them of his good qualities and the monks listened. However, in order to illustrate to them the uncountable years over which those good qualities had been nurtured, the Buddha told them the story of the *Culla haṃsa*[18] and the *Mahā Haṃsa Jātakas*[19] in which they had both been born as swans. Though not stuck in the mire of *saṃsāra,* on that occasion, too, when the Buddha had been caught in a noose and was in trouble, he had stood by him. The Buddha also related the story of the crab Suvan. Once when he, the Buddha, had been born a Brahmin in the Brahmin village of Sālindiya, the monk Anaňda had been born as a crab. A crow, in order to satisfy the cravings of his mate, instructed a cobra to bite the Buddha on his calf. The snake did so. But when the crow came to pick out his eyes, the crab caught hold of him. The snake, hearing the crow's cries, came to see what was happening; the crab caught hold of the snake, too, and forced him to suck back the poison. Though the two creatures both died, the Buddha's life was saved.

Although Devidat caused the killing of the king, who was a Stream-Enterer, and instigated archers to shoot at the Buddha, and rolled down boulders on him, since he did it all very craftily, his sinful deeds were not openly known. The people were unaware that he was responsible for all of this.

However, from the day that he instigated the elephant Nālāgiri everything became clear to them. "It is that fellow Devidat who has been at the bottom of the killing of the king, and it is he who sent the archers. It is that same fellow who threw down rocks on the Buddha's head. And the King keeps company with such a fellow!" Thus, they ridiculed him. Just as Devidat had destroyed his chance of *nirvāṇa,* so now the king, hearing their talk, stopped all offerings of alms and services to Devidat. He deprived him of a means of livelihood and forbade his visits. He ordered the people not to give even a grain of rice to Devidat, when he went on his begging rounds.

Devidat, deprived of the offerings and services of the people and having no other means of survival, decided to live by deceit. He went to the Buddha and said, "Command your monks to live in the forest until they die, to eat only what they get by begging, to refuse whatever invitations they get, to wear only robes made from cemetery rags, not to sleep on a bed, only at the roots of trees, and not to eat any fish or meat."

These were not the kind of commands that the Buddha would give. He refused. Devidat then said, "I have formulated rules in their highest form but the Buddha does not agree to enforce them. Anyone who wishes to remain suffering in *saṃsāra* is free to do so. Let all those who wish to be rid of suffering, follow me." Thus, himself caught up in *saṃsāric* suffering, he left the Order, and consigned those who followed him also to suffering.

Some recently ordained monks, who had not yet practiced the discipline and had not yet developed wisdom, heard this talk and said, "What the monk Devidat says is convincing." They followed him. Devidat, together with his following of five hundred monks, preached the five rules of monastic conduct that he had promulgated; he won the hearts of men of little wisdom. He did not get much from begging so he walked around asking for food; he attempted to spread disunity among the monks. The Buddha heard of these activities and said, "Devidat, do not do that. To cause a schism in the Order of monks is a grave sin." But Devidat disregarded those words and continued his activities.

One day he met the monk Anañda on his begging rounds and said, "Friend Anañda, from now on I spurn the Buddha and his Order and will set up on my own, keeping the fasts and monastic practices separately. Anañda reported this to the Buddha. The Buddha said, "Alas, what he does is most wicked. Many will be destroyed because of this one man."

> Sukaraṃ sādhunā sādhu sādhu pāpena dukkaraṃ
> papaṃ pāpena sukaraṃ pāpamariyena dukkaraṃ.*

"Good actions come easily to the good not the wicked. Sinful deeds come easily to the sinner. Noble ones do not engage in wickedness. Even if one were to pour palm beer into the mouth of a Stream-Enterer it would not go down his throat."[20] Thus, he preached.

One full moon night, Devidat gathered together his group of followers and seated them down within the sacred limits of the place of

*It is easy for good men to do good but for the wicked it is hard,
It is easy for the wicked to sin but for a noble one, that is hard.

ordination and said, "let those who find the five rules I laid down agreeable, follow me and take a ticket.[21] About five hundred monks, ignorant of the rules of the Order, took tickets from him. By observing a separate set of disciplinary rules, he caused a schism in the Buddha's Order. He then took those monks with him and went to the headwaters of the stream of Gaya. When the Buddha learnt they had gone there, he sent the two chief disciples to bring back those who were not yet fully committed to Devidat.

At that time, Devidat happened to be preaching a sermon. It was a little like an offering of flowers placed on a fishing net. He saw the two chief disciples arrive and putting on a show of great majesty, like the Buddha's. He said, "O Ṣāriputra, my back aches. I would like to lie down for a while. Will you preach in my place?" At that the two disciples sat down and, like lions roaring where jackals howled before, began to preach with great power and dignity. As if pouring nectar into a pot that formerly contained poison, they persuaded Devidat's monks to change their opinions; they showed them the path to *nirvāṇa*. Then the chief disciples vanished through the air accompanied by those five hundred monks.

After they left, Devidat's chief disciple Kokālika went to where Devidat was sleeping and said, "Monk Devidat, wake up. I warned you that the Buddha's chief disciples Säriyut and Mugalan were up to no good. But, as if I was not good enough, you invited them to preach. Now they have left with all your followers." Then, in order to put an end to the man's claim to Buddhahood and his own claims to be first disciple, without the slightest hint of respect or obedience, he struck the sleeping Devidat in the chest with his knee. It was as if he had decided to administer a medicine for Devidat's fake illness. The blow struck hard and as foul air issues out of a diseased body, so, hot blood spouted forth from his mouth.

The monks at Rajagaha saw the Senior Monk Säriyut come flying through the air accompanied by a retinue of monks. They rushed up to the Buddha saying, "Master, when the Senior Monk Säriyut left there were only two of them. They now return accompanied by five hundred!" The Buddha said to them:

Hoti sīlavataṃ attho paṭisanthāravuttinaṃ
Lakkhaṇaṃ passa āyantaṃ ñāthisaṅghapurakkhataṃ
Atha passasimaṃ kālaṃ suvihīnaṃ ca ñātihi."*

---

*The intentions of good men of pleasant speech are always fulfilled.
Behold the deer Lakhana returns with a host of relatives
The deer Kala returns alone, bereft.

"O monks, as told in the *Lakkanamiga Jātaka,*[22] when he and I were born as deer, he (Devidat) was the deer Kala, who allowed the entire herd that was in his charge to die. Not one was left; he returned alone. Whereas the deer Lakkhana carefully escorted back every deer in his charge. That was a good deed even on the part of an animal. Devidat was then the deer Kala. The Senior Monk Säriyut was the deer Lakkhana."

"Master," the monks continued, "This Devidat imitates you. Just as you preach with the chief disciples on either side of you so he now preaches with his Kokālika and others at his side, who are chief disciples only in name.

For it is said:

> Api vīraka passesi sakuṇaṃ mañjubhāṇakaṃ
> Mayūragīvasaṃkāsaṃ patiṃ mayahaṃ saviṭṭhakaṃ
> Udakathalacarassa pakkhino niccaṃ āmakamacchabhojino
> Tassānukaraṃ saviṭṭhako sevāle paliguṇṭhīto mato.*

"It is not just today that such things have happened. Even during my birth as a bird, living both in water and on dry land, this man, Devidat, born as the bird Saviṭṭhaka,[23] wished to do everything that I did. He ended up getting stuck in the slime and died. In this context the Buddha also related the *Kuruṃgamiga Jātaka,*[24] the *Parantapa Jātaka*[25] and other stories, describing how in the past, Devidat had made various attempts to kill him and failed. The Buddha suffered no harm but Devidat lost all honor and reputation as a result and whatever good qualities he had, deteriorated.

As it is said:

> Akkhi bhinnā paṭo naṭṭho sakhī gehe ca bhaṇḍanaṃ
> Ubhato paduṭṭha kammanto udakamhi thalaṃhi ca.**

In one of his births, this man happened to be out fishing and the fish hook got stuck in a post in the water. He thought it was an enormous fish, so leaving his clothes on the bank, he dived into the water.

---

*O Viraka, look at this sweet voiced bird with the neck of a peacock,
my husband Saviṭṭhaka,
Imitating birds that roam on land and water, eating fish,
this man of evil livelihood, died, ensnared in slime.

**He had his eyes destroyed, his clothes stolen, lost friends and all his goods
This man of evil livelihood.

He hit his face on the log and he lost the sight of both eyes. When he got back on the bank, he felt around but failed to find his clothes because a passerby had taken them. When he returned home, his wife and sister had quarreled and he had to pay for it.

The Buddha related numerous stories of the past lives for Devidat's benefit while he was at Rajagaha. But like rain that falls on a rock, they had little effect on Devidat. Though they were of no use to him, the sermons were of great benefit to a great many people. Thereafter the Buddha left Rajagaha for the city of Sävät and went to reside in the Devramvehera monastery.

Devidat was sick for nine months. When he was dying, he wished to see the Buddha and said to his disciples, "I would like to see the Buddha. Take me to him."

"When you were well and strong you were his enemy. Now, why do you wish to see him? We will not take you to him," they said.

"Do not destroy me. However much enmity I may have had towards the Buddha, he has never entertained even a single hair's breadth of enmity towards me.

As it is said:

> Vadhake devadattamhi core aṅgulimālake
> Dhanapāle rāhule cāpi sabbattha samamānaso.*

"This Buddha has the same feeling for me, who did these terrible crimes, as for that brigand Angulimālā, who came to kill him and chop off his fingers, or for that elephant Nālāgiri, huge as the Kāḷagiri-rock, who came roaring to kill him, or for the prince Rahal his son. Therefore take me to him without further talk of past enmity." He begged them again and again. So they put him on a litter and, like carrying a dead man, they set forth to see the Buddha.

The monks heard he was arriving and went to the Buddha and said, "Master, Devidat is coming to see you."

"He will not get to see me in this life," replied the Buddha.

Now why did he say that? It was because someone, who engages in five disciplinary practices that are contrary to the Rules of the Vinaya, cannot ever again set eyes on a Buddha in that lifetime.

The monks said, "He has come to such and such a place."

---

*For Devidat who tried to harm him, for the robber Aṅgulimālā,
for the elephant Dhanapāla, or for Rāhula his son,
his feelings towards all of them, are one.

But the Buddha replied, "No matter what he does, he will not get to see me. Whether he comes within four leagues, or three, or two, or one league of here, or whether he reaches the banks of the pond, or even if he walks into the Devramvehera monastery he will not get to see me."

Those who were bringing Devidat to the Buddha, set him down beside the pond at the entrance to the monastery and stepped in to take a bath. Devidat arose from his litter and stood up with his feet firmly set on the ground. Instantly both feet began to sink into the earth. Slowly he sank, first down to his calves, then to his knees, then to his hips, his chest, and finally to his chin. At that point he said,

Imehi aṭṭhīhi tamaggapuggalaṃ
Devātidevaṃ naradammasārathiṃ
Samanta cakkuṃ satapuññalakkhaṇaṃ
Pāṇehi buddhaṃ saraṇaṃ gatosmi*

"I take refuge in the Buddha, supreme in all the world, he who has all the marks of goodness." Like a sip of water put into the mouth of a dying man, he established himself in the Three Refuges and the Precepts even at this last stage. The Buddha then said, "If he remains a layman, there will be little chance for him to do good in the future, since he has already done much harm. But if he were to be ordained again as a monk, however, much Demerit he may have accumulated by his actions, there is still a chance of future blessings." With this in view he ordained him again.[26]

One might ask the question,[27] "Was it not because he was a monk and had received full ordination that he was able to cause a schism in the Order of Monks?" The answer is that, even if a schism had not occurred, it would have made no difference. He had drawn blood from the Buddha's body. Therefore, had he remained a layman it would still not have helped. But in consideration of blessings he might enjoy, at least in the future, the Buddha had him ordained. He in turn, made that his support and as a result, a hundred eons into the future he would become a *Pasē* Buddha.

Now, if by the mere fact of taking the Three Refuges, one can become a *Pasē* Buddha does that mean that becoming a *Pasē* Buddha is not such a hard thing to do? No. He became a *Pasē* Buddha because of a Fer-

---

*With my very bones and with both my hands
I take refuge in the Buddha, god of gods,
First among men, charioteer, who guides the willing,
He of the Omniscient Eye and the hundred marks of virtue.

vent Rebirth-Wish he had made over two incalculables and one hundred thousand eons ago. Now his renewed acceptance and his Taking Refuge in the Buddha was as if he poured fresh oil into a dying lamp to make it flare up anew.

Then the earth split asunder and Devidat descended into the Avīci-hell. He had to suffer now, fixed and immobile in hell, for the crimes he had committed against the motionless and unflinching Buddha. The Avīci-hell was four hundred leagues high. Though Devidat was short, his crimes mounted to a great height. As a result he was born [in hell] four hundred leagues tall. He was encased in a metal sheet up to his ears,[28] his feet were stuck in the earth up to his ankles. A steel spike as great as the trunk of a palm tree burning with the flames of hunger, came out of the west wall of the metal sheet, pierced through his back, splitting it apart, and entered out to the wall on the east side. Another similar iron spike came out from the south wall, pierced his right side, came out from the opposite end, and stuck in the north wall. Yet another spike from the metal sheet at the top, pierced through his head, splitting it, and emerging through his bowels down into the earth. Thus, suspended and held perfectly still, he boiled in hell.

The monks began to spread talk saying,[29] "Alas, Devidat came all this distance and did not get to see the Buddha. Instead all he got was to see the fires of hell and be dragged down below."

The Buddha responded, "This is not the first time, O monks, that he has been dragged down into the earth because of crimes committed against me. It has happened before. He related the *Khantivāda Jātaka,*[30] the *Culla Dhammapāla Jātaka,*[31] and other stories.

When Devidat was swallowed in the earth many were glad. They strung up flags, planted decorative banana trees, placed ornamental waterpots and engaged in great festivities. The monks informed the Buddha of this. The Buddha said again, "This is not the first time, O monks, that men have rejoiced at his death. In the past, once when he was born as the cruel king Piṃgala, he lived the life of a harsh and wicked man. Everybody rejoiced and celebrated his death. Only the palace guard wept. When the people asked him, 'How is it that you are the only one who weeps?' The guard replied, 'Every day, as I left the King's room he would give me three knocks. When I went in, I was given three more knocks. That is a total of six knocks a day. As a result, I have not a single firm spot left on my head. I weep because I'm afraid that the King of Death when he sees him, will refuse to take him, because he is so wicked, and as a result he may return to earth. My head that was now rested peacefully these past few days will once more be denied that peace. I weep when I think about that possibility.' " The Buddha then related the *Piṃgala Jātaka.*[32]

The monks did not know where Devidat had now been reborn so they asked, "Master where has he been reborn?" The Buddha said that he had been born in the Avīci-hell. He then continued, "O monks, those who sin, think about what they have done and suffer remorse in this world. In hell, too, they are subject to countless tortures and suffer bodily pain. Thus, they suffer in mind and body. Sinners like Devidat know no respite either in this world or in the next."

Some people suffer when they take a medicine, yet, after it is swallowed they are cured of their sickness and get relief. So this sermon about the sufferings in the underworld, though painful to listen to, once preached, enabled many to reach *nirvāṇa.*

Thus, good men should always keep the teachings in mind, refrain from the sins that are committed through the Three Doors of the Senses, and without difficulty, obtain worldly blessings as well as Spiritual Attainments.

Endnotes

DEVADATTA

Illustrates stanza 17 of the Yamaka Vagga.

> Idha tappati pecca tappati . . . bhīyō tappati dugatiṃ gatō
>
> He laments here, he laments hereafter,
> He who does wrong laments in both places,
> He laments even more when he goes to hell.

The Sinhala form of the name is Devidat. However, in the first part of the story, he is referred to as Devadatta, the more formal Pāli version of the name. There is an interesting shift midway through the story after which point the Sinhala name Devidat is used. One wonders if the shift was the work of later scribes or whether the author began his translation with the formal name, which was the one used in the Pāli DA, but unconsciously slipped into the more familiar local usage as the story progressed.

1. The parents of the young men who had become monks . . .

The implication here is that because they were kinsmen of the Buddha, they should in fact have shown their support by encouraging their sons to join the Order of a fellow kinsman.

2. Were they imaginging these things . . .

Illustrates the fallacy of believing that truth or knowledge comes from firsthand experience. If the experience is limited, the facts so acquired may be totally wrong.

3. He was told, "First the field must be cleared. . . .

The details show the author's complete familiarity with the process and techniques of rice cultivation. The DA version by contrast, reads, "First, the field must be plowed and after that such and such other things must be done, and these things must be done year after year." [Burlingame 1979, 233] The techniques and methods Dharmasēna describes have remained virtually unchanged in Sri Lanka for over a period of seven hundred years. The stress on the enormously hard labor involved in the process of production sharpens the contrast between that and the totally distant, unreal world of the rich noblemen.

4. . . . , they left accompanied by a fourfold escort.

A fourfold escort consisted of elephants, horses, chariots, and foot soldiers. They were the four components of princely armies.

5. . . . , we were stiff with pride . . .

The princes consciously humble themselves by asking that their retainer be ordained before them. As senior in the Order, they will then have to render services to him. This symbolic gesture underlines the Buddhist position, which ran counter to Brahmin attitudes and beliefs, regarding the importance of birth and high status.

6. As a tortoise . . .

Another illustration of the author's powers of detailed observation and his familiarity with the activities of creatures in the animal world.

7. That city had a long wall made of Morality, . . .

The doctrinal information is conveyed through metaphors that give us the architecture of a medieval city with its wall, moat, streets, and buildings. It is perhaps significant that the two main buildings referred to are the palace and the Hall of Justice. The archeological remains of the fourth century fortress at Sigiriya as well as what remains of the eighteenth century capital city of Kandy suggest that the royal palace and the "Audience Hall" or Hall of Justice were the central markers of medieval Sri Lankan cities.

The description of the main thoroughfare lined with market stalls is of particular interest, for it is replicated in the market fairs in Sri Lankan villages even today. The main road is lined with a motley collection of small stalls selling flowers, fruits, vegetables, foods, perfumes, medicines, and other goods.

8. He postponed the stage of full Enlightenment . . .

According to the Buddhist story, the monk Ānanda wished to serve the Buddha and attend on him till his death. Therefore, he delayed attaining to full Enlightenment in order to perform this special task.

9. From this point, Devadatta is referred to as Devidat, the Sinhala version of the name. I have kept the shift.

10. He practiced the Eight Meditative Attainments . . .

The Eight Meditative Attainments are the Eight *Samāpatti*. Devidat, like the others, engaged in certain meditative practices and acquired certain kinds of psychic powers that come from Trance States. However, he failed to achieve the true treasure, which was the "gold" of Enlightenment.

11. Mahasup is the Sinhala form for Mahā Kaśyapa one of the Senior disciples of the Buddha.

12. King Bimsara . . .

Here Devidat goes through the list of possible converts. He realizes that neither King Biṁbisāra nor the king of Kōsala is likely to follow him.

13. . . . , he took on the guise of a dwarf . . .

The word in the text is "kasub," which is usually translated as tortoise. Sorata in his dictionary refers to a possible meaning as "squat man" or "dwarf." I have chosen to use the latter in the context. Since Devidat had attained the *Samāpatti*, he had acquired supernormal powers that he displays here.

14. *Sērivānija Jātaka* story.

The story of the two rival merchants. See reference in notes to "Wearing the Ochre Robe."

15. "This Gōtama-monk has thrown me out. . . . "

Note the disrespectful manner of address. It is as if by refusing to call him a Buddha and treating him as just another ascetic, Devidat hopes to bring him down to his level.

16. . . . Nālāgiri, who usually consumed only eight pots of palm beer . . .

Palm beer or "*Rā*," as it is called in Sinhala, is an intoxicating brew made from the sap of the coconut palm. It is still the popular drink in rural areas. Literary accounts describe it as being given to elephants to incite them in battle.

17. . . . an elephant from the clan of Caddanta.

Refers to the *Caddanta Jātaka* story about a royal elephant who is killed by a hunter sent by a queen. The queen had been the elephant's wife in a former birth and had conceived a grudge against him because of an imaginary slight. However, when the hunter kills the elephant and brings her the tusks, the queen is filled with remorse and dies of a broken heart.

18. *Culla-Haṃsa Jātaka* story.

A king of wild geese is caught in a fowler's snare and he is deserted by all except his chief captain, who refuses to leave him. The fowler is so touched by this devotion that he decides to release the captive bird. However, they insist on being taken before the king of the country; after preaching the Doctrine to him, the two birds are set free.

19. *Mahā Haṃsa Jātaka* story.

A queen has a dream about golden geese and entreats the king to bring her one. The king has a decoy lake constructed and his fowler at length captures the king of the geese (the Bōdhisatva). The trapped goose utters a cry of pain as a signal to the others to fly away and all, except one of them, fly off. The goose king exhorts his companion also to leave before it is too late, but the friend resolutely remains saying, "No I'll not leave, thee, royal goose when trouble draweth nigh, But stay I will and by thy side will either live or die." [Cowell 1981].

The friend then offers the fowler his own golden feathers or himself captured alive, in exchange for the goose king's life. The fowler is so impressed that "being a mere bird he can do what for men is impossible. For they cannot remain constant in friendship," that he lets them both free.

20. This additional touch, introduced into the paraphrase of the stanza, is very typical of this translator/narrator.

21. . . . , follow me and take a ticket.

Another instance of the exercise of choice by means of a "ballot," a practice not uncommon among the Buddhist *Saṅgha*.

22. *Lakkanamigha Jātaka* story.

The story of two stags. One through stupidity, loses all his following whilst the other brings his herd home safely.

23. The story of Devidat born as Saviṭṭhaka appears in the *Vīraka Jātaka*. The Bodhisatva, as the crow Vīraka, dives into a swamp and catches fish. Saviṭṭhaka asks to become his attendant and feeds off the fish Vīraka catches. After a while, he decides to catch his own fish. He is warned that he does not belong to the species that can dive in the water, but he does so nevertheless and drowns.

24. *Kuruṃgamiga Jātaka* story.

The story of the Bōdhisatva born as an antelope and caught in a trap set by a cruel hunter. A woodpecker and a tortoise rescue their friend the antelope.

25. *Parantapa Jātaka* story.

The Bōdhisatva is born as a prince who can understand the speech of jackals. Devadatta is his father. The old king sends his son to meet a hostile enemy. The son begs not to go since he has seen a vision that he will be killed in battle. The father insists saying, "What is your life or death to me? Go."

The city is surrounded and the old king flees to the forest with his wife and attendant Parantapa, who finally seduces the queen and kills the king. His son, the Bōdhisatva, meanwhile, first retreats but then successfully defeats the hostile armies and rules the kingdom.

26. With this in view he ordained him again.

Illustrates the Buddha's all-pervasive compassion even toward his enemies.

27. One might ask the question, . . .

The implication behind the question is, why ordain him again, since the last time he was ordained he created a schism in the *Saṅgha?* As always, the rhetorical questions and answers enable the author to elucidate points of doctrinal interest and answer the kind of questions that might arise among his lay readers.

28. He was encased in a metal sheet up to his ears, . . .

The account here is so vivid and detailed it is almost as if the author is describing a painting on a temple wall. Sri Lankan temples are often decorated with just such paintings of heaven and hell. No doubt painters depicted what they had read about in early Buddhist texts and the paintings in turn became the source of subsequent descriptive accounts, thereby perpetuating the images in which heaven and hell were evoked in the culture.

There is a further ironical twist in modern times. The horribly macabre and sadistic killings that Sri Lankans on both sides of the recent civil war mete out as punishment to their enemies, seem a lurid reflection of some of these depictions. But whereas their forbears confined such sadistic fantasies to verbal or pictorial depiction, today, they are acted out in real life.

29. The monks began to spread talk saying, . . .

Note the constant questionings and implied criticisms of the Buddha's actions and the Buddha's responses to them. The criticisms are always surfaced and answered.

30. *Khantivādi Jātaka* story.

The story of how a wicked king cruelly maltreated an ascetic. However, the patience of the holy man endured to the end. The king ends up in hell.

31. *Culla Dhammapāla Jātaka* story.

A king, being jealous of his queen's affection for their child, has the boy mutilated and killed. He suffers punishment in hell.

Samandēvi

Just as a man scorched by the sun is attracted to the shade, or as a sufferer in *saṃsāra* seeks *nirvāṇa,* so to attract those afraid of the five sins, let me now tell you the story of Samandēvi.

How does it go?

Each day two thousand monks were provided meals at the home of the nobleman Anēpiḍu. Similarly, two thousand were regularly fed at the home of Visākhā. If anyone else in the city of Sävät, even the king, wished to give an offering of alms, they had to do so with the permission of these two people. And what was the reason for this? It was surely not because the occasions were lacking. It was because the monks would invariably ask, "Has the nobleman Anēpiḍu or the noblewoman Visākhā[1] been consulted, regarding this offering of alms?" And, if they replied they had not, then even if the offering had cost hundreds of thousands, it was like a dish without salt, not good enough. Because you see Anēpiḍu and Visākhā knew well the specific requirements and tastes of the monks, so food that was prepared under their instructions was always happily consumed by the monks. The result was that anyone who gave a gift of food invariably invited them as advisors. Thus, the two of them had hardly any time to attend to the monks who were hosted in their own homes.

Visākhā, finding that she did not have enough time, delegated her granddaughter for the task, knowing she would be very good at it. From then on, it was the granddaughter who attended to the requirements of the two thousand monks.

Similarly, the nobleman Anēpiḍu appointed his elder daughter Subadhrā for the task. Subadhrā made offerings to the monks, listened to their sermons, became a Stream-Enterer and set herself on the Path of Enlightenment. However, not yet completely free of sensual attachments,[2] she married and left. At which point, the younger daughter, Little Subadhrā was allotted the task. She, too, became a Stream-Enterer while performing her duties. But at the age when she was to about to partake of *nirvāṇa,* she also decided to get married. Then the youngest daughter Sumanā was given the task. In the course of performing her duties, she attained to the second stage of a Once-Returner. In doing so, she had rid herself of all sense desires and so did not get married.

Some time thereafter, she was smitten with an illness and could not eat. She sent for her father whom she wished to see. The nobleman happened to be in a certain household supervising an offering. He got her message and came immediately.

"What is the matter my child, Sumanādēvi?" he asked.

"I don't hear you, younger brother," she replied.

"My child, what is wrong? Why do you babble like this?"

"Younger brother, I do not babble." she said, and died as she was speaking. She was reborn in the Tusī heaven with a life-span of fifty-seven million six hundred thousand years, and free of all sickness for as long as she lived.

The nobleman, who was a follower of the Buddha, had rid himself of doubts and false beliefs but he had not yet reached the stage of one who is beyond grief. Therefore, weeping and lamenting, he cremated his child and overwhelmed by sorrow went to seek the ungrieving Buddha.

The Buddha asked him, "Why do you weep, nobleman?"

He replied, "My little daughter Sumanā is dead. I weep for her, master."

"Do you not know that all beings who are born must inevitably die just as surely as a *Bōsat*, who has been granted a 'prophetic revelation,' must necessarily become a Buddha? Why then do you cry?" the Buddha asked.

"Master I know it. But I weep because my daughter, at the point of death,[3] was out of her mind. She died raving. That is what grieves me most, Master."

"What did she say, nobleman?" asked the Buddha.

"Master, when I talked to her and called her child, twice she addressed me as 'younger brother.' Does that not clearly show she was raving?"

"Nobleman, she was not raving. You may be older in years and in terms of kinship but you are junior to her in goodness. You are a Stream-Enterer, your daughter is a Once-Returner. She is further along the Path than you and therefore your senior. That is why she addressed you thus."

"Master, where is she now?" he asked and was told she was now in the Tusī heaven.

The Buddha continued, "Listen O nobleman, those who have done good are happy in this world thinking about the good they have done. In the next world, too, they are happy and enjoy the highest pleasures. Thus, good actions bring happiness in this world and the worlds beyond. Therefore, do not delay in doing good."

At the end of this sermon, many were consoled and arrived at the city of *nirvāṇa*. Wise men, therefore, should rid themselves of all sins that bring no profit, do only good deeds that bring great rewards, and win the blessings of this world as well as Spiritual Attainments.

Endnotes

SAMANDĒVI'S STORY

Illustrates stanza 18 of the Yamaka Vagga

> Idha naňdati pecca naňdati . . . bhīyō naňdati suggatiṃ gatō

> He delights here, he delights hereafter,
> The good doer delights in both places,
> He is even more delighted when he goes to heaven.

1. "Has the nobleman Anēpiḍu and the noblewoman Visākhā . . . "

Anēpiḍu (Anāthapiṇḍika) and Visākhā were wealthy lay devotees of the Buddha. The former had built the monastery at Jētavanārāma for the Buddha.

2. However, not yet completely free of sensual attachment, . . .

There is no strong criticism of the two older sisters for not proceeding beyond the first stage of the path to *nirvāṇa* and deciding to get married instead. There is just the comment that they have not acquired sufficient detachment from worldly distractions and therefore they have made a different choice from the youngest sister.

3. " . . . But I weep because my daughter, at the point of death, . . . "

Buddhists believe that a person's last thought at the point of death is what conditions the place of one's immediate next life. Hence, for example, the nobleman Dhammika's request that the monks chant Protective Stanzas as he is dying. Anēpiḍu's grief is that, since his daughter was not in her right mind at the point of death, she could not have been reborn in a "happy" situation. The Buddha not only consoles him but also clearly states that she is his senior, in that she is further along the path than he, her father.

The Two Monks Who Were Friends

Moreover, if a person knows the Doctrine but fails to practice it, then it is of no use to him. He is like the man who never learned the martial arts and so finds a weapon useless. But for those who do act according to the Teachings, it is a great source of protection, like a ship that provides security for those on board. We shall illustrate this with the story of the two monks who were friends.

How does it go?

Two noblemen living in the city of Sävät heard the Buddha preach at the Devramvehera monastery. They then gave up their worldly wealth, accepted the teachings, and received Higher Ordination. As they were required to spend five years under the tutelage of an older monk, they spent that with a preceptor. When the five rainy seasons were over it was time to give up their pupil status so they went to the Buddha and asked which category of Practice they should adopt. They were given a detailed description of what the two categories were. At that point, one of them said, "Master, I took to the robes as an older man, therefore, I cannot perform the Practice of Scholarship. It would be better to teach me the Practice of Contemplation." He asked to be taught the various steps leading up to the stage of becoming an *arahat*.

As a lotus born of the water, growing in the water, yet does not mix with the water, so he gave up all interest in his clan or community. And as the lotus stands well above the water, so he was desirous of being elevated by becoming an *arahat*. Just as the lotus trembles at the slightest breeze so he trembled at the slightest touch of Defilements. As good seed sown in a fertile field, once it gets the necessary rainfall brings in a good harvest, so he used the labor of Right Effort and, in the fertile field of the Buddha's Teachings, sowed the seed of Moral Conduct, and directed the water of the Noble Path through the channels of Meditation in order to obtain the rice of Enlightenment. As grain grows and ripens in a field that has been ploughed and prepared, pleasing those who labor, so, with the industrious hard work of Right Effort, he prevented the weeds of Defilements from growing. Instead, he gathered the harvest of the Fruits of Enlightenment from the field of the Buddha's Teachings, and filled the storehouse of his mind with it.

The other monk, who had taken ordination while yet young, said, "I will fulfill the Practice of Scholarship." He made every effort, studied the words of the Buddha contained in the *Tripiṭaka*, followed the rules of Moral Conduct, and made that the guiding principle of his life. He developed a taste for preaching but did not develop full understanding and achieve Enlightenment. He preached to five hundred fellow monks who gathered around him and became the teacher of eighteen communities of monks.

Certain other monks went for instruction to the Senior monk who had obtained meditation exercises from the Buddha. Having followed his instructions, they, too, attained Enlightenment. After some time they went to the Senior monk, saluted him and said, "We wish now to go to the Buddha to inform him that our work as monks is completed."

"Go, O monks, worship the Buddha and the eighty disciples on my behalf, too. Greet also the monk who was my friend when we were laymen and say that I salute him," responded the Enlightened Monk.

The monks went to the monastery, saluted the Buddha, and the eighty great disciples, and went in search of the Scholar Monk, who had studied the *Tripiṭaka*. They told him, "Master, our teacher asked us to greet you."

"What is the name of this teacher of yours?" he asked.

"He is the monk who was your friend when you were laymen together."

On several such occasions the Enlightened Monk sent this message of salutations. At first, the Scholar Monk accepted the greetings but then later became irritated.[1] So when they (next) said "Our teacher monk sent his salutations to you," he asked in a manner indicating his dislike, "Who is this monk who happens to be everybody's teacher?"

"It is your friend the Enlightened Monk," they replied.

"What did you learn from him? Did you learn any text such as the *Dīgha Nikāya?* Have you been instructed in at least one of the texts of the *Tripiṭaka?*" he asked. Then he thought, "This monk does not know even a four-lined stanza and wears robes he picked up in a cemetery. The moment he became a monk, he took to the forest without learning to preach or chant. How has he now acquired so many disciples? Let him come here and I will test his skills."

Some time later the Enlightened Monk came to visit the Buddha. Since he did not know of the sinful thoughts of his former friend and paid no attention to the matter himself, he left his bowl and robes in that monastery, and went to pay his respects to the Buddha and the eighty great disciples. Afterwards he returned to where his friend the monk lived.

The Scholar Monk paid him the customary courtesies, set up seats of equal height for them both, and got ready to ask questions.

At that point the Buddha thought,[2] "This Scholar Monk, because he is learned, will question my son and harass him. If he does that, it will be a sinful act and he will be reborn in hell. That would be a pity." Thus, out of compassion for the Scholar Monk, the Buddha, very casually, as if taking a walk around the monastery, came to where the two monks were, and sat down in the seat reserved for him.

Wherever monks sit they must first prepare a seat for the Buddha, so the Teacher sat in the place reserved for him. He then asked the Scholar Monk a question regarding the first stage of Trance. Because of the Scholar Monk's conversance with the Teachings, he answered correctly. Then he questioned him about the second Trance State and on up to the eightfold Meditative Attainments in their entirety. He answered those, too. The Buddha then asked him questions on sections of the first stages of the Path. However great a scholar one may be, only if one has reached a stage of Enlightenment can one answer such a question. The monk, therefore, failed to answer it. When the question was asked of the Enlightened Monk, he was able to give the answer promptly, since he had already achieved Enlightenment. The Buddha applauded his answer. He then asked further questions about the Three Stages of the Path from the Scholar Monk. However, since he had not even reached the first stage he could not answer them. The Enlightened Monk answered each question without hesitation, since he had already reached those stages. On all four occasions, the Buddha applauded the Enlightened Monk. Hearing that applause, all the deities, from the earth goddess up to the gods in the Akanitā Brahma worlds, and the serpents in the Nāga world, the Suparṇas, all acclaimed him.

The disciples and fellow residents of the Scholar Monk heard the roars of applause and were displeased with the Buddha. They said, "Why did the Buddha do this? Four times he applauded this old monk who knows nothing. By contrast, he did not so much as say the word, 'good' let alone applaud our Scholar Monk, who is versed in the *Tripiṭaka*. After all he is a leader of five hundred monks." Thus, they criticized the Buddha.

The Buddha then asked, "What is it you say, monks?"

When they answered he said, "O monks, he who is your teacher is like a cowherd, a hired hand, who looks after cattle that he does not own. This, my son, is like the owner of the herd who, therefore gets to enjoy the five milk products."[3]

In addition the Buddha preached the following sermon.

"Listen, O monks. In my *sāsana,* a monk who is indolent may go to a teacher, study the words of the Buddha contained in the *Tripiṭaka* and teach it to many others. But if he himself does not engage in practicing the Doctrine, which a person who listens to such preaching should do, and if he does not meditate on subjects such as Impermanence, even for the short moment that it takes for a chicken to flap its wing, then such a monk is like a hired cowherd, who leads the cattle out at dawn, drives them to pastures and to water all day long, and at evening brings them back to their owner. Each day he collects a pittance of a fee, but never gets to share in the milk products. Such a monk gets only support and services from his disciples. He does not obtain the Fruits of monastic life, which are the Spiritual Attainments. This Scholar Monk is like that. The cattle owner by contrast, enjoys the produce of the herd that the other has cared for.

"Thus, of those who take great pains, listen to the Teachings of the Buddha and act on his advice, some will achieve Insight and reach the first Trance State and others will practice Insightful Meditation and reach the Path and the Fruits of full Enlightenment. Just as the cattle owner is entitled to the produce of his cattle, so they will be entitled to the benefits of a monk's life."

Thus, the Buddha first preached to monks in his *sāsana,* who though virtuous and of good moral conduct yet are indolent and do not practice the Meditation on Impermanence. Then he preached to monks who, though unlearned, meditate on the true nature of things, concentrate on the Objects of Meditation, and live a life of effort.

"A person who is vigilant and heedful,[4] if he concentrates on even a small portion of the Doctrine, such as the Category of One or the Category of Two and understands their objectives and knows the virtues that can arise from them, and if he lives in accordance with the Teachings of the nine Spiritual Attainments then as he mindfully practices this Doctrine,[5] made up of such factors as the four modes of Pure Conduct, the thirteen modes of Asceticism, the tenfold Objects of the Meditations on Impurities—all of which are collectively called the "Rules of Conduct of the Primary Part" and if he lives intent on the realization of Enlightenment, thinking, "I will comprehend the Path and the Fruits, this very day, this very moment,' then such a monk, by his proper conduct, will rid himself of the Defilements of Lust, Hatred, and Delusion. He will understand the Doctrine that must be comprehended clearly in terms of their Origins and Causes. He will possess a mind that is completely emancipated, achieved by suppressing one evil thought with another good thought (*tadaṅga*). He will suppress Defilements (*vikkhambhaṇa*), annihilate them totally (*samucchēda*), achieve mental tranquility (*paṭippassạddhi*), be saved from the cycle of becoming (*niṣṣaraṇa*), and achieve total emancipation (*vimutti*). He will not cling to the Five Aggregates that are triggered by the Fourfold Attachments, the twelve spheres of Perception (*āyatana*), and the eighteen Elements (*dhātu*) found both within oneself and without, and constituted in this life or the next. This great person, who has rid himself of all Defilements, then comes into possession of the Spiritual Attainments, those qualities of monkhood known as the Paths which can be acquired only by an expert such as an *arahat.*"

The Buddha concluded his sermon ornamenting it with a discourse on Spiritual Attainments like a builder who completes the construction of a house with a pinnacle of gems.

At the end of his sermon, many attained the four Paths and the four Fruits. Therefore, the wise should learn the Doctrine expounded by the Buddha, practice it, and comprehend the bliss of *nirvāṇa*.

Endnotes

THE TWO MONKS WHO WERE FRIENDS

Illustrates stanzas 19 and 20 of the Yamaka Vagga.

> Bahumpi ce sahitaṃ . . . na bhāgavā samaññassa hōti
> Appampi ce sahitaṃ . . . sa bhāgavā samaññassa hōti.
>
> One who recites a large number of texts but is not virtuous,
> is heedless, a cowherd counting other's cows,
> he does not share in the blessings of a recluse.
> One, who recites a small number of texts but is virtuous,
> Forsakes lust, hatred, delusion,
> with true understanding and serenity of mind,
> clings to nothing here or hereafter,
> such a one enjoys the blessings of a recluse.

1. At first, the Scholar Monk . . . later became irritated.

The Scholar Monk becomes jealous and irritated at the thought that his friend, who had none of his scholastic talents, has many pupils who bring these constant messages of greetings.

2. At that point the Buddha thought, . . .

Once again the Buddha anticipates that the Scholar Monk may commit an act of Demerit. In his compassion, he intervenes to stop it. The Buddha intervenes in this manner in many of the stories, for example, the case of Devidat.

3. In the DA, this story ends here with a quotation of two verses from the *Dhammapada*.

4. However great a scholar one may be . . .

Again a clear distinction is being made between scholarship that may lead even to Trance States; and Realization of Enlightenment, which is the province of those who have attained to the Stages of the Path or Spiritual Attainments.

5. This entire section of text would be totally incomprehensible to a lay audience. It was clearly intended for an audience of scholar monks.

6. "A man who is vigilant and heedful, . . ."

This section of the text consists of a list of abstract doctrinal categories and concepts from the *Abhidhamma Piṭaka*. It is not usual for the author to introduce material in this formal scholastic manner without explaining and elaborating the doctrinal concepts through simple images. But as the concluding image suggests, it was perhaps an exhibition of scholastic virtuosity on his part, for the benefit of an audience of scholarly monks familiar with the meanings of the terms. The graphic image of the builder putting the final touches to his construction with a gem-studded pinnacle, suggests this.

I have briefly translated the content of the terms and given the terms themselves in parentheses.

Appendix 1

Index to Jātaka stories referred to in the text. The references given below are to the volumes edited by Professor E. B. Cowell and published by the Pāli Text Society, 1981.

The Senior Monk Cakkhupāla

Vedabbha Jātaka (Vol. 1, no. 48, p. 121)

Cullaseṭṭhi Jātaka (Vol. 1, no. 4, p. 14)

Padamāṇavaka Jātaka Also called *Padakusala māṇavaka Jātaka* Fausboll (Vol. 3, pp. 501–514)

Suppāraka Jātaka (Vol. 4, no. 4, p. 86)

Kuṇāla Jātaka (Vol. 5, no. 536, p. 219)

Vessantara Jātaka (Vol. 6, no. 547, p. 246)

Maṭṭakuṇḍalī

Sudhābhōjana Jātaka (Vol. 5, no. 535, p. 202)

Kalandaka Jātaka (Vol. 1, no. 127, p. 280)

Uraga Jātaka (Vol. 3, no. 354, p. 107)

Culladhanuggaha Jātaka (Vol. 3, no. 374, p. 144)

Javanahaṃsa Jātaka (Vol. 4, no. 476, p. 132)

Naḷapāna Jātaka (Vol. 1, no. 20, p. 54)

The Senior Monk Nāgasēna

Ummaga Jātaka (Vol. 6, no. 546, p. 156)

The Monk Tissa, the Fat

Ummaga Jātaka (Vol. 6, No. 546, p. 156)

The Demoness Kāḷī

Phandana Jātaka (Vol. 4, no. 475, p. 129)

Ulūka Jātaka (Vol. 2, no. 270, p. 242)

The Monks of Kosambä

Laṭukika Jātaka (Vol. 3, no. 3, p. 115)

Vaṭṭaka Jātaka The story referred to in the text is entitled the *Sammōdamāna Jātaka* in Fausboll (Vol. 1, pp. 208–210)

Dīghiti Kōsala Jātaka (Vol. 3, no. 371, p. 139)

Swarṇa Karṭaka Jātaka (Vol. 3, no. 389, p. 183)

The Senior Monk Mahākāḷā

Mugapakha Jātaka (Vol. 6, no. 538, p. 1)

Wearing the Ochre Robe

Sēravānija Jātaka (Vol. 1, no. 3, p. 12)

The Chief Disciples

Ummaga Jātaka (Vol. 6, no. 546, p. 156)

The Senior Monk Nanda

Canda Kiṇara Jātaka (Vol. 4, no. 485, p. 179)

Dharmapāla Jātaka (Vol. 4, no. 447, p. 32)

Suppāraka Jātaka (Vol. 4, no. 463, p. 86)

Devadatta

Sērivānija Jātaka (Vol. 1, no. 3, p. 12)

Culla Haṃsa Jātaka (Vol. 5, no. 533, p. 175)

Mahā Haṃsa Jātaka (Vol. 5, no. 534, p. 186)

Lakkanamiga Jātaka (Vol. 1, no. 11, p. 34)

Kuruṃgamiga Jātaka (Vol. 2, no. 206, p. 106)

Parantapa Jātaka (Vol. 3, no. 416, p. 249)

Khantivāda Jātaka (Vol. 3, no. 313, p. 26)

Culla Dhammapāla Jātaka (Vol. 3, no. 358, p. 117)

Piṃgala Jātaka (Vol. 2, no. 240, p. 165)

Vīraka Jātaka (Vol. 2, no. 204, p. 103)

Glossary

Abhidhamma. The *Abhidhamma Piṭaka* is the third division or section of the Buddhist canon (the *Tripitaka*) and contains the metaphysical philosophy of the Buddhist Teachings. Thus it is the most complex and abstract part of the Scriptures and consists of the following seven books: The Dhammasaṅganī; Vibhaṅga; Dhātukathā; Pudgalapajñapti; Kathāvatthu; Yamaka; Paṭṭhāna.

Aggregates (p. khandha, s. & sk. skandha). In its widest sense, the term refers to the elements or substrata of sensory existence, the sensorial aggregates that condition the appearance of life in any form; all existing things, substances, the material universe, everything of which impermanence may be predicated. They are enumerated as form, sensation, perception, mental formation, and consciousness. These are the five elements or attributes of sentient being.

Amu. A grain that requires less water for growing than rice. Amu is considered 'inferior' to rice.

Anāgāmin. Also called a "Non-Returner," because he will not be born again in the human world before he attains *nirvāṇa*. *See also* Stages of Enlightenment.

Bhāvanā. Translated as Contemplation or Meditation. It is one of the three ethical foundations of Buddhism. The other two are, Acts of Giving *(dāna)* and Moral Conduct *(sīla)*.

Bimbā. Referred to in the story of Prince Nanda is the wife of Prince Siddhārta before he became the Buddha. She is more popularly known by the name "Yasodharā," though Bimbā is the older usage. G. P. Malalasekera is of the opinion that Bimbā was her real name and Yasodharā only an epithet. (*Dictionary of Pali Proper Names*, Vol. 2. p. 741).

Bōdhi Tree. The tree under which the Buddha attained Enlightenment and therefore revered by Buddhists. It is a species of ficus *(ficus religiosa)* called *"Bō"* in Sinhala.

Bōdhisatva. An aspirant to Buddahood. He is one who cultivates the Perfections *(pāramitā)* during his various existences and finally achieves Enlightenment as a Buddha.

Bōsat. The Sinhala form of the word Bōdhisatva.

Brahma heavens. The "radiant *brahmas*" as they are called, live in two categories of heavens: that of the "Corporeal *brahmas*," of which there are sixteen placed one above the other, and the heavens of the "Formless *brahmas*" of which there are four. *Ābhassara* and *Subhakīrṇa* (mentioned in the text) are two of the sixteen; each have a god by that name. The *brahmas* are of a higher order of gods than the *devas*, since they are free from sensual passions. However, Brahma heavens like all other heavens are not eternal. They, like the human world, are subject to final destruction.

Buddha. An Enlightened One, who by his own wisdom and insight has realized the state of *nirvāṇa*. See also Three Forms of Enlightenment.

Buddha Rays (s. Budu räs). The rays believed to emanate from the Buddha's person.

Chain of Causation (p. *paṭicca samuppāda*). The term given to a well-known Buddhist doctrine called "Dependent Origination," which sums up the principal causes of existence in their order of succession. It also embodies the Buddhist statement of a solution to the problem of suffering and so is a fundamental part of the Teachings.

Chintāmaṇi. A "wishing-gem" that is supposed to give its owner whatever he or she desires.

Consciousness (p. *viññāna*). As a metaphysical concept in the Buddhist teachings, it has eighty-nine subdivisions under three broad categories; Meritorious Thoughts *(kusalaviññāna)*, Demeritorious Thoughts *(akusala viññāna)*, and Indifferent Thoughts *(avyākata viññāna)*.

Council of Monks (s. *saṅgāyanā*; p. *saṅgīti*). The term literally means "chanting together." It refers, however, to three historical convocations of the Buddhist clergy held for the purpose of fixing the text of the Buddhist Scriptures. The first was held at Rajagaha immediately after the Buddha's death (543 B.C.) with the Senior monk Kāśyapa presiding. The second was at Vesāli under the patronage of Kālāsoka (443 B.C.), and the third at Pāṭalīputta in the time of King Dhammāsoka in (309 B.C.) under the patronage of the monk Moggaliputtatissa.

Crores. Ten millions or one hundred lakhs. It comes from the Indian word *karōr.*

Cullaseṭṭhi Jātaka. It is the story of a man by that name, who picks up a dead rat and sells it to a person who owns a cat. (It happened to be a full moon day of religious observances, therefore, no killing took place and no other meat was available.) With the proceeds, he keeps on buying and selling various goods, maintaining always a small margin of profit. Ultimately he becomes very wealthy.

Daṁbadiva. The Sinhala name for India. *See also* Jambudīpa.

Damsak Pävatumsuta (p. Dhamma Cakka Pavattana Sutta). The sermon called "The Establishment of the Doctrine." It literally means to set in motion the wheel of the Doctrine or establish the Law. This was the first sermon the Buddha preached after he attained Enlightenment: it contains the fundamentals of his Doctrine such as the Four Noble Truths.

Dāna. Generosity or the act of giving, one of the three ethical principles fundamental to Buddhism. The other two are *sīla,* Moral Conduct and *bhāvana,* Contemplation or Meditation.

Defilements (s. & sk. *kleśa*). Translated also as Impurities. There are ten *kleśa:* craving, hate, ignorance, vanity (egocentricity), erroneous beliefs, doubt, sloth, arrogance, lack of shame to sin, and lack of fear to sin.

Demerit (s. akusal). Bad or wrong acts that have negative karmic consequences in the future.

Devramvehera. The Sinhala name for the Jetavanārāma, a monastery built by the nobleman Anāthapiṇḍika (s. Anēpiḍu) and located near the city of Sāvatthi (s. Sävät). It was one of the major monasteries where the Buddha spent the longest time during his years of teaching.

Dhamma (s. & sk. *dharma*). The fundamental Law or Doctrine of existence and salvation as expounded by a Buddha. It is also commonly used for the discourses, conversations, or Teachings of the Buddha Gōtama.

Dhammapada. A Buddhist scriptural text in stanza form. This text is held in high esteem as a simple compendium of the salient teachings of the Buddha. It is one of the texts of the *Sutta Piṭaka.*

Dhammasaṅganī. The first book of the *Abhidhamma Piṭaka* consisting of doctrinal categories and philosophical formulations. It was highly venerated. We are told in the chronicles that King Mahinda (A.D. 913–923) had it inscribed in gold. King Vijayabāhu (A.D. 1059–1114) studied it and translated it.

Dhutāṅgas. Very severe ascetic practices which are considered by some to aid progress on the Path. There are thirteen such practices. *Nesajjika* or meditation while seated without lying down, practiced by the monk Cakkhupāla, is one of them.

Divine Eye (s. *diväsa*). Enlightened Ones or *arahats* have the power of clairvoyance, thought-reading and the recollection of their own and others' past lives in earlier incarnations. This is referred to as acquiring the Divine Eye; is one of the supernormal powers obtained by intense meditation and the attaining of Trance States.

Divine Ear. Clairaudience, another of the supernormal powers, which is acquired by attaining Trance States.

Dog Asceticism (s. *balu tapas*). During the time of the Buddha, there were a group of ascetics who imitated dogs and wandered about crawling on all fours. In Sri Lanka, the term has come to mean fake asceticism.

Dukkha Khanda Sutta. A sutta or stanzas on the Aggregates of Suffering. See note on Aggregates.

Eight Meditative Attainments (p. *aṭṭha samāpatti*). This is a Buddhist philosophical term and refers to eight attainments, endowments, or modes of abstraction induced by ecstatic meditation.

Enlightenment. The Buddhist term for supreme understanding. It is the bliss that arises from extinguishing the fires of lust *(rāga)*, ill will *(dōsa)*, and delusion *(mōha)*. It is the ultimate goal for all Buddhists. *See also* nirvāṇa.

Fervent Rebirth-Wish (s. *prārtanā* or *pätuma*). Buddhism has no provision for prayer, because the Buddha is not a deity. Therefore, a *prārtanā* or wish for something in the next life is the nearest equivalent. A *prārtanā* is often, however, more than a wish or a prayer. It is a moral resolve to achieve specific goals in the next life, such as a Bōdhisatva's *prārtanā* to become a Buddha, made over a succession of rebirths. The wish is made after the performance of a pious act. Since it is most often related to the next life or future lives, I have decided to translate it as "Fervent Rebirth-Wish."

Field of Merit (s. *pin-keta*). Generally refers to the Buddha and the Sangha who are deemed worthy recipients of lay generosity *(dāna)* and other meritorious acts. They are like a ready field prepared for the sowing of good deeds by lay devotees.

Fivefold Supernatural Powers or Faculties *(abhiñña)*. They are the five faculties possessed by *arahats*, that is, different magical powers, the Divine Ear, the knowledge of former existences, knowledge of the thoughts of others, and the Divine Eye. Sometimes they are referred to as the six *abhiññas* in which case there is the addition of the knowledge that causes the destruction of human passions.

Five Impediments (p. *nīvaraṇa*). The five obstacles or hindrances to a religious life. They are lust, malice, sloth, pride, and doubt.

Five Precepts (p. *pañca sīla*). The five basic rules or precepts of Moral Conduct that a Buddhist must observe if he is to proceed along the path to Enlightenment. They are abstention from killing, stealing, adultery, lying, and the taking of intoxicating liquor.

Five Senses. Sight, sound, smell, taste, and touch.

Garuḍa. An enormous mythical bird that feeds on snakes.

Gautama (s. Gōtama). The name of the last Buddha whose dispensation is the present, therefore, referred to also as "our Buddha." He is but one of a long line of Buddhas and will be followed by the Buddha Maitreya.

Granthadhura, Vidarśanādhura. Monks can engage in one of two categories of religious practice. They can devote themselves to the scholarly study of the Scriptures and thereby gain understanding, or they can engage in meditation and the cultivation of Insight, by which means they achieve Enlightenment. The former is termed a Scholar of the Texts *(granthadhura)* and such Textual scholarship is generally undertaken in the monasteries. The latter is termed *(vidarśanādhura)*, one who has made Contemplation the primary concern.

Gav. A specific measure of distance equivalent to four miles. I have translated it as league for lack of a more precise equivalent.

Gōtama. See Gautama.

Higher Knowledge (p. *abhiññā*). Also translated as Wisdom or Higher Insight depending on the context, and refers to that special wisdom or supernormal powers of apperception acquired by long training in life and thought. Can also refer to the supernatural faculties possessed by *arahats. See also* Fivefold Supernormal Powers.

Higher Ordination (s. *upasampadā*). Admission to the privileges of a recognized *bhikkhu*. Buddhists who join the Order first have to serve time as novices. After various requirements have been fulfilled, they receive higher ordination and become full-fledged members of the *Sangha* or Buddhist Order.

Impediments. *See* Five Impediments.

Impurities. *See* Defilements.

Jambudīpa (literally, the island of the Rose-Apple). The ancient name for India.

Kalpa. The term used to define vast periods or a cycle of time. All universes are subjected to a process of destruction and renovation. A mahākalpa is the period that elapses from the commencement or restoration of a universe to its complete destruction. I have translated it as "eon" for lack of a better term.

Kalpalatā. A wish-fulfilling vine that grows in heaven. So also is the *Kalpavṛkṣa* or wish-fulfilling tree that also grows there.

Karma (literally, action or deed). Thus, good and bad *karma* refer to acts of Merit and Demerit and their consequences. There are two broad categories of *karma*. *Paṭisandhi karma* are actions that give rise to only one result and nothing thereafter. *Pavatti karma* are actions whose multiple consequences occur in a succession of future births.

Kasiṇa. Aids or objects of meditation such as colors or elements. They are ten in number. Concentration on a *kasiṇa* is a means of inducing contemplation.

Kiṁbulvat. The Sinhala name for Kapilavāstu, the city which was the Buddha's hometown.

Knowledge of the Path (s. *mārgajñāṇa*). Enlightenment or understanding of the sublime truth of the Buddha's Doctrine, that is, the Four Noble Truths. They are Suffering, the Cause of Suffering, the Destruction of Suffering, and the Eightfold Path that leads to the destruction of suffering or *nirvāṇa*.

Lakh. A term for the number one hundred thousand.

Maitreya. The name of the Bōdhisatva presently in the Tusita heaven, who will be the next Buddha.

Mahāmēru. The mountain at the center of a *Sakvaḷa* believed to be more than two million miles (168,000 *yodun*) high, half of which is below the earth. On top of it lies the Tusita heaven of the gods and at its base the kingdom of the *asura* or demons.

Maheśvara. The Supreme Being or God. It is also used as a name for Shiva.

Mahā Sihivatan Sutta. *See* Sihivatan Sutta.

Māra. The god/demon of destruction and death is Māra. Sometimes they are referred to as five: Dēvaputra Māra, Kleśa Māra, Abhisanskara Māra, Skandha Māra, Mṛtyu Māra.

Meditative Insight (s. *vivasun*). The knowledge or insight that comes from contemplation.

Merit (s. *kusal*). Good or right actions that have good karmic consequences.

Moral Conduct (p. *sīla*). Right Living and ethical conduct. It is one of the three basic practices required of a Buddhist for achieving Enlightenment. *See also* dāna and bhāvana.

Nāga. Hooded snakes who, in Buddhist mythology, occupy a nether region under the rock Tikūṭa Pabbata that supports Mount Mēru. They also haunt the earth and are considered naturally inimical to man, though they were friendly to the Buddha. The Buddha preached to them his Doctrine and many of them were converted to the Path.

Nesajjika. One form of severe ascetic practice. See dhutaṅga.

Nirvāṇa. Supreme Enlightenment, the cessation of all desire, ill will and delusion, and the end to rebirth. The ultimate goal for a Buddhist.

Pacceka Buddha (s. *pasē budu*). One who attains Enlightenment but does not teach the Doctrine to others. *See also* Buddha.

Päḷalup. Pāṭaliputra in Buddhist history.

Paṇḍukambala Śailāsanaya. The name for the throne of the god Sakra. It is supposed to heat when a good man suffers so Sakra is made aware and can intervene to help.

Pasē Budu. The Sinhala term for a Paccēka Buddha.

Path (s. *mārga*). See Path and Fruits.

Path and the Fruits (s. & sk. *mārga-phala*). The stages of Enlightenment in Buddhism are termed *mārga-phala* (Path and Fruits). These are the four stages of the path *(mārga)* and their specific forms of realization or fruits *(phala)*. The four stages are that of the *Sotāpanna* (Stream-Enterer), that is, one who has entered the stream of salvation; the *Sakadāgāmi* (Once-Returner), that is, one who might be born once more as a human being before achieving *nirvāṇa;* the *Anāgāmi* (Non-Returner), that is, one who will not be born again as a human before he attains nirvāṇa; and Arahat (the Purified One). As one achieves each stage, one also arrives at a realization or the fruition of that stage. The four *mārga* and four *phala* together are called "*mārga-phala*." I translate the term sometimes as the Path and its Fruit (which is the popular Buddhist usage) or as "Spiritual Attainments," depending on the context. The meaning remains unchanged.

Paṭṭhāna. The name of the last book of the *Abhidhamma Piṭaka. See also* Abhidhamma.

Paṭisandhi karma and Pavatti karma. *See* karma.

Perfections (s. & sk. *pāramitā*). To become a Buddha one must spend many lifetimes practicing the Perfections or principal virtues. There are ten: generosity, moral conduct, renunciation, wisdom, courage, forbearance, truthfulness, determination, compassion, and equanimity. Each can be further subdivided into the ordinary, the inferior, and the unlimited form of the Perfection—hence, the reference also to thirty *pāramitā*.

Planes of Existence (p. *pañcagati*). There are five of them: that of the heavenly or divine, the earthly or human, the animal, the ghostly or spirit world, and the demonic or hell.

Practice of Scholarship. *See* note on granthadhura.

Practice of Contemplation (p. *vidarśanādhura*). *See* note on granthadhura.

Prātimokṣa. The collection of the Rules of Discipline of the *Vinaya Piṭaka.*

Preta. Spirits of dead relatives who dwell in hell or in a state of perpetual punishment. They are wasted in appearance and look like dry leaves. They are said to haunt places where they lived as men and need to be propitiated by their living kinsmen often with offerings of polluted food (because of their low status.) If not propitiated they can cause harm to the living.

Precepts. The Buddha laid down three categories of precepts or rules for Buddhists to follow. They are the Five Precepts (s. *pan-sil*), which all lay Buddhists must observe; the Eight Precepts or *(aṭa-sil),* which are more rigorous rules that laymen observe once a week or once a month; the Ten Precepts or *(dasa-sil),* which are to be observed by Buddhists who give up the lay life.

Precept and Practice. They are the two basic conditions for a Buddhist life. A Buddhist must understand the Precepts and practice them.

Protective Stanzas (s. *pirit,* p. *paritta*). They are stanzas that are recited ceremonially by Buddhist monks to invoke blessings and protection for individuals or groups. Water and thread, magically infused with protective power by the recital of *pirit,* is then distributed to the participants. The water is drunk and the thread is worn as a talisman around the wrist or neck. This is a practice common in Sri Lanka even today.

Purification of Morality (s. *sīla-visuddhi*). It is the first of the seven categories or stages of Purification that form the substructure of the *Vimutti Magga* (the Path to Freedom), a text preserved in Chinese and in the Pāli version of Buddhaghosa.

Rāhu. One of the Asura demons who is supposed to cause eclipses by swallowing the sun and moon.

Rainy season (s. *vas;* p. *vassāna*). The rainy season known for monks as the period of *vas* is a time when monks go into retreat. They take up residence in one place, and engage in religious duties such as preaching. During this period, the lay devotees undertake to provide the monks with food and to see to their needs.

Rebirth-Wish. *See* Fervent Rebirth-Wish

Riyan. A measure equal to one cubit or eighteen inches.

Salkalaṇa Tree. A mythological tree that remains hidden and appears only in the time of a Buddha or a *cakravartin* or universal monarch.

Sakvaḷa. Buddhism refers to a complete system of worlds or universes that include the sun and moon and all the worlds as far as the light of the sun extends, as well as a series of heavens and hells. Such *Sakvaḷas* are thought to be innumerable.

Sākya. The clan of the Buddha. It was a *kṣatriya* not Brahmin caṣte group.

Saṃsāra. Refers to the continuous cycles of birth, decay, and death that Buddhists consider characterize the human condition and make it one of suffering. Enlightenment provides release from this *saṃsāric* cycle.

Samskāra. All conditioned things; essential conditions or psychological structures requisite for acts, speech and thought.

Saṅgāyanā or Councils. *See* Council of Monks.

Sāriyut. The Sinhala form of the name Sāriputta, who was one of the Buddha's two chief disciples.

Sāsana. The term includes the Buddha's Teachings, the Order of Monks, and the devotees. The nearest equivalent in English would be the concept of a church as in "the church of Christ." However, the connotations of the word "church" are so Christian that I have refrained from using it.

Satkuḷa rock. Believed to be situated in the foothills of the Yugandhara mountains of the Himalayas.

Sävät. The Sinhala term for Sāvatthi, the capital of the kingdom of Kōsala in Northern India. The Buddha spent many years at the Jetavanārāmaya monastery located in this city.

Sevenfold Noble Possessions (p. *satta ariyadhana*). They are: Faith; Moral Conduct; Modesty; Fear of Evil; Learning; Self-denial; Wisdom.

Sihivaṭan Sutta. The Sinhala name for the Satipaṭṭhāna Sutta, the teachings on Mindfulness or meditative practices that lead to Enlightenment. There are four Satipaṭṭhāna—pertaining to the body, the sensations, the mind, the phenomena.

Spiritual Attainments (s. *nava lovuturā dahaṃ*). Also translated in Buddhist literature as the nine Transcendental or Supramundane States. They consist of the attainments of the four stages of the Path *(mārga)*, the four Fruits *(phala)*, and Enlightenment (nirvāṇa), a total of nine. Blessings for a Buddhist, therefore, can be of two kinds: *lovī*, that is, worldly, or *lovuturā*, that is, supramundane or transcendental, such as the spiritual attainments of the stages of Enlightenment. I have chosen to use the simpler phrase Spiritual Attainments to translate the concept. *See also* Path and Fruits.

Stages of Enlightenment. *See* Path and Fruits.

Stream Enterer (s. *sōvān;* p. *sotāpanna*). *See* Path and Fruits.

Sumana. In the Sri Lankan context, Sumana would be identified as the god Saman, one of the guardian deities of the Island. In the "Demoness Kāḷī" story, he is seen as performing a similar function, that of guarding the entrance to the temple.

Supramundane States. *See* Spiritual Attainments.

Tavtisā (p. *Tāvatiṃsa*). It is the second of six heavens in Buddhist cosmology and is the abode of the thirty-three gods headed by Sakra.

Tusī. The Sinhala form for the Tusita heaven, another one of the six Buddhist heavens.

Teacher of the Three Worlds (s. *tilō-guru*). Another term of reference for the Buddha, who preached his Doctrine in the heavens, on earth, and in the spirit world.

Ten Acts of Merit (s. *dasa pinkiriya*). The ten meritorious acts are the following: charity or the giving of alms, observing the moral precepts, meditation, transference of merit to other beings, accepting merit transferred by others, attending on worthy people, evoking a serene mind towards Enlightened ones, teaching the Doctrine, hearing the Doctrine, cultivating Insight.

Tadaṅga Prahāna. The practice of suppressing a sinful thought with a corresponding positive one.

Three Cycles of Existence (p. *tivaṭṭa*). They are the cycles of *karma (kamma vaṭṭa)* or *karma* formations, the round of Defilements *(kilēsa vaṭṭa)* consisting of Ignorance, Clinging, and Craving, and the round of Consequences *(vipāka vaṭṭa)* consisting of Consciousness and Corporeality.

Three Jewels (s. *trivida-ratna,* also *tun-ruvan*). They are the Buddha, the Dhamma, and the Sangha, commonly referred to as the Triple-Gems.

Three Aspects of Practice for a Disciple. Understanding of the Doctrine *(pariyatti),* Practice *(paṭipatti),* and Realization *(paṭivedha).*

Threefold Virtues (s. *tun susiri*). They are virtuous acts performed by Body, Word and Mind. Generosity, Moral conduct, and Contemplation.

Three Worlds. The three worlds in Buddhism refer to heaven or the formless realm *(arūpa),* the human world or the world of form *(rūpa),* and the spirit world, hell, or the realm of lust *(kāma).*

Tīrthakas. A sect who held wrong beliefs. Buddhist texts do not dismiss those who held other views as heretics or unbelievers, but rather as misguided ones who must be converted by debate and discussion. The texts refer to constant debates between Buddhist monks and those of other sects, for conversion could only occur through such debate and discussion.

Trance States (s. *dhyāna*). States achieved through the attainment of full concentration during which there is the complete though temporary suspension of the fivefold sense activities. However, this state of Consciousness is one of full alertness and lucidity.

Trance State of Cessation (p. *nirōdhasamāpath*). One of the many categories of Trance States that can be achieved by concentrated Contemplation.

Tripiṭaka (literally, the Three Caskets or repositories). The Buddhist doctrinal canon is in three books or repositories known as the *Tripiṭaka.* They consist of the *Sutta piṭaka* or the repository of the doctrinal expositions, the *Vinaya piṭaka* or the repository of the rules of monastic discipline, and the *Abhidhamma piṭaka* or the repository of the transcendental doctrine, in which the teachings are abstracted, condensed, and systemetized.

Vaiṣrāvaṇa. *See* Vesamuṇi.

Vēda. The four sacred books of the Brahmins. They are the Rg vēda, the Yajur vēda, and the Sāma vēda, and the Atharva vēda.

Vesamuṇi (vaiṣrāvaṇa). The god of the northern quarter in early Buddhism. In Sri Lankan folk Buddhism, he is known as Vesamuni, overlord of demons.

Vidarśanādhura. *See* Granthadhura.

Vigilence (s. *nopamāva,* p. *appāmada*). A concept central to Buddhism and translated also as Mindfulness, Awareness, or Heedfulness.

Vinaya piṭaka. The books of the Doctrine that contain the rules of conduct for the Buddhist order of monks. It is one of the three *piṭakas* or caskets that contain the entirety of the Buddhist Teachings.

Vivarana. Vivaraṇa literally means a declaration. It is generally translated as a "warrant" in the Buddhist literature as it also means an 'assurance' that a specific wish or event will come to pass in a future life. I translate the term as 'prophetic declaration.'

Yodun. A measure of distance equal to about sixteen miles or four gav.

Yon (p. *yavana*). The word is believed to be derived from the Greek word Ionian to refer to the peoples of the Greco-Muslim kingdoms established after Alexander's conquests of India.

Yugandhara. A mountain range believed to be in the Himalayas, again a cosmological rather than a geographical entity.

Bibliography

Buddhadatta Thera. Ambalangoda P., ed. *Dhammapadatthakatha*. Colombo: M. D. Gunasena and Co., 1956.

Burlingame, E. W. *Buddhist Legends translated from the original Pāli text of the Dhammapada Commentary.* Parts I–III. London: Published by the Pāli Text Society, 1979. (First published as volumes 28–30 of Harvard Oriental Series) Cambridge Ma.: Harvard University Press, 1921.)

Carter, John Ross and M. Palihawadene, trans. and ed. *The Dhammapada*. New York: Oxford University Press, 1987.

Cowell, E. B., ed. *The Jātaka or Stories of the Buddha's Former Births*. 4 vols. London: Published for the Pāli Text Society by Routledge & Keagan Paul Ltd., 1981.

Dimock, E. C. et al. *The Literatures of India: An Introduction*. Chicago: University of Chicago Press, 1974.

Dutt, Sukumar. *The Buddha and Five Centuries After.* Calcutta: Sahitya Samsad Press, 1978.

Fausboll, V., ed. *The Jātaka: Together with its Commentary.* 4 vols. London: Published for the Pāli Text Society by Luzac & Co., 1962–1964.

Fausboll, V., ed. *Jatakattha Vannana*. 4 vols. London: 1896.

Geiger, Wilhelm. *Pāli Literature and Language*. Authorized English translation by Balakrishna Ghosh. 2d ed. Calcutta: University of Calcutta, 1956.

Ñaṇavimala Thera, Kiriëllē ed. 2d edition *Saddharma Ratnāvaliya*. Colombo: M. D. Gunasena and Sons, 1971.

Godakumbura, Charles. *Sinhalese Literature*. Colombo: The Colombo Apothecaries Co. Ltd., 1955.

Gunaratna, L., ed. *Saddharma Ratnāvaliya*. Colombo: Ratna Book Publishers, 1975.

Hettiaratchi, D. E. ed. *Dhampiya-aṭuvā-gätapadaya*. Colombo: Sri Lanka University Press, 1974.

Jayatilleke, Sir D. B. ed. *Saddharma Ratnāvaliya*. Colombo: Anula Press, 1934.

Malalasekera, G. P. *Dictionary of Pali Proper Names*. London: Luzac & Co.

Norman, H. C. ed. *The Commentary on the Dhammapada*. 4 vols. London: Published for the Pāli Text Society by Luzac and Co., Ltd., 1970 (first published, 1906).

Obeyesekere, Ranjini, and Gananath. "The Tale of the Demoness Kali: A 13th Century Text on Evil," *Journal of the History of Religion*. Chicago: 1990.

Obeyesekere, Gananath. *A Meditation on Conscience*. Colombo: Published for the Social Scientists' Assoc. of Sri Lanka, Navamaga Press, 1988.

Obeyesekere, Ranjini. "The Act of Translation," *The Massachusetts Review* 29 no. 4 (Winter 1988–89): 262–267.

Olivelle, Patrick. *The Origin and the Early Development of Buddhist Monachism*. Colombo: Gunasena & Co., 1974.

Reynolds, C. H. B. ed. *An Anthology of Sinhalese Literature upto 1815*. London: Published for the UNESCO National Commission of Ceylon by George Allen & Unwin Ltd., 1970.

Rhys Davids, C. A. F. trans. *Sacred Writings of the Buddhists: Psalms of the Sisters*. New Delhi: Cosmo Publication, 1986.

Richman, Paula. *Women, Branch Stories, and Religious Rhetoric in a Tamil Buddhist Text*. New York: Maxwell School, Syracuse University, 1988.

Saddharmaratnāvaliya. 2 vols. Edited by the Sinhala Department of the University of Colombo. Colombo: Published for the Sri Lanka Oriental Languages Association by the Government Publications Bureau, 1985.

Siri Ratnasāra Thera, Kahavē. ed. *Dhammapadattha-katha*. Revised by Mahagoda Siri Ñanissara Thera. Parts I–II. Colombo: Published by the Trustees of the Simon Hewavitarne Bequest. The Tripitaka Publication Press, 1919.

Wickramasinghe, M. de Z. ed. *Nikāyasaṅgrahaya* by Jayabāhu Dēvarakṣita. C. M. Fernando, trans. Colombo: 1890; 1908.

Index